About the Author

Educated at Goldsmiths College (University of London) and subsequently at the London School of Economics, Mark Curtis was a Research Fellow at the Royal Institute of International Affairs (1989–92) and has been a Visiting Fellow at the Institut Français des Relations Internationales in Paris and the Deutsche Gesellschaft für Auswärtige Politik in Bonn. He is the co-author of a book on European security and the author of various journal and press articles on international affairs. He currently works for the international development charity ActionAid.

THE AMBIGUITIES OF POWER

British Foreign Policy since 1945

MARK CURTIS

Zed Books Ltd
LONDON & NEW JERSEY

The Ambiguities of Power was first published by
Zed Books Ltd, 7 Cynthia Street, London N1 9JF,
UK, and 165 First Avenue, Atlantic Highlands,
New Jersey 07716, USA, in 1995.

Copyright © Mark Curtis, 1995

Cover designed by Andrew Corbett
Set in Monotype Garamond by Ewan Smith
Printed and bound in the United Kingdom
by Biddles Ltd, Guildford and King's Lynn

A catalogue record for this book is available from
the British Library

US CIP data is available from the Library of
Congress

ISBN 1 85649 347 4 cased
ISBN 1 85649 348 2 limp

CONTENTS

INTRODUCTION

In attempting to understand Britain's role in the world, two approaches are possible. In the first, one can rely on the mainstream information system, consisting primarily of media and academia, where commentators are presumed to provide analyses of current affairs independent of the reasoning and priorities of the state. This is deemed to be consistent with notions of a 'free press' and 'political science'. In the second approach, by contrast, one can consider the facts of the real world.

The two approaches lead to vastly different conceptions of the nature of British foreign policy and international affairs. By adopting the second approach it is possible to reach a coherent understanding of the reality of British foreign policy which differs markedly from one that would arise from a dependence on the mainstream information system. Indeed, as will be shown in this study, the so-called information system interprets Britain's role in the world according to precepts acceptable to the ruling groups that control policy – as fundamentally benevolent.

It appears to be a widely held assumption that Britain (and indeed the Western states as a whole) promotes certain grand principles – peace, democracy, human rights and economic development in the Third World – as natural corollaries to the basic political and economic priorities that guide its foreign policy. It is evident that the Western states have achieved a level of freedom and prosperity for their own citizens unsurpassed in history. From this there is a tendency to believe that – particularly in relation to states elsewhere – the Western states' role in the world is essentially benign. It is perhaps not surprising to find assumptions as to such basic benevolence regarding foreign policy among those who have actually made policy. For example, according to former Labour Foreign Secretary Michael Stewart, 'British interests [in the postwar world] could only be protected as part of the general interests of mankind, and one of the chief of these was the preservation of peace. ... Our task, therefore, was to discover how best a nation of our rank could co-operate with others for the general good.'[1] Even the colonial period is not excluded from such a notion. Thus Churchill once noted 'the reputation of the British empire as a valiant and benignant force in the history of mankind'.[2] For Harold Macmillan the empire was 'a strong instrument' 'for the preservation of peace and the spread of civilisation throughout a great part of the globe'.[3]

More interesting, the vast majority of allegedly independent commentators within the information system similarly promote the notion of Britain's basic benevolence. Consider the following observations by leading academics. One professor of government at the University of Manchester describes Britain as 'a defender of political freedom' without further comment.[4] A professor of international relations at the London School of Economics claims that the Attlee Labour government's conception of the Commonwealth was as 'a new theatre for the spread of welfare and equality'.[5] Similarly, the chairman and the deputy director of one of Britain's leading academic institutes write in their study of British foreign policy as follows:

> Britain has had the good fortune not to have been faced with sharp discontinuities in its modern history, or with the painful process of coming to terms with defeat, division or dishonour ... British history, as popularly understood, is the story of the extension of English ideas and influence, of the sustained defence of liberty against Continental despotism, of the benign character of the nineteenth-century Pax Britannica, and of the maturing of Empire into a free association of states ... Withdrawal from Empire and accommodation to the European continent has been a gradual but successful process, completed without large-scale colonial wars or domestic disruption, maintaining the basic traditions of British foreign policy and leaving Britain with a valuable legacy in terms of its international reputation.[6]

They also state:

> The promotion of democratic values through foreign policy is most directly demonstrated by government attitudes to human rights outside Britain. In the nineteenth century the Royal Navy extended the anti-slavery campaign from Britain to the Atlantic and Indian Oceans, enforcing basic standards of civilised behaviour. ... Human rights issues are no less controversial or difficult today, though British governments have far less capability to intervene in the affairs of other countries.[7]

In similar vein, another leading British foreign policy analyst writes of the period before the Second World War thus:

> The outstanding characteristic of British foreign policy and diplomacy is found in what Sir Harold Nicolson called its 'civilian' character. It was the policy of a satisfied and prosperous state with no military influence upon its domestic politics. Co-operation instead of conflict, profitable trade and cheap diplomacy instead of costly and wasteful warfare, peace rather than war, became the guiding principles of British foreign policy. Britain, as it has been put, had 'the moral opportunity' to develop a peaceful foreign policy; she took this opportunity. Thus her interests happily merged with those of others; her policy was based upon self-interest but was also happily in conformity with moral dictates and humanitarian aspirations. It was possible to assume ... that what was good for the world was good for Britain, which amounted in fact to saying also that what

was good for Britain was good for the world ... The concepts of 'civilian diplomacy' and of 'harmonisation' did not lose their relevance even after the eclipse of the British Empire.[8]

The assumption and active promotion of the concept of Britain's basic benevolence in foreign policy does not preclude a recognition that, occasionally, 'mistakes' can be made and ill-considered policies implemented, or – taking the argument one step further – a recognition that, occasionally, policies are pursued that deliberately deviate from promoting the grand principles mentioned above. Yet fundamentally the assertion, or assumption, is that the world role of Britain and the West, despite occasional deviations, is at root benign, both in motivation and in effect. Little is seen to be wrong with the basic policy priorities and the major institutions and domestic structures of society that shape them. If anything is required it is merely a degree of reform to rectify occasional 'errors' by wayward individual policy-makers or the consistent monitoring of policy through the instruments available to an open society, in the secure knowledge that, fundamentally, all is well. In short, if we dislike a particular government's policies, we can vote for another one at the next election.

The concept of Britain's basic benevolence is, however, unsustainable in view of the historical and contemporary facts of the real world; it is also of immensely serious import. The Western states' role in international affairs remains the most serious issue with which the contemporary world is confronted. In the current era, there is little doubt who wields primary military and political power and who controls the international economic system: the United States, the European Union and Japan and the business corporations based in these states. Yet the basic political and economic priorities of the leading Western states – especially Britain and the United States, the two leading Western powers of the postwar period – are fundamentally in contradiction with the grand principles assumed to be generally consistent with foreign policy. Since 1945, rather than occasionally deviating from the promotion of peace, democracy, human rights and economic development in the Third World, British (and US) foreign policy has been systematically opposed to them, whether the Conservatives or Labour (or Republicans or Democrats) have been in power. This has had grave consequences for those on the receiving end of Western policies abroad. It also, logically, has implications for those concerned with creating a better society at home.

It would be surprising if the citizens of every country were not told by their leaders that their state stands for benign grand principles, whether that state is a Scandinavian democracy or the most vile of regimes elsewhere. Clearly, that cannot be true since, if it were, then terrible human rights abuses and mass killings would not be permanent features of our world. Responsibility for the world's horrors is always ascribed by state leaders to others. The widespread starvation and poverty that afflict large tracts of the world can more conveniently be depicted as the result of others' policies. In the West, blame can be accorded to despotic Third World leaders who lack even the pretence of concern for their populations. The criticisms may be valid, but they ignore the role of those who often helped install these despots in the first place and who keep them in power through military or economic aid and political support. Such criticisms also ignore the existence of an international political and economic order (organised and controlled by the West) which systematically contributes to, and often directly causes, this suffering.

Another possible view is that the prevalence of poverty and economic underdevelopment (and even of large-scale human rights abuses and war) is somehow in the natural order of things, outside human control and therefore insoluble by human devices. Television images of poverty and starvation often convey the impression that huge numbers of the world's population are simply irredeemably poor. This picture absolves those primarily responsible in the North and South from promoting any fundamental changes in the structure of domestic and international society: conveniently, since that structure happens to work in their favour.

In the real world, the basic fact is that Britain is a major, systematic contributor to much of the world's suffering and horrors and this contribution arises from the basic economic and political priorities that governments pursue at home and abroad. These fundamental policy stances are the result of planning broadly determined by the domestic structures of society which define 'national interests'. One of the most striking facts is that it is relatively easy to demonstrate the reality of British foreign policy. The method used here is to look at the facts of history and the contemporary world, using formerly secret government documents now in the public domain and a variety of other sources from independent organisations, the press and academia.

However, this immediately gives rise to an apparent inconsistency: if it is relatively easy to show that Britain's fundamental priorities contribute significantly to widespread suffering, why is this not a consistently stated notion and a generally held assumption? The answer again concerns the nature of domestic society and forms a crucial component of the system. Despite their rhetoric and, indeed, their power, it is not primarily state leaders who form our understanding of the world but rather the intermediaries between the state and the public who communicate world events to the public – either on an everyday basis through the media or on an often more analytical level in academia. Given time and access to the resources, it is simple to show that the picture of Britain's world role presented by these intermediary mainstream media and academic commentators is geared not to providing accurate descriptions based on fact but rather to serving implicitly the interests of the ruling groups or elites that control policy. There are major, notable exceptions to this, yet the assertion holds true to the extent that it is justified to refer to this as a 'propaganda system'. This propaganda system will be documented in the following pages.

It is a system that functions extremely well, indeed to the degree that it would be misleading to believe that these intermediaries are consciously aware of their role. At one level, it is perfectly easy to understand why supposedly independent commentators might connive with state leaders to produce the required ideology: opportunities for career advancement – in any career – depend essentially on not rocking the boat by threatening established beliefs. Such a conceptualisation most clearly explains conscious deceit on the part of the individual and thus is more in line with a conspiracy theory. By contrast, what occurs more generally is that the fundamental tenets of state ideology – including the grand principles mentioned above, concerning the state's basic benevolence – are necessarily internalised by those communicating them to the public, and they become convenient basic beliefs and ready-made assumptions. (Whether the individual commentator actually believes the stories and interpretations which are peddled is largely irrelevant to this enquiry since – in an institutional analysis – what matters is the final product.) The information system, from which we obtain our knowledge of international affairs, is therefore fundamentally geared to obscuring the realities of state policy in favour of conforming to the necessary ideology. This conceptualisation transcends notions of an individual's or an organisation's 'political bias' and can be applied across virtually the entire information system.

As regards the promotion of the principles noted above – peace, democracy, human rights and Third World economic development – much of Britain's history is embarrassing by virtually any standards, with the defeat of Nazism in the Second World War intervening as an outstanding exception. Since Britain led the world in enslaving what is now known as the Third World by a series of human slaughters and military conquests before instituting an economic imperialism that enforced virtual (and real) slavery on tens of millions of people while using their resources for Britain's enrichment, it is perhaps a wonder that any allegiance to the actions of the British state (patriotism) can still be invoked by state leaders to create support for British policies in the Third World. In 1991, however, during a House of Commons debate on the future of the army, it was still possible for a member of parliament to refer to 'glorious battle honours won over centuries of gallantry and sacrifice'.[9] The words recall Churchill's previously cited assertion about the benign effects of the British empire and his description of 'what is called colonialism' as 'bringing forward backward races and opening up the jungles' (Churchill also noted: 'I was brought up to feel proud of much that we had done').[10] The periodic bouts of nationalist fervour enacted by the public (during the Falklands and Gulf wars, for example) are surely quite irrational from any individual standpoint and are more easily understood by reference to the propaganda system's inherent ability to convey a basically benevolent picture of Britain's world role. Given the facts about the recent history of British foreign policy in the Third World – let alone those about the colonial era – this is a major propaganda achievement.

The central features of British foreign policy in the Third World since 1945 have included brutal military interventions, large-scale abuse of human rights, and opposition to economic development benefiting the poor. Analysis of the historical record reveals that the early postwar interventions in, for example, Malaya and Kenya were far more brutal than customarily presented and that the pursuit of elementary 'national interests' has contributed systematically to human rights abuses throughout the postwar period, for example in South Africa, Indonesia, Chile and Uganda. Other aspects of British policy studied in this book are rarely, if ever, considered in other academic works: for example, the 1953 intervention to overthrow the government of British Guiana, and the removal, beginning in 1965, of the population of Diego Garcia. Consideration of declassified planning documents (see Chapter 4) throws much new light on British interventions and covert operations in the Middle East, especially in Iran, Oman, Jordan and Kuwait.

This study also attempts to elucidate the special relationship with the United States, which became the dominating fact of British foreign policy after planners understood, as early as the 1940s, that Britain could no longer pursue a satisfactory world role independently. The special relationship has entailed consistent (though varying levels of) British support for the foreign policy of the United States, which after 1945 assumed the primary role in constructing a world order on Western guidelines, a role that involved numerous acts of overt and covert aggression for which Britain consequently became (and remains) the primary apologist and supporter. British support for postwar US interventions in Southeast Asia and Latin America is considered in Chapter 6 of this study, whilst in the final chapters I argue that, in the current era, Britain's traditional policy priorities remain predominant. This I show by reviewing British policy in, amongst others, the Gulf War and Indonesia/East Timor and by considering the current international economic order, in which Britain remains a highly significant actor.

By contrast, the view of British foreign policy offered by allegedly independent commentators has, in the overwhelming majority of cases, invariably accorded with state ideology, thus concealing real motivations and their often severe human consequences. In consequence, opposition to state policies has been overcome and public support more easily established. The depiction of Britain's benevolence serves to convince the general public that little or nothing is fundamentally wrong with state policies and priorities, thus reducing the inspiration to work for structural change and marginalising the public further from playing any significant role in the political process. The public is reduced to the status of a mere onlooker, playing no meaningful role in policy-making whilst state leaders profess their commitment to democracy.

To prove the arguments raised here, two things need to be done above all, and have been attempted in the following pages. The first is to examine what British policies and their motivations and effects have actually been and are currently, using historical and contemporary evidence rather than internalised assumptions and ready-made beliefs. The second is to show the vast gulf that exists between the reality of British actions and the descriptions of them by supposedly independent commentators in the information system. The picture of British foreign policy that emerges is vastly different from that customarily presented or assumed. Yet there are very good reasons for concealing reality, since the maintenance of the existing domestic and international power structures and privileges is at stake.

Notes

1. Michael Stewart, *Life and labour: An autobiography*, Sidgwick and Jackson, London, 1980, p. 142.

2. Cited in David Cannadine, *Blood, toil, tears and sweat: Winston Churchill's famous speeches*, Cassell, London, 1989, p. 105, from a speech made in February 1931.

3. Harold Macmillan, *Tides of fortune, 1945–1955*, Macmillan, London, 1969, p. 228.

4. Dennis Austin, 'A South African policy: six precepts in search of a diplomacy?', in *International Affairs*, Vol. 62, No. 3, Summer 1986, p. 392.

5. F.S. Northedge, *Descent from power: British foreign policy 1945–1973*, George Allen and Unwin, London, 1974, p. 221.

6. Christopher Tugendhat and William Wallace, *Options for British foreign policy in the 1990s*, Routledge/Royal Institute of International Affairs, London, 1988, pp. 9–10.

7. Ibid., p. 91.

8. Joseph Frankel, *British foreign policy 1945–1973*, Royal Institute of International Affairs /Oxford University Press, London, 1975, pp. 119–20.

9. Nikki Knewstub, 'Seven Tories vote against defence cut proposals', *Guardian*, 16 October 1991.

10. Churchill to Eisenhower, 8 August 1954, in Peter Boyle (ed.), *The Churchill–Eisenhower correspondence 1953–1955*, University of North Carolina Press, Chapel Hill, 1990, p. 167.

PART ONE

THE POSTWAR SYSTEM

CHAPTER I

AIMS AND PRIORITIES

In the first few years after the end of the Second World War the essential framework of international politics in the postwar world, and Britain's place within it, was established. It is therefore instructive to take a close look at the developments of those early years and, in particular, at the motives and interests of the Western powers that primarily shaped them, namely, the United States and Britain.

The British empire and great power status

Of paramount importance to British leaders immediately after the Second World War was the maintenance of great power status. Ernest Bevin, Foreign Secretary in the Attlee Labour government, observed in 1945 the traditional British actions that had secured such a status in the first place, by drawing an instructive parallel with contemporary Soviet designs. He told the Soviet Foreign Minister that 'just as a British admiral, when he saw an island, instinctively wanted to grab it, so the Soviet government, if they saw a piece of land, wanted to acquire it'.[1] Whilst the Soviet Union was doing precisely this throughout Eastern Europe, one extra territory to be grabbed as part of the British postwar booty was Cyrenaica, part of the former Italian colony of Libya. 'In view of the potential strategic value of Cyrenaica for His Majesty's Government, it is highly desirable that the territory should be brought under British influence,'[2] Bevin wrote in August 1945, reflecting the fact that this land-grabbing was one aspect of a policy designed to render Libya a British client state. The Foreign Office noted that Libya would need 'to be the client of some power' and that it would need to 'be kept to some extent under our tutelage'.[3] This policy had significant consequences, contributing to a heightening of tensions between the Soviet Union and the West and, much later, to the rise of an anti-Western revolutionary regime under Qadafi, which overthrew the client regime in 1969.

A proposed redrawing of the boundary between Italian Somaliland (a colony of defeated Italy) and Kenya (a colony of Britain) provided a further illustration of how Britain intended to pursue a traditional pastime in the new era. 'If either Greater Somalia or Italian Somaliland is under non-British administration', the Foreign Office noted in 1945, it would be 'desirable' to return to Kenya the territory ceded from it to the Italian colony in 1942. However, if Britain were to gain control of Somalia and Italian Somaliland, 'then it may be administratively convenient' to include this territory under British jurisdiction, also adding in 'part of the present Northern frontier district of Kenya' as well.[4]

In a reversal of fortunes for the British empire, during the Second World War capturing territory had become a German and Japanese pursuit; Japan's military conquests of many of Britain's Asian colonies endangered the resumption of British control over them after the war's end. The political adviser to Admiral Louis Mountbatten explained that the British aim was 'the restoration of our political position south of the Tropic of Cancer'.[5] The adviser observed that it would be unfortunate if the Japanese simply surrendered to the British rather than allow Britain to regain the territories by fighting. 'If we are prevented by Japanese surrender from fighting battles for the recovery of the S[outh] E[ast] A[sia] C[ommand], it is of paramount importance that we should make the best possible showing in our re-occupation of territories which the Japanese have overrun.'[6] A similar reasoning applied to the British colony of Hong Kong. The Colonial Office remarked that 'a most embarrassing situation may ... arise in the event of Hong Kong being liberated by Chinese forces'[7] rather than British. Unless, that is, there were an agreement with the Chinese leader to hand back the territory to Britain.

There were further dangers to continued colonial control. Britain was particularly worried that if other European powers were to lose control over their colonies this could affect the British position in theirs. The Foreign Office, referring to the French mandates in the Levant, for example, noted the 'potential effect on our interests in Egypt and Iraq' of 'an exaggerated attitude on the part of the Levant states',[8] meaning their desire for independence.

There was also the potential threat of international control of the colonies under the auspices of the newly established United Nations (UN). Britain's view was that such UN control would be a 'retrograde step' and would mean that 'control would be exercised by a body the majority of whose members was both prejudiced and ignorant on colonial affairs'.[9] The Foreign Office explained in 1950, in reference to the United Nations: 'the present is a critical time period in the development of the colonial empire and ignorant or prejudiced outside interference could do untold harm.'[10] Generally, 'the United Nations is not an ideal instrument for shaping international policies on purely British lines', the Foreign Office noted. 'It is clear that many of the objectives of British foreign policy are being pursued independently of the United Nations and some, indeed, perhaps in spite of it.' The UN represented clear dangers to customary British foreign policy, notably from what were referred to as the 'backward nations of Asia and the Middle East'. Britain also pointed out the drawbacks of democracy in the organisation, declaring that 'the possibility, under the system of "one state, one vote", for small nations to exert undue influence may endanger the ability of the United Kingdom and Commonwealth to preserve their essential interests from United Nations interference'.[11]

On the other hand, the UN could at times be helpful to Britain: 'much of the work of the United Nations may be usefully directed to serve the purposes of the United Kingdom'.[12] Bevin explained, for example, that the 'security' of the route through the Mediterranean and Middle East was 'vital to the safety of the British empire'. This needed to be retained 'under the World Organisation' but Britain should 'refuse to share' it with the USSR, a member of the UN Security Council.[13] Similarly, with regard to military facilities in Cyrenaica, London School of Economics historian John Kent assesses the British position thus: 'there would be no objection to sharing these under the aegis of the United Nations provided they were controlled by Britain or a state on whose friendship the British could rely'.[14] There was, thus, no distinction made between control by Britain and control by the United Nations. (This stance helps to explain Western leaders' eagerness in the 1990s to have the UN function now as it was supposed to do after the Second World War: to operate, that is, under their control.)[15] The 'ignorant or prejudiced outside interference' of the UN in the pursuit of basic foreign policy priorities necessarily had to be prevented, a stance that has remained consistent throughout the postwar period up to the 1990s.

At the root of Britain's aim of upholding its great power status – and central to an understanding of the nature of the world order being constructed under Anglo-American guidelines – lay the desire to use the world's economic resources for its own benefit. As the Governor of Kenya had explained, Britain was in Africa to 'develop and civilise this continent as part of what I may call Western European civilisation and economics'.[16] The consequences if Britain were to lose overall control over its domains were spelt out in a top-secret Treasury document of April 1950: 'Any general withdrawal by the United Kingdom on the political and military fronts would have an adverse effect on our economic position'.[17] A Foreign Office memorandum written at the same time similarly concluded:

> ... if the United Kingdom were voluntarily to abandon her position of political influence in selected areas, she would probably find herself not only without economic access to those areas but unable, through loss of prestige, to prevent a further involuntary decline in her influence elsewhere and consequently a general decline in the strength of the Western powers.[18]

Similarly, it was the re-establishment of Britain's 'commercial position' in China and Japan, Bevin wrote in a secret memorandum in 1950, that guided British policy in the Far East immediately after the war.[19] And similarly, one might add, elsewhere.

A 1950 Foreign Office document entitled 'British overseas obligations: A regional survey' reveals Britain's postwar economic interests and priorities in various of the world's regions. 'Africa', the document stated 'is an important source of raw materials in peace and war ... these materials are of particular importance now and in the long term to the United Kingdom as they both earn and save dollars.' Southeast Asia, meanwhile, was 'a substantial economic asset and a net earner of dollars'; the document noted that the colony of 'Malaya alone had a surplus of $145 million in 1948'. As regards the Middle East, its oil resources were of 'paramount importance'. 'United Kingdom oil companies have made large net profits since the war (£50 million by the A[nglo] I[ranian] O[il] C[orporation] alone in 1948).' The report noted that these profits were offset by 'the retention in the Middle East of a major part of the profits for the purpose of oil expansion and development' but that 'this development should however yield rich results in due course'. Furthermore, 'the oil produced is ... essential to the United Kingdom and earns commodities from other countries which might otherwise cost dollars. This dollar expenditure too should yield rich dividends in the future.' 'It is estimated that the denial of the Middle East to the United Kingdom would involve a loss in United Kingdom export trade of about £150 million sterling per annum.'[20] As regards the United States, meanwhile, their concerns in the Middle East were 'based upon their interest in oil producing areas, eg, Saudi Arabia and Persia, and upon their growing realisation that there is a growing market both for commercial enterprise and for ancillary services, eg, civil aviation'.[21]

Rich pickings were therefore to be had, provided control over the international system and the world's economically important regions could be maintained, by military interventions or covert operations if necessary. Ensuring 'economic access' to the world's resources – the overall stimulant to British and other European colonialism – would continue in the aftermath of the Second World War, to provide the basis for policy. In this Britain was joined – in fact overtaken – by the United States; US planning documents also clearly reveal that the harnessing of the world's economic resources to the Western economies, and specifically to the economy of the USA, was the central aim of the new world order under construction (see below).

In pursuing its first-order priorities, Britain initially attempted to establish a 'third force' between the United States and the USSR. This was a scheme, of vast proportions, for a joint Western European exploitation of colonial resources. A Foreign Office paper drawn up in July 1945 remarked thus:

> ... it is essential that we should increase our strength in not only the diplomatic but also the economic and military spheres. This clearly can best be done by

enrolling France and the lesser Western European powers and, of course, also
the Dominions, as collaborators with us in this tripartite system.[22]

The scheme aimed at establishing 'an African Union under European
auspices'; this 'would not fear comparison either in manpower or in
agricultural and mineral resources with either the United States or the
Soviet Union'.[23] As John Kent has commented, the Foreign Secretary,
Bevin, viewed Africa 'as a valuable source of manpower and raw materials;
with a commitment to colonial development the Foreign Secretary saw
potential benefits for imperial trade as well as imperial defence'. Bevin
observed that 'it would be necessary to mobilise the resources of Africa
in support of West European Union', and that 'two great mountains of
manganese are in Sierra Leone etc. US is very barren of essential minerals
and in Africa we have them all.' Bevin's aim for the Middle East, meanwhile, was to develop 'a prosperous producing area which would assist
the British economy and replace India as an important market for British
goods'. The aim of using colonial resources for the benefit of the British
economy was also made explicit in the proposed establishment of the
Colonial Development Corporation. This would 'promote ... the production of foodstuffs, raw materials and manufactures where supply to
the UK or sale overseas will assist our balance of payments'. The plan
was supported by the Chancellor of the Exchequer, who noted that 'the
development of our African resources in particular is ... of prime importance and must be a major consideration in planning our economic
activities'. Harold Wilson, then President of the Board of Trade, concurred,
remarking that successful colonial 'development' might uphold Western
Europe's position *vis-à-vis* the United States. Field Marshal Montgomery
claimed that British living standards could be maintained by Africa's
minerals, raw materials, land and cheap coal, the problem being that the
African was 'a complete savage' incapable of developing these resources
himself.[24]

Similar reasoning – urging exploitation disguised as development – had
been outlined by the British Treasury in 1945. 'We have to devise
techniques for bringing influence to bear upon other countries' internal
decisions,' one paper read. 'We should be able to exert a very great
influence upon the structure of that development' and 'we could usefully
begin with parts of the world in which we already have great influence –
the colonial empire, the Middle East and India.' The Treasury further
commented: that ' ... we need not overtly use the sterling balances as a
weapon; but the fact remains that if those countries want to be repaid in
goods they will be very well advised to accept our advice on the general
course of their development.'[25]

These plans conceived at the highest levels of state provide some
interesting insights into British priorities and reasoning in the postwar

period. Note that African resources are 'ours', a consistent assumption of colonial governments. Pacific islands captured by Britain are referred to as 'our islands',[26] whilst uranium supplies in the Congo, then a colony of Belgium, are referred to as 'their' (i.e. Belgian) minerals.[27] Even the latter became 'ours', at least partly, as 'the English-speaking combination' of the USA, Britain and Canada undertook 'measures to assure to ourselves exclusive supplies and control of these raw materials', in the words of the Foreign Office. This had the fortunate added effect of bringing 'into the English-speaking orbit the countries with whom we have negotiated agreements'. The drawback, a Foreign Office memorandum noted, was that:

> ... if and when these [measures] become known to the Soviet government they will increase their suspicion; and that government's probable desire to make similar agreements with e.g. Czechoslovakia will increase the drift towards ... rival spheres of influence. ... we shall ... have to reckon with an appeal by the Soviet or some other government to the fourth article of the Atlantic Charter which pledges its signatories to further the enjoyment of all states ... of access on equal terms to the raw materials of the world.[28]

'We must be prepared for a real hubbub when the Russians hear we are trying to corner the raw material,' read a Foreign Office minute of 1945, revealing its real attitude to the principle of 'equal access' to the world's resources discussed below.[29]

'Development' for the colonies in reality meant development for the West. In effect, Western 'development' programmes entail the transfer of resources from poor to rich, a basic goal that has been achieved on a significant scale in the decades since 1945 as well in the colonial era, providing a source of much Third World poverty. Britain's application of its postwar scheme for colonial 'development' provides ample evidence of this. According to historian David Fieldhouse:

> The basic fact is that between 1945 and 1951 Britain exploited those dependencies that were politically unable to defend their own interests in more ways and with more serious consequences than at any time since overseas colonies were established. ... Between 1946 ... and 1951, total Colonial Development and Welfare expenditure throughout the whole empire was only about £40.5 million or around £8 million a year. In the same period colonial sterling balances held in London ... rose by some £150 million. In addition, in 1951 West African marketing boards held £93 million on deposit in London. That is, one way or another, the colonies were lent or given some £40 million by Britain but were forced to lend or tie up in London about £250 million. This was disinvestment on the grand scale, the most accurate assessment of the extent of British imperial exploitation.[30]

Fieldhouse notes that by using the sterling area – the large part of the world where the British pound was the trading currency – as a device for supporting the pound, 'the colonies were compelled to subsidise Britain's postwar standard of living'. Equally, the system of bulk buying of Third World commodities by Britain – at prices set in London which were well below the world market price – became a weapon 'to extract wealth from peasant producers'.[31]

By 1949, however, and despite these achievements, it was clear that the 'third force' scheme – which would institutionalise this exploitation further – could not be realised due to Britain's overall weakness relative to the superpowers and the pressure to decolonise, and the idea was officially abandoned. British foreign policy subsequently embarked upon a dual track. The first was a so-called transfer of power in the colonies, where possible to elements who could be relied upon to continue to give Britain favoured treatment, in particular by guaranteeing British access to their economies and raw materials. This was a first step in the establishment of the postwar partnership between the Northern states and the elite elements who presided over policy in the South; working together they could secure their own interests, at the expense only of the Third World populations. Britain 'must ensure that any major obligations it gives up are taken over by its friends', the Foreign Office outlined in a 1950 memorandum.[32] Professor Cranford Pratt of the University of Toronto observes that 'all that Hailey, Cohen and their colleagues [the British planners who drew up the plans for decolonisation] advocated can be interpreted as shrewdly designed to protect and advance British economic and political interests in these changing circumstances'.[33] Indeed, there was often an understanding that, by granting independence, British interests could be even more safely assured than under formal colonialism, since the new project of nominal independence could foster the collaboration of hitherto excluded elements such as educated elites. The 1947 Cohen–Caine report on the colonies 'was a plan to convert (or reconvert) formal into informal empire as the need arose' and therefore 'such colonial reform would extend the life of colonial control'.[34] We return to these British objectives in Chapter 3.

The second change of track for British foreign policy – the seeds of which were already present, particularly as regards Europe – was the establishment of a 'special relationship' with the United States, entailing basic support for US foreign policy goals. This, it was understood, could enable Britain to salvage its international status, help ensure a US commitment to Western European security, and in addition enable the continuation of colonial plunder. It is to the British alignment with US policy that I now turn.

The 'junior partner' under US hegemony

The essential framework of the postwar world was very much the product of Anglo-American power, signified by the Atlantic Charter and the establishment in the 1940s of the Bretton Woods financial system, the

International Monetary Fund (IMF) and the World Bank. US foreign policy priorities after the end of the Second World War were centred on the economic organisation of the new international system. Throughout the war and in the postwar years, US leaders consistently reiterated the same aim: the creation of an 'open door' in international trade and investment, whereby all states would be granted 'equal access' to the world's economic resources and raw materials, unfettered by trade barriers and other obstacles in the way of international business. US leaders stated that 'the United States regards barriers or onerous restrictions imposed by governments on the investment and withdrawal of foreign capital as likely to deter investment and economic development generally'.[35] Also, 'American enterprises in other countries should be assured the right of access to raw materials and markets and to labour supply of the host country on the same terms as business enterprises operated therein by its citizens or by citizens of third countries'.[36] The consistently repeated goal was the establishment of an international economic order that would not 'hamper the natural and normal flow of economic and commercial activity throughout the world'.[37]

Since the United States had emerged from the Second World War as the world's most powerful nation, it alone was in a position to construct and, to a large extent, impose such an order. Despite the rhetoric about 'equal access' under the rubric of 'free trade' and the 'open door', it was clear that US business interests would be the prime beneficiaries from such a system. This was not, of course, surprising. Britain had supported free trade during its period as the world's hegemonic power, since its overall competitive position then had ensured that it would be the prime beneficiary. When it began to lose that competitive edge Britain adopted a system of 'imperial preference', safeguarding its economic interests from now more competitive rivals – the most important being the United States and Germany – through protectionist measures.

Whilst it became customary for media and academic commentators to note US 'pre-eminence' or even 'hegemony' in the postwar world, what this meant in practice was far from innocent. US goals were outlined by the US State Department's Policy Planning Staff in a top-secret report in February 1948.[38] The report noted that the US has 'about 50% of the world's wealth but only 6.3% of its population. ... In this situation we cannot fail to be the object of envy and resentment.'

> Our real task in the coming period is to devise a pattern of relationships which will permit us to maintain this position of disparity without positive detriment to our national security. To do so, we will have to dispose with all sentiment and day-dreaming; and our attention will have to be concentrated everywhere on our immediate national objectives. We need not deceive ourselves that we can afford the luxury of altruism and world-benefaction.

As part of this reasoning, the report observed: 'we should cease to talk about vague and – for the Far East – unreal objectives such as human rights, the raising of living standards and democratisation. The day is not far off when we are going to have to deal in straight power concepts.' Similar notions were contained in a secret 1954 report to the President from a special Hoover Commission subcommittee. The report contained the following statement:

> ... hitherto accepted norms of human conduct do not apply. ... to survive, long standing American concepts of 'fair play' must be reconsidered. We must ... learn to subvert, sabotage and destroy our enemies by more clever, more sophisticated and more effective methods than those used against us.[39]

In rather clear terms these reports reveal the US priorities that were to underlie its global pre-eminence. Their relevance to subsequent US policy and the development of the postwar world is striking. The aim of maintaining a global 'disparity' of wealth – a fundamental requirement – is a concept crucial to understanding the nature of postwar North–South relations. The irrelevance of human rights to the leading Western powers is another leitmotif of postwar history, with equally horrifying consequences. Dispensing with what the State Department report called 'romantic and universalistic concepts', US leaders were to make 'straight power concepts' the order of the day. For the establishment of a 'truly stable world order can proceed ... only from the older, mellower and more advanced nations of the world'.

The fact that these nations were democracies provided some problems in the straight exercise of power, since their governments were at least finally accountable to the public. But, as a former US Under Secretary of State explained:

> ... there are very few things that a democracy cannot do if given a particular combination of circumstances and necessity. It is impossible to draw a sharp line between democratic principles and immoral actions, and an attempt to do so constitutes a dangerous and unnecessary handicap.[40]

In fact, little effort was made to draw such a distinction, as the leading Western states, led by the United States, embarked upon numerous acts of violence to secure their primary goals.[41]

Britain, with little choice but to accept the new, US-led order, opted for the role the US intended it to play, that of a 'junior partner in an orbit of power predominantly under American aegis' (John Balfour, of the British embassy in Washington).[42]

In 1953 Churchill wrote to US President Dwight Eisenhower: ' ... my Number One is Britain with her eighty million white English-speaking people' – those of the right colour in the British domains – 'working with your one hundred and forty million'.[43] But the formalisation of the relationship with Britain as the junior partner was begun by a Labour government and continued by subsequent Labour and Conservative governments alike. Great power status and the special relationship reinforced each other. The Foreign Office noted in 1950 that 'so long … as the United Kingdom maintains her position as a world power and increases her economic strength and stability the United States may be expected to continue to welcome her as an intimate, but not exclusive, partner'. But 'a disastrous weakening of the British position' might result in the US being 'forced to consider possible alternative lines of policy'.[44]

In realising its plans for a 'truly stable world order' under its hegemony, general US policy in the years immediately following the Second World War was to support the Europeans in maintaining control over their colonies. At the end of the war there was 'clear agreement with the Americans that in British territories in the Far East which are in an American command, the policies to be followed on the liberation of those territories shall be laid down by H[er] M[ajesty's] G[overnment] and accepted by the American force commander'.[45] In 1950, the Foreign Office observed that 'there is basic agreement on the long term objectives of colonial policy as conceived by the United Kingdom and United States',[46] including in Africa, where the UK had been successfully engaged in a programme of economic exploitation of vast proportions. The US Policy Planning Staff noted in 1948 possible 'arrangements whereby a union of Western European nations would undertake jointly the economic development and exploitation of the colonial and dependent areas of the African continent'. This, it noted, 'has much to recommend it'.[47] The main reason for this was that 'the United States realises the importance to her own economy, in peace and war, of many British colonial resources and the possibilities of their further development'.[48] '"Black" Africa', the State Department explained, 'is an important source of raw materials. … Manganese, cobalt, columbite, industrial diamonds, chrome ore, uranium, rubber, palm oil, asbestos, graphite, vanadium, mica, copper, tin and many other materials of considerable importance to the United States are produced there.'[49] Former South African prime minister Jan Smuts agreed, declaring: 'Africa should be developed as an appendage of Europe with the European peoples taking the lead. The African native has shown individual capability, however, the natives do not have the drive which is characteristic of Europeans.'[50]

A top-secret document of 1950 dealing with Anglo-American ministerial talks on the 'colonial question' revealed US priorities:

> The United States believes in the advancement of the economic and, where suitable, the strategic advantages to France and the United Kingdom of their colonies and trust territories. The United States expects that equal economic treatment will be given to American capital and American nationals who engage in trade in the African colonial areas … The United States desires to have

access to raw materials, air and sea facilities, air routes and communications points and to guaranteed right of equal economic treatment in the African colonial territories.[51]

US support for the continued exploitation of the Third World and the upholding of the Europeans' colonial position extended to France as well as Britain and the economic motives for this were clearly paramount, as is shown in the US stance towards Indochina, where from 1946 France was fighting a bloody war of reconquest against the Vietnamese independence movement. The US Secretary of State observed in 1947: 'we have fully recognised France's sovereign position in that area and we do not wish it to appear that we are in any way endeavouring [to] undermine that position'.[52] At the same time US officials acknowledged that, as the US Consul in Vietnam put it, the 'French record in past, especially past two years, impingement on and unilateral derogation of native rights, certainly inspires no great confidence that French will willingly grant more than such minimum as will satisfy world opinion'.[53] The Vietnamese, the consul stated, 'have, under the French "colonialist" regime of the past 60 years, witnessed the creation of a most efficient machine of exploitation and self-interest, centring in the Bank of Indochina and the fabulous import–export firms, but also extending throughout all grades and ranks of French commerce and officialdom'.[54]

US planners further noted that Indochina could be a 'most lucrative economy'[55]. The US government should 'encourage American business interests to initiate and enlarge their efforts in trade and industrial relations, stressing the positive contribution American business can make and disabusing the peoples of Southeast Asia of the idea that American business means exploitation per se'.[56] Britain also supported the French position in the area; the Joint Chiefs of Staff noted in 1950: 'nothing is more important than to make sure that the French restore order and establish a stable and ultimately independent friendly government in Indo-China'.[57] Britain's primary reasons were the same as those of the US:

> In the UK view, the economic development of South and Southeast Asia should contribute not only to the welfare of Southeast Asia but also to the balance of world trade by developing sources of raw material for the United States and Europe.[58]

The UK, the United States and France agreed that it is 'important for the economy of Western Europe that Western European trading and business interests in Southeast Asia should be maintained', since the 'countries of Southeast Asia are rich in natural resources and certain countries in the area at present produce surplus foodstuffs'.[59] These economic priorities and interests underlay the US war against Vietnam in the 1960s and 1970s, conducted under the mantle of the 'communist threat' and the idea that the Vietnamese were stooges of the Kremlin, but with the United States's major interests being well understood and well documented.[60]

As regards French colonies elsewhere, the US position envisaged that 'North African states under France's benevolent tutelage develop into friendly partners which will be bulwarks of a strong France'.[61] 'We are not seeking to disrupt their empire or to place in jeopardy their position in North Africa,' the Policy Planning Staff noted.[62] This position was taken in the knowledge that 'French North Africa and North Africa as a whole are anachronisms in the present period of history, since they are among the last areas in which imperialism of the old school is practised, as a prestige instrument and for economic reasons'.[63] The message was clear: a new form of control – replacing old-style imperialism – was required. The United States envisaged 'evolution toward self-government while concurrently safeguarding economic development of country and legitimate French interests in area by integration into French Union': self-government, that is, under French control.[64]

But effective control of the world economy meant control over the world's oil reserves and thus the Middle East. Britain believed that the area was 'a vital prize for any power interested in world influence or domination'.[65] For the United States the oil resources of Saudi Arabia were 'a stupendous source of strategic power and one of the greatest material prizes in world history'.[66] At the end of the Second World War Britain had been the pre-eminent power in the Middle East; its oil companies held major concessions in the Gulf states and the British government wielded effective political domination over them. The United States initially supported the British position in the area in the knowledge that, as the State Department put it, 'it was long the British policy to keep the people flanking the sea route to India in a state of primitive economy'.[67] 'The peoples of the region', it noted, 'remain for the most part ignorant, poverty-stricken and diseased.'[68] In 1945 the United States noted that:

> our petroleum policy toward the United Kingdom is predicated on a mutual recognition of a very extensive joint interest and upon a control, at least for the moment, of the great bulk of the free petroleum resources of the world. ... US–UK agreement upon a broad, forward-looking pattern for the development and utilisation of petroleum resources under the control of nationals of the two countries is of the highest strategic and commercial importance.[69]

As the postwar period progressed, the US began to displace Britain as the primary controlling power, however, and attempted to secure primarily for itself that 'control ... of the great bulk of the petroleum resources of the world'. This was realised above all in the CIA- and MI6-sponsored coup in Iran in 1953, which gave US oil corporations an increased share of that country's oil revenues (see Chapter 4). A 1953 internal US document declared: 'United States policy is to keep the sources of oil in the Middle

East in American hands'.[70] The 'older, mellower and more advanced' nations of the world were continuing to exert their control over Middle Eastern resources, but the share of the profits gradually reflected who was the new hegemonic power.

Given the stakes involved, everything feasible was to be done to prevent interference with Western control over these resources, a basic requirement that continues into the present. As regards Saudi Arabia – in which 'an American company has an oil concession of great potential importance to American strategic as well as commercial and political interests' – the US had 'every interest' in 'maintaining peace and order in the country', meaning helping to maintain in power elements who would continue its favoured treatment.[71] Perhaps this was one reason why 'among increasing numbers of Arabs there is ... a conviction that we are backing the corrupt governments now in power, without regard to the welfare of the masses',[72] who were being kept in check 'through police and other repressive measures'.[73] Clearly, little has changed throughout the decades, which is no small indicator of the success of the policy; and it helps, additionally, to maintain that 'disparity' of wealth that was such a central US aim.

One way of maintaining stability was to provide arms to the Saudi regime, another practice of key importance in the present era, and one that helps to 'keep the goodwill of the king and other important Saudi Arabs', as it was put in 1947.[74] The United States made it clear that its policy was to confine arms sales to countries of the Middle East to reasonable quantities required for the maintenance of 'internal security', that is, control over the population.[75] The alleged Soviet threat also proved useful: the West could claim that the presence of its military forces in the region was intended to deter Soviet aggression. But the reality was somewhat different. As the State Department noted, 'the Dharan airbase [in Saudi Arabia] is the most important "strategic facility" in the area, and its rehabilitation ... would be very helpful in strengthening our position in a country whose oil resources are of such vital importance'.[76] Similar reasoning applied to the 'sheikhdoms, sultanates etc' south of the Persian Gulf, 'where oil development might be tied up with the installation of "ghost" airfields, which would provide defence in depth and also be accessible by sea'.[77]

Aside from Saudi Arabia, 'the position of the rulers of the Persian Gulf might be thought of as that of independence regulated, supervised and defined' by the British government, as the US Department of State put it.[78] As regards Kuwait, the Foreign Office policy was clear:

If the way were ... opened to Egyptian and Iraqi penetration there would be a real danger that Kuwait would be rapidly infected with all the ultra-nationalist maladies from which those two countries are at present suffering. Kuwait would become involved in Arab League affairs and in all the rivalries and intrigues which now divide the Arab states. This involvement of Kuwait in Middle East politics would be to the advantage neither of the United States nor ourselves.[79]

Kuwait would therefore be nurtured as an outpost of the new empire, supplying its oil, and the revenues from its oil, to the West, while it was kept out of regional politics altogether, a necessity in view of the 'ultra-nationalist maladies' that were infecting the region and threatening Western control.

Thus the Foreign Office was correct in stating, '... there is ... no difference between the USA and the United Kingdom in their broad conception of the sort of economic world which is wanted,' as the two collaborated to achieve primary goals.[80] Yet US support for Britain was coupled with a desire on the part of the United States to exercise its overall hegemony in the new system, a wielding of power that involved some fundamental British sacrifices and that often outraged British planners. The British embassy in Washington noted the USA's general 'trend towards hegemony',[81] and the Foreign Office remarked on 'American imperialism in the South East Pacific',[82] wondering whether the USA 'must increasingly feel that – although they may avoid the word "colonial" – a quasi-colonial status alone can protect any part of Asia'.[83] Bevin, as Foreign Secretary, noted in 1950 that in the Far East 'the United States have tended to be a law unto themselves since the end of the war';[84] the Foreign Office, referring to the Philippines and Thailand by 1951 as 'American stooges' (in fact, somewhat correctly) noted: 'it is very difficult to escape the conclusion that the United States is seeking to determine the future of Asia without taking Asia into account', a practice with which the memorandum's authors were surely familiar. The world, the memorandum continued, was one 'which is still governed by power and by fear', a not unreasonable assessment – then or now – given an understanding of the motives and priorities of some of the powers who have shaped it.[85]

In a 1945 memorandum, Bevin viewed the exercise of US foreign policy as 'power politics naked and unashamed'. There was 'a great difference' he believed, in the 'spheres of influence' approach 'from anything that has existed hitherto'. He continued thus:

Whereas under the old Monroe system economic institutions and the system of government afforded liberty of trade and intercourse to other countries of the world, present tendencies are quite different. If you take Russia, for instance, all the argument and pressure that is going on indicates that in the whole life of the communities concerned there is an attempt to incorporate it into the Russian complete economy while the United States, notwithstanding their claim to establish multilateral agreements with trade, appear to me to be taking similar steps so far as the Far East and South America are concerned by financial and economic methods.[86]

This appraisal of US policy could in fact be applied to the entire non-Soviet world which, it is clear from the documents, it was fully the United States's intention to subsume under its overall hegemony.[87]

At the inaugural meeting of the Board of Governors of the IMF and the International Bank for Reconstruction and Development (the World Bank) the US representatives 'were shown to be using all the methods prevalent in their own domestic political arena to organise a cohesive bloc of subservient followers, and to push through decisions against which there was a substantial volume of serious, cogent opposition'.[88] Britain complained in 1945 that 'at this moment of weakness we were being forced to abandon traditional habits by ruthless exercise of economic power'.[89] One way in which this occurred was by the combined force of the US government and US business interests. For example, the British embassy in Washington made this observation:

> ... federal regulated civil aviation lines can rely upon constant official support to secure the foreign bases and facilities necessary to enable them to girdle the globe. The weight of administrative backing can readily be mobilised for the establishment of American-controlled telecommunications systems in un-developed regions and for securing the maximum possible American share in the exploitation of Middle East oil resources.[90]

In this vein, the US Secretary of State 'recently informed Mr Bevin that the United States government expect [Britain] and the New Zealand government to waive their claims to twenty-five Pacific islands'.[91] The New Zealand government commented that 'no-one had worried much about what country these disputed islands belonged to until the growth of civil aviation plans shortly before the war'. Some of the islands over which 'the United States now asked that their sovereignty be recognized actually formed part of New Zealand metropolitan territory (the Northern Cook Group)'.[92]

This was correctly described as 'the outward thrust of American business interests which see in the advent of peace an opportunity for acquiring a predominant position for themselves not merely in the Western Hemisphere but in other continents'.[93] The US government would provide the conditions for these aims to be realised, invariably referred to as 'containing' Soviet expansion or defending the 'free world'. The non-Soviet world was to be organized along these lines but there were still substantial threats to overcome.

Notes

1. Record of a conversation at the US Ambassador's residence, Moscow, 17 December 1945, in Great Britain, FCO, *Documents on British Foreign Policy Overseas*, Series I, Volume II, London, HMSO (hereafter *Documents on British Foreign Policy*), p. 735.

2. Memorandum by Bevin and Hall, 25 August 1945, *Documents on British Foreign Policy*, Ser. I, Vol. II, p. 30.

3. W. Roger Louis, 'Libyan independence, 1951: the creation of a client state', in Prosser Gifford and W. Roger Louis (eds), *Decolonisation and African independence: The transfer of power, 1960–1980*, Yale University Press, London, 1988, pp. 170, 183.

4. Foreign Office brief, 13 July 1945, *Documents on British Foreign Policy overseas*, Ser. I, Vol. I, p. 269.

5. Dening to Sterndale-Bennett, 13 July 1945, *Documents on British Foreign Policy*, Ser. I, Vol. I, p. 271.

6. Dening to Sterndale-Bennett, 2 August 1945, *Documents on British Foreign Policy*, Ser. I, Vol. I, p. 1256.

7. Arrangements for the Administration of Hong Kong in the event of Its Liberation by Regular Chinese forces, enclosure in G. Gater to A. Cadogan, 28 July 1945, *Documents on British Foreign Policy*, Ser. I, Vol. I, p. 1184.

8. J. Anderson to Shone, 15 July 1945, *Documents on British Foreign Policy*, Ser. I, Vol. I, p. 294.

9. United Kingdom/United States ministerial talks, 8 May 1950, *Documents on British Foreign Policy*, Calendar to Ser. II, Vol. II, pp. 491–2.

10. Brief by Wright for Bevin, 6 May 1950, *Documents on British Foreign Policy*, Ser. II, Vol. II, p. 245.

11. Permanent Under-Secretary's Committee, 'The United Kingdom and the United Nations', 25 April 1950, *Documents on British Foreign Policy*, Calendar to Ser. II, Vol. II, pp. 137–47.

12. Permanent Under-Secretary's Committee, 'The United Kingdom and the United Nations', 25 April 1950, *Documents on British Foreign Policy*, Calendar to Ser. II, Vol. II, pp. 138.

13. Memorandum by Bevin, 10 September 1945, *Documents on British Foreign Policy*, Ser. I, Vol. II, p. 81.

14. John Kent, 'The British empire and the origins of the cold war', in Ann Deighton (ed.), *Britain and the first cold war*, Macmillan, London, 1990, p. 172.

15. For example, US National Security Adviser Brent Scowcroft remarked during the 1990–91 Gulf crisis: '… what we are seeing is the UN beginning to operate as it was foreseen to operate when it was established in 1945–6'. Martin Walker, 'The eagle soars again', *Guardian*, 1 September 1990; See also Thatcher's speech at the Aspen Institute, quoted in *Independent*, 6 August 1990, and George Bush's address to Congress, United States Information Service, *Official Text*, p. 4.

16. Cranford Pratt, 'Colonial governments and the transfer of power in East Africa', in Prosser Gifford and W. Roger Louis (eds), *The transfer of power in Africa: Decolonisation 1940–1960*, Yale University Press, London, 1982, p. 261.

17. Brief by E. Plowden for S. Cripps, 25 April 1950, *Documents on British Foreign Policy*, Ser. II, Vol. II, p. 131.

18. Memorandum for the Permanent Under-Secretary's Committee, 27 April 1950, *Documents on British Foreign Policy*, Ser. II, Vol. II, p. 171.

19. Memorandum by Bevin, 30 August 1950, *Documents on British Foreign Policy*, Ser. II, Vol. IV, p. 119.

20. Permanent Under-Secretary's Committee, 'British overseas obligations: Regional survey', 27 April 1950, *Documents on British Foreign Policy*, Calendar to Ser. II, Vol. II, pp. 310–17.

21. Minute by Mason, 4 April 1946, *Documents on British Foreign Policy*, Ser. I, Vol. IV, p. 208.

22. Orme Sargent, 'Stocktaking after V.E. Day', 11 July 1945, in Graham Ross (ed.), *The Foreign Office and the Kremlin: British documents on Anglo-Soviet relations 1941–45*, Cambridge University Press, Cambridge, 1984 (hereafter *The Foreign Office and the Kremlin*), p. 211.

23. Duff Cooper, Britain's ambassador to Paris, cited by John Kent, 'Bevin's imperialism and the idea of Euro-Africa, 1945–49', in Michael Dockrill and John Young (eds), *British foreign policy, 1945–56*, Macmillan, London, 1989, p. 52.

24. Kent, 'Bevin's imperialism', pp. 52–66.

25. Memorandum by Richard Clarke, 11 May 1945, in Alec Cairncross (ed.), *Anglo-American economic collaboration in war and peace 1942–1949*, Clarendon Press, Oxford, 1982 (hereafter *Anglo-American economic collaboration*), p. 110.

26. Minute by Mason, 19 July 1946, *Documents on British Foreign Policy*, Ser. I, Vol. IV, p. 320.

27. Cabinet Office to Joint Staff Mission, 4 May 1946, *Documents on British Foreign Policy*, Ser. I, Vol. IV, p. 281.

28. Foreign Office memorandum, 11 September 1945, *Documents on British Foreign Policy*, Ser. I, Vol. II, pp. 534–5.

29. Minute by A. Clerk Kerr, 12 September 1945, *Documents on British Foreign Policy*, Ser. I, Vol. II, p. 541.

30. D.K. Fieldhouse, 'The Labour governments and the empire–commonwealth, 1945–51', in Ritchie Ovendale (ed.), *The foreign policy of the British Labour governments, 1945–1951*, Leicester University Press, Leicester, 1984, pp. 95, 98.

31. Fieldhouse, pp. 96–7.

32. Memorandum for the Permanent Under-Secretary's Committee, 27 April 1950, *Documents on British Foreign Policy*, Ser. II, Vol. II, p. 163.

33. Pratt, p. 255.

34. W. Roger Louis and Ronald Robinson, 'The United States and the liquidation of British empire in tropical Africa, 1941–1951', in Gifford and Louis (eds), *The transfer of power in Africa*, pp. 42, 51.

35. Executive Committee on Economic Foreign Policy, 'Statement of United States credit and investment policy', 11 August 1948, *FRUS*, 1948, Vol. I, Part 2, p. 957.

36. R. Loree to Secretary of State, 8 February 1949, *FRUS*, 1949, Vol. I, p. 632.

37. State Department to British Embassy, 1 September 1945, *FRUS*, 1945, Vol. VI, p. 1297.

38. Policy Planning Staff, 'Review of current trends: US foreign policy', 24 February 1948, *FRUS*, 1948, Vol. I, Part 2, pp. 510–29.

39. Cited in US Congress, Senate, Church Committee, *Final report*, No. 94–755, Vol. 4, 94th Congress, 2nd Session, 1976, p. 53.

40. R. Lovett, Record of a meeting of the State-Defence Policy Review Group, State Department, 16 March 1950, *FRUS*, 1950, Vol. I, p. 197.

41. For US foreign policy in the postwar period see especially Noam Chomsky, *Deterring democracy*, Vintage, London, 1991; Chomsky and Edward Herman, *The Washington connection and Third World fascism*, South End, Boston, 1979; Gabriel Kolko, *Confronting the Third World: United States foreign policy 1945–1980*, Pantheon, New York, 1988; William Blum, *The CIA: A forgotten history*, Zed, London, 1986.

42. Balfour to Bevin, 9 August 1945, *Documents on British Foreign Policy*, Ser. I, Vol. III, p. 17.

43. Churchill to Eisenhower, 5 April 1953, *Churchill–Eisenhower correspondence*, p. 34.

44. Permanent Under-Secretary's Committee, 'Anglo-American relations: Present and future', 22 April 1950, *Documents on British Foreign Policy*, Ser. II, Vol. II, p. 82.

45. Arrangements for the administration of Hong Kong in the event of its liberation by regular Chinese forces, Enclosure in G. Gater to A. Cadogan, 28 July 1945, *Documents on British Foreign Policy*, Ser. I, Vol. I, p. 1185.

46. Brief by Wright for Bevin, 6 May 1950, *Documents on British Foreign Policy*, Ser. II, Vol. II, pp. 244–5.

47. Policy Planning Staff, 'Review of current trends: US foreign policy', 24 February 1948, *FRUS*, 1948, Vol. I, Part 2, p. 511.

48. Permanent Under-Secretary's Committee, 'The United Kingdom and the United Nations', 25 April 1950, *Documents on British Foreign Policy*, Calendar to Ser. II, Vol. II, p. 139.

49. Bureau of Near Eastern, South Asian and African Affairs, 'Regional policy statement on Africa south of the Sahara', 29 December 1950, *FRUS*, 1950, Vol. V, p. 1588.

50. Memorandum by McGhee, 7 March 1950, *FRUS*, 1950, Vol. I, p. 188.

51. United Kingdom/United States ministerial talks, 8 May 1950, *Documents on British Foreign Policy*, Calendar to Ser. II, Vol. II, pp. 494–5.

52. Secretary of State to the Embassy in France, 3 February 1947, *FRUS*, 1947, Vol. VI, p. 67.

53. Consul in Saigon to Secretary of State, 26 September 1947, *FRUS*, 1947, Vol. VI, p. 141.

54. Consul in Saigon to Secretary of State, 20 November 1947, *FRUS*, 1947, Vol. VI, p. 149.

55. Consul in Saigon to Secretary of State, 11 July 1947, *FRUS*, 1947, Vol. VI, p. 112.

56. C. Reed to Director of the Office of Far Eastern Affairs, 13 August 1948, *FRUS*, 1948, Vol. I, Part 2, p. 608.

57. Chiefs of Staff, 'Defence policy and global strategy', 7 June 1950, *Documents on British Foreign Policy*, Ser. II, Vol. IV, p. 424.

58. Tripartite Drafting Group, 'Southeast Asia', 1 September 1950, *FRUS*, 1950, Vol. III, p. 1174.

59. Agreed tripartite minutes on Southeast Asia, 22 May 1950, *FRUS*, 1950, Vol. III, p. 1083.

60. See Noam Chomsky, *For reasons of state*, Pantheon, New York, 1973; Chomsky and Edward Herman, *After the cataclysm: Postwar Indochina and the reconstruction of imperial ideology*, Spokesman, Nottingham, 1979; Gabriel Kolko, *Vietnam: Anatomy of a war, 1940–1975*, Allen and Unwin, London.

61. Secretary of State to Embassy in France, 10 June 1947, *FRUS*, 1947, Vol. V, p. 688.

62. Memorandum by the Policy Planning Staff, 'French North Africa', 22 March 1948, *FRUS*, 1948, Vol. III, p. 687.

63. Summary of remarks by McGhee, 25 October 1950, *FRUS*, 1950, Vol. V, p. 1573.

64. Secretary of State to Embassy in France, 10 June 1947, *FRUS*, 1947, Vol. V, p. 686.

65. Introductory paper on the Middle East by the UK, undated [1947], *FRUS*, 1947, Vol. V, p. 569.

66. Memorandum by the Chief of the Division of Near Eastern Affairs, undated [1945], *FRUS*, 1945, Vol. VIII, p. 45.

67. Department of State memorandum, 'Specific current questions', undated [1947], *FRUS*, 1947, Vol. V, p. 547.

68. Memorandum by the Chief of the Division of Near Eastern Affairs, undated [1945], *FRUS*, 1945, Vol. VIII, p. 46.

69. Memorandum by the Acting Chief of the Petroleum Division, 1 June 1945, *FRUS*, 1945, Vol. VIII, p. 54.

70. NSC 5401, quoted in Mohammed Heikal, *Cutting the lion's tail: Suez through Egyptian eyes*, Andre Deutsch, London, 1986, p. 38.

71. Report by the Subcommittee on rearmament, 21 March 1946, *FRUS*, 1946, Vol. I, p. 1159.

72. Office of Near Eastern Affairs, 'Regional policy statement: Near East', 28 December 1950, *FRUS*, 1950, Vol. V, p. 274.

73. Conclusions of a conference of Near Eastern Chiefs of Mission, undated [1949], *FRUS*, 1949, Vol. VI, p. 170.

74. Department of State memorandum, 'Specific current questions', undated [1947], *FRUS*, 1947, Vol. V, p. 553.

75. Statement by the United States and United Kingdom, undated [1947], *FRUS*, 1947, Vol. V, p. 613.

76. G. Merriam to E. Ramsey, 25 February 1948, *FRUS*, 1948, Vol. V, p. 225.

77. Memorandum by the Chief of the Division of South Asian Affairs, 9 October 1947, *FRUS*, 1947, Vol. V, p. 562.

78. Department of State memorandum, 15 March 1946, *FRUS*, 1946, Vol. VII, p. 65.

79. Letter from B. Burrows, Head of the Eastern Department of the Foreign Office, in US Ambassador in the UK to Secretary of State, 19 August 1949, *FRUS*, 1949, Vol. VI, p. 1571.

80. Permanent Under-Secretary's Committee, 'Anglo-American relations: Present and future', undated [1950], *Documents on British Foreign Policy*, Calendar to Ser. II, Vol. II, p. 208.

81. Memorandum by Balfour, 28 November 1945, *Documents on British Foreign Policy*, Ser. I, Vol. IV, p. 10.

82. N. Butler to Balfour, 23 July 1945, *Documents on British Foreign Policy*, Ser. I, Vol. I, p. 850.

83. Minute by R. Milward, 23 May 1950, *Documents on British Foreign Policy*, Ser. II, Vol. II, p. 196.

84. Memorandum by Bevin, 30 August 1950, *Documents on British Foreign Policy*, Ser. II, Vol. IV, p. 120.

85. Telegram from E. Dening, 23 January 1951, *Documents on British Foreign Policy*, Ser. II, Vol. IV, pp. 323-4.

86. Memorandum by Bevin, 8 November 1945, *Documents on British Foreign Policy*, Ser. I, Vol. III, pp. 311-12.

87. See especially Noam Chomsky, *Deterring democracy*, pp. 45-58; Gabriel Kolko, *The politics of war: The world and United States foreign policy, 1943-1945*, Random House, New York, 1968, pp. 281-313.

88. Earl of Halifax to Bevin, 27 March 1946, *Documents on British Foreign Policy*, Ser. I, Vol. IV, p. 193.

89. British Mission (Washington) to Cabinet Office, 3 October 1945, *Documents on British Foreign Policy*, Ser. I, Vol. III, p. 182.

90. Balfour to Bevin, 9 August 1945, *Documents on British Foreign Policy*, Ser. I, Vol. III, p. 16.

91. Memorandum by Balfour, 28 November 1945, *Documents on British Foreign Policy*, Ser. I, Vol. IV, p. 7.

92. Note of a meeting in the Foreign Office, 22 January 1946, *Documents on British Foreign Policy*, Ser. I, Vol. IV, p. 57.

93. Memorandum by Balfour, 28 November 1945, *Documents on British Foreign Policy*, Ser. I, Vol. IV, pp. 3, 5.

CHAPTER 2

THREATS AND REMEDIES

The real threat

The secret planning documents are often explicit about the absence of any real threat from the Soviet Union to Western interests in the Third World. A December 1950 Foreign Office paper entitled 'Russian strategic intentions and the threat to peace' declared that 'only three Middle Eastern countries – Turkey, Persia and Afghanistan – are exposed to direct Soviet attack', and then stated that such an attack was almost inconceivable in all three cases. 'Short of general war ... an attack on Turkey is unlikely owing to the Western guarantees which she enjoys.' Regarding Persia (Iran), 'the Soviet government must be aware that any attack on her would carry a grave risk of general war, and it is more likely that Soviet efforts to gain control of Persia will be confined to propaganda, diplomatic and subversive activity'. Meanwhile, 'there is little danger of a direct attack on Afghanistan'.[1] Similarly, another document noted that 'the success of indirect or subversive action by the Soviet government ... in any of the Arab states or in Israel is also improbable in the immediate future'.[2] Such reasoning is highly significant. The understanding that even 'indirect' Soviet action would probably be unsuccessful in 'any of the Arab states' does not exactly conform with standard doctrine – enunciated to the public then and throughout the period following the Second World War – of the prospective domination of the Middle East by the Soviet Union.

Whilst US and British foreign policies in the postwar period until the collapse of the Soviet Union were invariably portrayed by officials and commentators as responses to Soviet designs and as part of the so-called Cold War, the documents reveal a different story. This is not to say the Soviet Union was not perceived as a threat at all or that the East–West confrontation was a figment of the imagination. Yet Western foreign policies in the postwar world can be understood primarily as responses to the Soviet Union only by accepting state pronouncements at their word and ignoring facts; in reality, the actions (or the threat of actions) of the Soviet Union were often a minor factor, even a nonexistent one, in motivating and deciding Western policy in the major areas. In the real world, the primary threats to Anglo-American interests in the Third World have arisen from independent nationalist movements, from *within* states. These movements commonly rejected traditional foreign control over their economic resources, the exploitation of these resources by Western business corporations, and the related impoverishment of the general population at the hands of a tiny, all-powerful ruling elite. Revolutionary aims were typically the development of economic resources for national priorities, and independent, egalitarian socioeconomic progress, offering the prospect of real gains for impoverished populations. The revolutions that occurred in Vietnam, Cuba and Nicaragua, for example – all customarily described primarily as arenas of East–West conflict – were more properly nationalist struggles for independence and meaningful social and economic development (see Chapter 6).

The British Treasury observed in 1945 that the new economic order could work 'only if there is a high US national income and a rapid and non-autarkic economic growth of the underdeveloped countries and we must manifestly do all in our power (even at some inconvenience to ourselves) to secure these'. Mention was made of the 'danger to us of autarkic industrialisation undertaken for its own sake'; that is, presumably, nationalist economic development for the benefit of the local population, rather than for 'international trade', essentially meaning the Western business interests well placed to profit from it.[3] What Britain admitted to be the 'inconsistent' application of the principle of equal access to raw materials in the case of uranium supplies[4] revealed something of the meaning of 'equal access' generally. 'Equal access' to the world's economic resources in practice meant access for the powerful states, and the principle of other states using their own resources for genuine national development represented a clear threat to the new economic order.

In pursuit of this policy Anglo-American power engaged in numerous military conflicts and covert operations, consistently throughout the postwar period, in Malaya, Vietnam, Nicaragua, Kenya, Kuwait, the Dominican Republic, British Guiana, Iran and many other places. The idea of 'doing all in our power to secure' these economic interests became a frightening reality for those on the receiving end. Policy was invariably explained by reference to the 'Soviet threat', but in reality the foremost priority was maintaining 'trading and business interests'.[5]

Of chief importance were the Middle East (described by Britain as 'a source of oil, which is an essential dollar-saver and a potential dollar earner') and Southeast Asia ('very important in peace, as a dollar-earner and as a sterling source of essential raw materials').[6] The United States noted in 1947:

> It is important to maintain in friendly hands areas which contain or protect sources of metals, oil and other national resources, which contain strategic objectives, or areas strategically located, which contain a substantial industrial potential, which possess manpower and organised military forces in important quantities.[7]

The essential requirement for the furtherance of these interests was 'stability' in the states and regions concerned, a euphemism consistently used by Western leaders and essentially meaning state power residing in the hands of political elements favourable to the West and acquiescing in effective Western control over the country's resources. The US State Department noted in 1950 that 'North Africa enjoys stability, even though such stability is obtained largely through repression'. However, 'if the Arab nationalist leaders were to attain power, it would inevitably create a situation of instability in this area'.[8] 'Instability' – the wrong elements being in power – in the Western view may lead to unacceptable nationalist or 'autarkic' development. A similar term is 'moderate', often applied to governments in the Middle East and meaning those on favourable terms with the West, as opposed to 'extremists', those who threaten Western hegemony and the Western right to control their resources. 'Security' can be understood in a similar sense. Currently – as throughout the postwar era – the term 'Middle Eastern security', for example, describes oil resources being under the West's control or under the control of its friends. Similarly, the US State Department noted in 1947 that the 'security' of North Africa 'is at the present time maintained by France', meaning the region was controlled by France in the face of nationalist 'threats' thereto.[9] In the 1940s during the Greek Civil War, the 'communists' were described as attempting to destroy 'internal order', a phrase meaning that they were threatening the West's political control over the country.[10]

The word 'democracy' had similar overtones in the case of Vietnam. Thus the State Department in 1948 called for the establishment of 'our conception of a democratic state' in Vietnam and at the same time noted, 'we have not urged the French to negotiate with Ho Chi Minh, even though he probably is now supported by a considerable majority of the Vietnamese people'.[11] US officials admitted that Ho Chi Minh 'is the only Viet [sic] who enjoys any measure of national prestige'[12] and also the 'unpleasant fact' that Ho Chi Minh 'is the strongest and perhaps the ablest figure in Indochina'.[13] Churchill wrote to Eisenhower in 1954, '... there is, I am told, no doubt which way the Viet Nam population would vote if they were freely consulted.'[14] The US 'conception of a democratic state' US ruled out support for the country's most popular leader.

The often-stated absence, or negligible impact, of a Soviet and/or 'communist threat' and the real threat of nationalism can be considered region by region. The documents are often explicit. In the most important region – the Middle East – the State Department noted in 1950 that 'the Arab states are all oriented towards the West in varying degrees, opposed to communism and generally successful at present in minimising or suppressing existing communist activities through restrictive measures'. Communist parties were 'non-existent in Yemen and Saudi Arabia; outlawed in Iraq, Egypt, Syria and Lebanon and apparently unorganised in Jordan'.

Rather, 'throughout the Arab states, at the present time, extreme rightist or ultra-nationalist elements may exercise greater influence and form a greater threat to maintenance of a pro-Western orientation than the communists'. Noting the 'anti-Western orientation of ultra-nationalist elements', the report states that 'the Soviet government does not appear to be exercising direct pressure upon the governments of these states'.[15]

Indeed, the documents are replete with examples of the fact that communism was not a major threat in the Middle East.[16] The aim of securing control over Middle Eastern oil resources was jeopardised, rather, by the possibility that 'the rising nationalism of the peoples of the Middle East should harden in a mould of hostility to the West'.[17] There thus had essentially been no change from the threat of the prewar period, when Britain was the hegemonic power in the region, the West's problem then being to 'develop' the Middle East 'in order to prevent further degeneration into acute nationalism hostile to British influence'.[18]

The situation was much the same elsewhere. On Africa, the State Department commented in 1950: 'today "Black" Africa is oriented towards the non-Communist world. Communism has made no real progress in the area.'[19] 'In some territories', however, it noted the existence of a 'growing spirit of nationalism on the part of the natives, which should not, however, be confused with communism'.[20] In North Africa 'communism presents no menace at the present time', Assistant Secretary of State McGhee observed in 1950. Rather, nationalism 'constitutes the real force of the future in this area'.[21] 'By far the greatest number of nationalists', it had been noted in 1947, 'reject any association with communism'.[22]

The same could be said of Asia. 'Nationalism is the strongest force in Asia,' McGhee stated in 1950.[23] In the Far East, the head of the US Policy Planning Staff stated: '... the problem is not one primarily of Russians but of the basic relations of Americans with Asiatics.'[24] Similarly, 'communism does not immediately threaten the governments of South Asia', the State Department commented in 1950. 'The prospect for the period 1950 to 1955 is that, barring intra-regional warfare or widespread famine in India, the non-Communist elements now governing in South Asia can be expected to retain power.'[25] In Southeast Asia, meanwhile, the US State Department reported in 1950 that 'since the end of the war, the dominant theme in the greater part of Southeast Asia has been nationalism and desire for freedom from colonial tutelage'.[26] A survey conducted in the same year concluded that 'in most of Southeast Asia there is no fear of communism as we understand it'.[27]

So if there was little or no communist or Soviet threat to the Middle East, 'Black' Africa, North Africa, the Far East, South Asia and Southeast Asia, there were not many areas left where communism or the Soviet Union could be supposed to be on the march. However, the threat to the realisation of the new economic order posed by nationalism was often similar in nature to the threat which, in the understanding of Western planners, was posed by the Soviet Union and communism. With regard to the Third World, this threat was not primarily of the nature publicly stated, which stressed Soviet *military* designs. A Foreign Office memorandum stated in 1950: '... it is obvious that when an area falls into Communist hands, its economic and trading value to the Western world becomes greatly reduced, while Western capital assets are liquidated with little or no compensation.'[28] This would be a 'blow to the principle of multilateral trade on which we depend'.[29] Thus one of the feared consequences of China's becoming communist was that Britain's economic interests there would be jeopardised. A few months after the 1949 communist revolution in China, Foreign Secretary Bevin stated: '... it is problematical whether private trading interests will survive very long if the full rigour of Communist theory and practice is applied.'[30] Bevin noted that 'the condition of United Kingdom business interests in China has gravely deteriorated' and urged the British embassy in China 'to make representations to the Chinese government about the position of British economic interests' there.[31] Similarly, the Soviet Union's control of Eastern Europe signified 'an economic blackout in these areas for all other nations'.[32] Equally, in 1945 the US ambassador in Iran was concerned with threats to the USA's economic interests:

> Soviet domination of Iran Govt would be definitely harmful to American interests for the following reasons: (1) It would mean exclusion of American airlines from Iran; (2) It would orient Iranian trade toward Russian to detriment of our commercial interests; (3) It would end all possibility of an American oil concession in Iran; (4) Most important of all it would mean extension of Soviet influence to shores of Persian Gulf creating potential threat to our immensely rich holdings in Saudi Arabia, Bahrain and Kuwait.[33]

Since nationalism and communism could pose similar threats to Western economic interests, they could often be presented as precisely the same thing; this was particularly convenient for public relations purposes. If nationalist development could simply be presented as 'communist', it could more easily be ascribed to the machinations of the Kremlin, which was presented as being behind communist movements everywhere. Western leaders thus obtained a ready-made cover for their interventions: they could be described as a response to the Soviet Union. It would after all have been much more difficult to present actions as simple interference in the internal affairs of states, particularly where national liberation movements enjoyed widespread popular support and held out the prospect of meaningful social and economic progress for the impoverished. The positing of a worldwide conspiracy had obvious advantages: essentially nationalist struggles in even the smallest of places could be depicted as part of a global Cold War confrontation.

It was therefore crucial to present the supposed Soviet threat in stark terms. The 'threat' became an article of faith – a basic assumption – and it became sufficient for Western leaders merely to state that the Soviet Union was enacting its designs here or there, without the need to present much, or any, evidence. Interestingly, however, this article of faith also permeates many of the secret planning documents. It would certainly be incorrect to describe the promulgation of the 'Soviet threat' as a conspiracy deliberately fabricated for public consumption. Though there are clear specific cases where supposed Soviet machinations were purposely concocted by Western leaders,[34] it was more generally the case that the basic ideological framework in which the concept was promoted was internally digested by those actually making policy. This internalisation of state ideology was also largely effected by 'independent' commentators in the media and academia, an internalisation that further served to reinforce the required doctrine.[35]

Take, for example, the following comments, which show the degree to which the basic assumptions were accepted at the highest levels. What is interesting is that these are top-secret documents intended only for internal distribution and not for public relations purposes. One major report, for example, drawn up by the British Foreign Office in December 1950, suggests that the Soviet threat is unrelenting. The Soviet Union attempts to aggravate 'all possible' causes of friction between the non-communist states. Soviet leaders will 'always' seek to exploit 'any' form of discontent. Soviet leaders will 'relentlessly' seek the establishment of world communism. Four examples are given of 'the Soviet technique of weakening non-Communist countries by promoting armed rebellion or civil war': Greece, Burma, Indochina and Malaya. In fact, however, the Soviet Union never provided any aid to the armed rebellions in Greece, Burma or Malaya. Its contribution at that stage in the way of material support to the Indochinese independence movements was marginal. The report describes the attack by North Korea on South Korea in 1950 as an example of 'Soviet-inspired aggression', even though no evidence has ever emerged that the Kremlin inspired the action. The report continues by stating that when the Soviet Union fails to achieve 'its ends by the use of force as in Korea, the Soviet government is accustomed to draw in its horns and to revert to attempts to gain its ends by negotiation instead' – a sure sign of its malevolent designs, the using of the despicable weapon of negotiation![36]

US planners had similar concerns. In 1951 the National Security Council remarked on the Kremlin designs of 'dividing the Western powers, undermining US mobilisation, obstructing the NATO program and frustrating prospective German and Japanese rearmament ... with the ultimate objective of paralysing opposition to communism'. In order to do all these things the Soviet Union had a staggering weapon at its disposal: 'the

Kremlin may adopt the tactic of encouraging the West to hope for a settlement of outstanding issues by *mutual agreement*!'[37]

In short, these top-secret documents are based on certain fundamental assumptions about the 'Soviet threat' which operate independently of any evidence and are patently incorrect by any objective indicators. Several explanations are possible. The first is to describe the reports as propaganda consciously directed to other elements in government, which appears unfeasible since they all shared the same assumptions. The second is to conclude that the reports are the results of sheer ignorance (or mis-perception), which is unlikely since Soviet inaction was obvious. The Soviet Union's failure to aid rebels in Greece, Burma or Malaya, for example, was surely known. Rather, we might conclude that these examples provide evidence of the internal digestion by planners of key basic assumptions: akin, perhaps, to the articles of faith which require acceptance in all collective belief systems, even if they can be proved false. This elevation on the part of foreign policy planners of the notion of the 'Soviet threat' to an article of faith served crucial ends by concealing foreign policy goals and the fact that the real threat to Western interests in the Third World came from nationalism.

The standard version of history presented by academia follows a similar pattern. Here, the overriding basis of the postwar foreign policies of the leading Western powers is seen as the 'containment' of Soviet expansion-ism: Soviet aggression (or the threat of aggression), it is alleged, forced the Western powers into defensive foreign policies and huge military build-ups in defence of Western interests against an expansionist adversary. The postwar era is thus summed up in the term Cold War, understood simply as a confrontation between two superblocs – NATO and the Warsaw Pact. Western efforts to counter Soviet designs could therefore largely be viewed as praiseworthy, whilst Western foreign policy was generally viewed as uncontaminated by any motives of straightforward economic exploitation of other lands.

US foreign policy in the Third World since 1945 is invariably viewed by British academics as being utterly dominated by the need to contain the Soviet Union, with almost no exceptions. Thus F.S. Northedge, Pro-fessor of International Relations at the London School of Economics, writes of the 'dominant place occupied by the world struggle against Communism in the American mind'.[38] The highly reputed analyst Lord Beloff notes in 1986 that 'the world-wide struggle against Communism ... remains the inevitable core of American policy'.[39] For David Watt, former Director of the Royal Institute of International Affairs, the Anglo-American special relationship is 'conditioned on Britain's remaining the single most effective adjutant in the task of containing the Soviet Union and its allies'.[40]

As regards British foreign policy, the propaganda system does allow for non-communist, nationalist forces to be accredited as the main threat to British interests in some states during the decolonisation process. Yet the real danger represented by these nationalist forces – that they would deprive Britain of the ability to plunder their economies for its own benefit – is rarely alluded to beyond occasional vague references to the threat to 'Britain's economic interests'.[41] That Britain's (and the USA's) 'economic interests' in the Third World in the postwar period have been synonymous with the systematic exploitation and impoverishment of local populations is effectively unmentionable in respectable circles. Linked with this is an inability to elucidate what the British policy of establishing friendly regimes after independence actually meant. Frankel, for example, notes that 'British reasons for establishing post-imperial regimes were by no means exclusively power-political; they included concern for the welfare of the people and for the protection of British interests'.[42] In the real world, concern for the welfare of the people in the post-independence Third World was not actually uppermost in British planners' minds and, indeed, was incompatible with the maintenance of Britain's 'economic interests'.

A leading British foreign policy analyst at the University of Cambridge, David Reynolds, has noted Britain's postwar desire to 'remain a world power by more informal means'. 'One stratagem for doing this', he notes, 'was through the Commonwealth, envisaged as a more enlightened and informal version of the British Empire.' Reynolds places himself at the extreme liberal end of the propaganda system by briefly mentioning the exploitation of colonial territories between 1945 and 1951, including the passage from Fieldhouse noted above. However, this mention is unaccompanied by further elucidations elsewhere in his study (which deals with foreign policy until the Thatcher period) of the systematic exploitation of the Third World carried out after 1951. This section is also introduced by noting that in British plans for 'colonial economic development', 'altruism was genuinely a factor', as was the concept of 'noblesse oblige'. Further, we are informed that, as regards Britain's 'informal empire' in the Middle East, 'Bevin was the leading exponent of a new mutuality, resting on "a common basis of partnership"'. This 'mutuality' and 'partnership' actually existed, as noted above, between British leaders and feudal despots – many of which continue today.[43]

Two particular aspects of the standard version of history were crucial in reinforcing state propaganda. First, Western military interventions overseas could invariably be portrayed as 'responses' to the actions of the other 'side'. Indeed, even if Soviet machinations were not presented as directly responsible for Western 'responses', the wider East–West struggle was readily upheld as providing the general setting for such interventions. Second, the toleration of horrifying social conditions, terrible human rights abuses, authoritarian governments or political repression in pro-Western Third World states could be explained away on the grounds that the alternative was communism and/or Soviet domination. Or, the Western states could not properly address themselves to these problems since the Soviet threat was an even greater evil. For example, one of Britain's leading 'independent' research institutes, the International Institute for Strategic Studies, commented as follows in its 1988–89 review of world affairs:

> If the principles of democratisation and commitment to human rights and free markets are not distorted by, or subordinated to, the need to contain a Soviet 'threat', the US would be freed from the need to become the 'world's policeman'. It will be able to see the problems of the world's impoverished nations – their critical debt burdens, fragile political processes and related human rights violations – in their own terms, rather than through an East–West prism.[44]

Such a presentation of reality provided crucial advantages to Western planners; it masked the real priorities and goals of Anglo-American power and hid from public view a proper understanding of their often horrifying consequences.

Consolidating the West

The US construction of a world order in which its trading and business interests would be predominant depended on the incorporation within it of the world's most productive economic areas: Western Europe and Japan. Without their buying power for US exports, their own production of goods for import by the USA and their technology and know-how, the US goal of expanded international trade and a multilateral world economy would be doomed to failure. It was therefore necessary to draw the major economically productive areas of the world closer together, effectively under US domination; this was referred to as 'consolidating the West'.

The process of 'consolidating the West' began in earnest in the late 1940s and early 1950s and was stimulated by the fact that the early postwar years had been disappointing in certain key respects. The Western European states had received a considerable boost to their economies after 1947 through the injection of US funds into European recovery by the Marshall Plan. Yet achievement of the degree of Western economic consolidation envisaged by the US remained noticeably deficient. Already, the Soviet Union and Eastern Europe had been cut off from the world economy. Areas of the Third World were threatening to overthrow direct colonial tutelage and the primacy of Western interests in those states.

In 1950 British officials stressed that 'while it might be impossible for the present to organise all parts of the world along the lines of the Atlantic community, one of the best ways of giving strength to the free world [sic] was to have a really united and powerful system of Western consolidation'.[45] The method of implementing this plan was quite simple: by taking recourse in the 'Soviet threat'. Some US and British internal documents and public statements had put forward hysterical propositions about the nature of Soviet intentions. The need to maintain the 'Soviet threat' principle to achieve the consolidation of the West was made quite explicit. The Foreign Office noted in 1950: 'it must ... be appreciated that the Western system is coming into being under the pressure of Soviet policy. ... It is probably fair to say that it is a system desirable in itself.' Then the paper notes that 'if Soviet pressure were relaxed as a result of some major tactical deviation, the development of the system might be arrested in proportion as the compelling cause of the danger from the Soviet Union diminished'.[46] A related evaluation was reached by the Foreign Office with regard to the United Nations; 'if there were no Soviet opposition to bind all the members together, friction between the different groups would be only too likely to develop'. The conclusion was that 'the consolidation of the West, under Anglo-American leadership, might well be in jeopardy'.[47]

It was understood, therefore, that there were clear advantages to 'Anglo-American leadership' of a 'consolidated West' in the promotion of the 'Soviet threat'. The usefulness of such a principle regarding control over Third World economic resources has already been noted: the 'Soviet threat' is used as a justification for intervention. This principle would have other crucial advantages, notably aiding the control of 'dissent' within the Western states. The British Chiefs of Staff gave mention in 1950 to 'a most insidious and mortally dangerous form of attack, namely the Fifth Column, whose aim is to rot resistance from within. ... This involves being increasingly tough with communism within our own countries and in our dependent territories.'[48] According to the Foreign Office, 'consolidation of the West cannot be solely a matter of agreement between governments. It must also involve an internal consolidation of the peoples of the Western countries and a rejection of Communist influence.'[49]

US documents reveal similar concerns, emphasising the necessity to 'vigorously prosecute a domestic information program, designed to insure public understanding and non-partisan support of our foreign policy'. Also important was 'a program for suppressing the communist menace in the United States [and to] cooperate closely with governments which have already taken such action and encourage other governments to take like action'.[50] The term 'communist' could of course be applied wholesale to any undesirables.

Italy was one state that required 'consolidation'. Bevin stated that part of the 'general aim of our policy towards Italy' was to 'make use of her for our own purposes as a "bastion of democracy" in the Mediterranean'.[51] The Foreign Office assumed that this 'was as much an American as a British objective and that the United States authorities should be encouraged to take their full share in the undertaking'.[52] This they subsequently did in the first major CIA operation in the postwar world, involving an assortment of political funding and propaganda to ensure the defeat of the Communist Party and an acceptable outcome to the 1948 elections.[53]

Japan was a further case. 'We are quite prepared to let the United States take the lead in controlling Japan,' the Far Eastern Department of the Foreign Office declared.[54] Before the end of the war in Asia, the Foreign Office had observed that after Japan's defeat 'it should be possible for the allies ... to decide and control the nature and extent of [Japan's] exports and imports'. It was also 'desirable to consider what place in [the] world economy is to be taken by Japan after defeat; to what extent, if any, Japan's productive capacity is to be used to supply the needs of, for example, South East Asia for essential consumption goods'.[55]

Control over Japan and the economic organisation of East Asia were key factors in determining the US engagement, beginning in 1950, in the Korean War, which is generally regarded purely as a Cold War confrontation. A 1948 CIA study noted that 'the key factor in [the] postwar development of Japan is economic rehabilitation'. For this purpose Japan 'must have access to the Northeast Asiatic areas – notably North China, Manchuria and Korea', with the key elements being markets and raw materials. The US aim was to 'connect up' the South Korean economy 'with that of Japan', in the words of Secretary of State Marshall in 1947. A year before war broke out the head of the Policy Planning Staff noted the USA's 'terrific problem' of how 'the Japanese are going to get along unless they reopen some sort of empire towards the South'. Thus Northeast and Southeast Asia together were to form a triangular relationship with Japan and the West, serving the role of providers of markets and raw materials to the industrialised powers. Independent nationalist development in Southeast Asia (and elsewhere) had therefore to be countered. 'What Korea got', leading US Korea specialist Bruce Cumings notes, 'was a highly penetrative American regime, which left – or sought to leave – few important economic decisions just to the Koreans themselves.' Thus the 1948 aid agreement between the USA and South Korea provided for the flow of US dollars and goods and in return the USA 'elicited pledges to open the country to foreign traders, reduce barriers to foreign exchange, facilitate "private foreign investment" and develop Korean export industries'. 'The neocolonial aspects of this agreement', Cumings notes further, 'would have been controversial had its full content been revealed.' The Korean War was fought to defend this system in South Korea and to incorporate it into the US-controlled sphere in East Asia, thus ensuring that the economic rehabilitation of the major regional client – Japan – could be pursued, with South Korea as 'a hinterland for Japanese industry and a frontyard of Japanese defence'.[56]

There has never been any real evidence that the Soviet Union encouraged, let alone planned, North Korea's invasion of the South in 1950. Rather, according to Cumings, who has produced the most extensively documented analysis of the origins of the Korean War, it was 'a local affair, the denouement to struggles going back to the colonial period'. The North Korean invasion 'sought to break the American *and* the Soviet embrace, and come up with a unified nation that could resist them both'. In the UN on the day of the invasion the USA's Western allies 'took the general line that this was a fight between Koreans' and was 'in the nature of a civil war'. But the allies were, according to Cumings, 'effectively silenced', with the USA preferring a different analysis. 'The real history of Korea in this period', Cumings states, 'fits what we now call a "North–South" conflict, the main agenda being decolonisation and a radical restructuring of colonial legacies'; it is a description that could be applied to virtually all the countries of concern to Western policy in the early postwar period, as well as after.[57]

As regards Europe, Germany was the key to Western consolidation. Here the essential aim was to ensure that 'the great productive machine of Germany could be utilised in the interests of the West'.[58] To do this 'it was important to tie her in to the West in all sorts of relations and by all sorts of ties so that whether she wanted to or not Germany could not look East'.[59] Britain's desire to wield influence over the western sectors of Germany in order to harness the economic resources of the Ruhr region was a major contributory factor in Germany's division. The US Policy Planning Staff had noted in 1948 that 'whereas a European federation would be by all odds the best solution from the standpoint of US interests, the Germans are poorly prepared for it. To achieve such a federation would be much easier if Germany were partitioned, or drastically decentralised.'[60] According to British academic Ann Deighton, 'the determination became to hang on to the areas over which the West retained influence while trying to ensure that responsibility for any future break was put squarely on the Russians'.[61] Central to this policy was a Western refusal to countenance elections throughout Germany – in 1952, for example, when Soviet proposals for all-German elections were rejected – and thus the chance for a reunification of the country.

Germany's centrality to the programme of Western consolidation is highlighted in another, crucial way. At a meeting of US, British and French foreign ministers in May 1950, consideration was given to 'how to make full use of the German economic potential'.[62] The answer was German rearmament, justified in the light of the 'Soviet threat' but rooted firmly in a plan of action being conceived in the leading Western capitals. Germany specialist Matthias Peter comments that:

> The German rearmament question was much more a problem within the American-led process of reconstructing and consolidating Western Europe than a military means of deterring Soviet aggression. While the long-term strategic importance of German divisions is not denied, Germany's remilitarisation was

also a device to increase security by stabilising the Western European economies.[63]

The mobilisation of German industry's idle capacity for use in its own and its Western partners' defence effort would both aid the economic reconstruction of Western Europe and, at the same time, lock Germany's economy further into the economy of Western Europe.

The formation of the North Atlantic Treaty Organisation (NATO) in 1949 was one important element in this process. It was ostensibly a military organisation and a pact to defend the Western states against possible Soviet aggression. However, its relevance elsewhere was not lost on its designers. The Foreign Office stated that the British government was 'likely to find [NATO] the most suitable basis for Western consolidation'; crucial to this was the economic component – NATO 'should not necessarily be devoted exclusively to military purposes'. Whilst 'some caution' was necessary in 'developing the non-military side' of the organisation, NATO formed the 'best basis for the future development of cooperation in the Western world'. It was therefore important that 'no useful opportunity should be missed of building up [NATO's] non-military side'.[64] Further, 'it was clear that this body should deal with economic problems which have a direct relationship to the pact and which do not come within the competence of the OEEC' – the Organisation for European Economic Cooperation – then the main organ of Western economic cooperation.[65]

Before we return to the question of rearmament as a device for stimulating economic growth, two other of the Cold War's defining elements can be considered: the Marshall Plan and the Truman Doctrine, both of 1947. The Marshall Plan provided large-scale US aid to the Western European states impoverished by the Second World War. The Truman Doctrine provided aid to Greece and Turkey, which at the time were presented as facing a significant communist threat. Both the Marshall Plan and the Truman Doctrine were further devices for ordering the non-Soviet world according to US guidelines and for securing prominent US goals. A US document reveals the extent of the economic dilemma at the time: 'The volume of United States foreign financing will, under present programs and policies, taper off rapidly during the latter part of 1948 and 1949. Similarly, the ability of foreign purchasers to finance US exports out of gold and dollar holdings will diminish as these reserves are drawn down.' 'The conclusion is inescapable that, under present programs and policies, the world will not be able to continue to buy United States exports at the 1946–47 rate beyond another twelve months.'[66] The injection of US aid into Western Europe through Marshall Plan funds was an obvious way of helping to solve this problem.

Note that communism in Western Europe was not the main problem. The Policy Planning Staff noted that it did 'not see communist activities as the root of the difficulties of western Europe. It believes that the present crisis results in large part from the disruptive effect of the war on the economic, political and social structure of Europe and from a profound exhaustion of physical plant and of spiritual vigor.'[67] As regards Greece and Turkey and the Truman Doctrine, US military aid was 'a powerful influence in orienting the recipient nations toward US policy' and would contribute to the 'internal order and integrity of the countries concerned'.[68] The extension of US aid was 'a question of political economy in the literal sense' and such aid was considered 'only in cases where the prospective results bear a satisfactory relationship to the expenditure of American resources and effort'.[69]

The explicit links between the 'consolidation' of the West under US auspices, rearmament and the promulgation of the 'Soviet threat' are further made clear in perhaps the most important US document of the period, if not the whole of the Cold War: National Security Council Directive 68 – NSC68 – finalised in April 1950.[70] Close consideration needs to be paid to it because it shows in clear terms the motivations of planners and their agenda for securing long-term goals.

The overall problem, as noted above, was that the economic consolidation of the West was not proceeding satisfactorily. NSC68 is clear on this point. It noted that 'despite certain inadequacies and inconsistencies, which are now being studied in connection with the problem of the United States balance of payments, the United States has generally pursued a foreign economic policy which has powerfully supported its overall objectives'. However, 'the question must nevertheless be asked whether current and currently projected programs will adequately support this policy in the future, in terms both of need and urgency'. Then the report considers the economic dilemma. 'The last year', it notes, 'has been indecisive in the economic field. ... The free nations have important accomplishments to record, but also have tremendous problems still ahead.' The specific problem was that Western Europe 'faces the prospect of a rapid tapering off of American assistance without the possibility of achieving, by its own efforts, a satisfactory equilibrium with the dollar area. It has also made very little progress toward "economic integration", which would in the long run tend to improve its productivity and to provide an economic environment conducive to political stability. In particular' – the report notes, supporting the evidence regarding Germany above – 'the movement towards economic integration does not appear to be rapid enough to provide Western Germany with adequate economic opportunities in the West'. Then the report crucially notes that 'there are grounds for predicting that the United States and other free nations will within a period of a few years at most experience a decline in economic activity of serious proportions unless more positive governmental programs are developed than are now available'.

A key question was therefore how to resolve these economic difficulties and mobilise the Western economies through 'more positive governmental programs'. The answer was rearmament, with the 'Soviet threat' as justification. The 'threat' had therefore to be presented in stark terms and NSC68 makes no bones about the issue. 'The Soviet Union, unlike previous aspirants to hegemony, is animated by a new fanatic faith, antithetical to our own, and seeks to impose absolute authority over the rest of the world.' The citizens of the USA 'stand in their deepest peril', the issues facing them are 'momentous', they are threatened with the 'destruction not only of this Republic but of civilisation itself'. 'Soviet efforts are now directed toward the domination of the Eurasian land mass' and 'the only apparent restraints on resort to war are ... calculations of practicality'. The Soviet Union, which is 'inescapably militant', 'does not hesitate to use military force aggressively if that course is expedient in the achievement of its design'.

Thus was presented the need for drastic countermeasures. The response to the ominous Kremlin designs that was recommended in the conclusion of the report was to embark upon 'a more rapid build-up of political, economic and military strength' throughout the West, principally involving the initiation of a massive rearmament programme. The report noted that 'unless the military strength of the Western European nations is increased on a much larger scale than under current programs and at an accelerated rate, it is more than likely that those nations will not be able to oppose even by 1960 the Soviet armed forces in war with any degree of effectiveness'. The advice was taken up, with crucial consequences. The real beginning of the postwar arms race can be traced to this report; over the next few years the United States and the major Western European states embarked upon huge increases in defence spending.

The 'Soviet threat' was so hysterically portrayed in NSC68 that even some of those involved in its formulation rejected its central tenets. A memorandum circulated in the Policy Planning Staff noted that 'there is little justification for the impression that the "cold war" ... has suddenly taken some drastic turn to our disadvantage'. Even the 'demonstration of an "atomic capability" on the part of the USSR' – it exploded its first atomic bomb in 1949 – 'adds no new fundamental element to this picture'. The memo included one particularly significant statement:

> this is not to say our international situation is secure, or is one that could justify complacency. ... But its basic elements are ones which were established largely by the final outcome of hostilities in 1945. Nothing that recently occurred has altered these essential elements.[71]

The US Bureau of the Budget also refuted the NSC68 thesis, noting that 'NSC68 is based on the assumption that the military power of the USSR and its satellites is increasing in relation to that of the US and its allies'.

... it is hard to accept a conclusion that the USSR is approaching a straight-out military superiority over us when, for example, (1) our Air Force is vastly superior qualitatively, is greatly superior numerically in the bombers, trained crews and other facilities necessary for offensive warfare; (2) our supply of fission bombs is much greater than that of the USSR, as is our thermonuclear potential; (3) our Navy is so much stronger than that of the USSR that they should not be mentioned in the same breath; (4) the economic health and military potential of our allies is, with our help, growing daily; and (5) while we have treaties of alliance with and are furnishing arms to countries bordering the USSR, the USSR has none with countries within thousands of miles of us.[72]

Similarly, the Assistant Secretary of State for Economic Affairs stated:

one of the assumptions of the report is the notion that the USSR is 'steadily reducing the discrepancy between its overall economic strength and that of the US. ... I do not feel that this proposition is demonstrated, but rather the reverse. ... the expansion in the US economy was double that of the USSR during 1949, and that was probably somewhat below our rate of expansion for the previous year. ... the broader economic case is clearly not proven. In fact, all the evidence in the report points the other way, that the actual gap is widening in our favour.[73]

The massive rearmament programme needed to be sold, however, since there were crucial underlying motivations. Former Under-Secretary of State and future Deputy Secretary of Defence Robert Lovett pointed out, referring to the threat posed by 'international communism': 'if we can sell every useless article known to man in large quantities, we should be able to sell our very fine story in larger quantities'.[74] This parallel was perhaps instructive. In one revealing section, NSC68 alludes to the irrelevance of the Soviet Union as a motivating factor in the proposed programme. 'Our overall policy at the present time', it states correctly, 'may be described as one designed to foster a world environment in which the American system can survive and flourish. ... This broad intention embraces two subsidiary positions. *One is a policy which we would probably pursue even if there were no Soviet threat.*' This is described as 'a policy of attempting to develop a healthy international community', meaning the process of reinvigorating or 'consolidating' the Western economies. 'It, as much as containment, underlay our efforts to rehabilitate Western Europe.'[75]

Lovett crucially pointed out that 'the economy of the United States might benefit from the kind of military build-up which we were suggesting'.[76] NSC68 itself also mentions this possibility, by noting that an increase in US gross national product 'would permit, *and might itself be aided by*, a build-up of the economic and military strength of the United States and the free world'. 'Foreign economic policy', the report stated correctly, 'is an instrument peculiarly appropriate to the cold war.' According to NSC68, 'from the point of view of the economy as a whole, the program [of rearmament] might not result in a real decrease in the standard of living, for the economic effect of the program might be to increase the gross national product by more than the amount being absorbed for additional military and foreign assistance purposes'.[77] A National Security Council report written a year after NSC68 and after the beginning of the re-armament programme reported on this 'industrial expansion program of very large proportions' and concluded that 'the economy has responded well to the stimulus of the defence program'.[78]

The rearmament programme was therefore ostensibly a military one designed to counter the 'Soviet threat' but also happened to promote the rehabilitation of the Western economies. Recourse to the 'Soviet threat' could foster the Western unity (or 'consolidation') required for the pro-gramme to be widely supported and sustained. Of fundamental importance, however, was the *type* of economic development required. An important element in NSC68 is that 'sacrifices' will be required from the public to enable more and more resources to be devoted towards the military. 'A large measure of sacrifice and discipline will be demanded of the American people,' it stated. 'They will be asked to give up some of the benefits which they have come to associate with their freedoms.'[79] To maintain popular acquiescence in the programme, therefore, required a positive frightening of the populace into believing the Russians were about to dominate the 'Eurasian land mass', take over the world etc. The State Department had voiced concerns about this by noting that 'what we need to do is to make the "cold war" a "warm war" by infusing into it ideological principles to give it meaning'. This was essential 'if we are going to get the support we need from the American and friendly peoples'.[80]

Yet, crucially, the immediate beneficiaries of the rearmament programme were to be the large corporations within the military–defence sector of the economy. With guaranteed industrial production and a guaranteed market (the Department of Defence) they were able to achieve high levels of output and reap large profits. Gains could be made throughout the economy as a whole but the relative gains would be made by these industries, in effect resulting in a redistribution of national resources away from the general population (in terms of health, education and social service spending, for example) – the public's 'sacrifices' and 'discipline' – towards the military–defence sector. Recourse to the 'Soviet threat' would have similar effects domestically, then, as in relation to the Third World; populations could be marginalised in favour of the pursuit of higher economic priorities benefiting business elites. That the rearmament pro-gramme seemed 'to point to a gigantic arms race, a huge build-up of conventional arms that quickly become obsolescent, a greatly expanded military establishment'[81] was therefore hardly to be despised. Such a programme could only be sustained by consistently portraying the Soviet Union as aggressive, about to invade, militarily superior etcetera. This basic assumption was promulgated with remarkable success throughout the postwar era, with the indispensable aid of 'independent' commentators.

These considerations explain much about the development of the postwar arms race and current military planning. Western military build-ups are always described as 'responses' to potential threats or adversaries, otherwise there could be little justification in diverting resources away from social needs. The actual facts of the postwar arms race reveal different motivations. Thus the United States provided by far the greater stimulus to the arms race than the Soviet Union; if anything, it was the Soviet Union that consistently responded to US weapons innovations rather than the other way round.[82] Of the key turning points in the arms race – signified by the development of major new offensive weapons systems – only the intercontinental ballistic missile was deployed first by the Soviet Union (in 1957). All the other major innovations – the A-bomb, H-bomb, multiple warhead missiles etcetera – were developed and deployed first by the United States, and it maintained considerable military superiority (for what it was worth) throughout the period, whilst state propaganda declared the opposite. The domestically rooted imperatives of increased arms spending are also revealed in the current era, with state leaders on both sides of the Atlantic searching for convincing rationales to present to the public for embarking on new weapons programmes and directing resources away from social programmes.

The framework of the postwar system

Officially, the dominating fact of the postwar world was the Cold War: the East–West confrontation essentially between the United States and Soviet Union. There was indeed such an East–West conflict but it cannot provide a basis for understanding the foreign policies of the leading Western powers. Instead, the secret planning documents and the factual details of Western foreign interventions suggest that the postwar world can be understood as being primarily centred around two other conflicts.

The first was a West–South conflict, involving numerous military inter-ventions and covert operations geared to preventing independent social and economic development in the Third World from taking place outside overall Western control.

The second dominating fact was the conflict between the USA and the other Western powers. This involved the US need to assert its hegemony *within* the industrialized world and over its commercial rivals: the defeated states of Germany and Japan and the other Western European nations (even though the 'consolidation' of the West initially required US support for the European empires). In the pursuit of both these aims, the East–West conflict – which had some basis in reality – provided the crucial ideological background.

In the Cold War, the United States and the Soviet Union became tacit collaborators: each could use the threat of the other to justify its actions. In the Soviet Union, whose regime ruled by force and without a domestic mandate through real elections, recourse could be made to Western imperialism which was attempting to undermine the revolution and destroy the Soviet way of life. Internal dissenters could be castigated as agents of imperialism. The Cold War – for which only the USA was responsible, according to Soviet ideological requirements – provided a convenient pretext for disciplining the domestic population and for mobilising and militarizing society to counter the gigantic threat from the West. The Soviet occupation of, and subsequent repression and intervention in, Eastern Europe could be conveniently legitimised by reference to the fact that this was the traditional invasion route of Western armies to Russia. The Soviet regime's continued rule over its domains was therefore aided by the premiss of the continuing Western threat.

For the West, on the other hand, the 'Soviet threat' proved useful in a number of ways (several dimensions of this have been noted above). On the domestic scene, socialism could be discredited as being synonymous with Soviet-style 'communism': there could be no viable alternative, it was claimed, either to capitalism as already practised in the West or to Marxism-Leninism in the East. It was instructive that when the Soviet system finally collapsed in the early 1990s, Western leaders pronounced the death of socialism at home. The failures of the Soviet dictatorship's economic and political system were meant to signify the inherent failings of socialism and state planning generally, and there was deemed to be no alternative to Western 'free market' capitalism. Such declarations hid a basic fact: there was little, if anything, that was socialist about Soviet society. Soviet leaders used the term, professing they were perfecting a new social system, to legitimise their dictatorial rule, as ideology is commonly used to rationalise repression. Western leaders participated in the charade, for their own reasons.

For US foreign policy, maintenance of the 'threat' was crucial, as noted above. In fact, the gains to both sides by recourse to the threat of the other were too good to be missed and what developed might be viewed as an effective understanding between the United States and the Soviet Union as to respective 'spheres of influence'. For the Soviet Union, this meant Eastern Europe, for the United States practically the rest of the world; it was an unequal division but one that reflected respective power. The system was relatively stable, though there were clear dangers that it might not last. Most important, there was the prospect of nuclear war during the Cuban missile crisis of 1962 and the Arab–Israeli war of 1973. However, throughout the postwar era the Soviet Union was decidedly cautious in intervening in the Third World – essentially US territory. There was only one Soviet invasion, of Afghanistan in 1979. Major supplies of

arms and materiel were delivered to the governments of Angola and
Ethiopia in 1975–77, after both had been invaded by neighbouring states
(South Africa and Somalia). Indeed, almost all Soviet involvement in the
Third World came in response to external (Western) aggression against
national liberation movements. A leitmotif of the Cold War is that the
states that became heavily dependent on Soviet aid and/or were deemed
outposts of the Soviet empire – Cuba, Nicaragua, Angola, Vietnam etcetera
– underwent essentially nationalist revolutions, confronted Western aggression and consequently turned to the Soviet Union for aid. Once evidence
of Soviet involvement was presented (and sometimes even when it was
not), Western actions could be presented as 'responses' and the wars
could be be portrayed as merely part of the East–West conflict, thereby
further legitimising aggression.

The division of the world into spheres of influence is recognised in
both the British and US secret planning records. In 1945, the Foreign
Office noted that Soviet aims might be tantamount to an 'acceptance of
something like a division of the world into spheres of influence and a
tacit agreement that no one of the partners will hamper or indeed criticise
the activities of the other within its own sphere'.[83] Britain appeared
especially keen on this state of affairs, seeing such an understanding as
enabling it to maintain its empire. Britain hoped that the UN would help
formalise Britain's control over its sphere of influence, whilst other powers
could maintain control over theirs. Thus the Foreign Office observed that
'the great Powers should each be primarily responsible for organising
effective arrangements in the different parts of the world which are of
particular interest to them'. 'Of particular interest' to Britain was the
Middle East, which happened to contain the world's great energy reserves
and control of which would facilitate control of the world's economy.[84]

Early British policy in Iran was to encourage the government in Tehran
to grant an oil concession in the north of the country to the Soviet
Union, since then Britain's concession in the south of the country might
be more secure. The US ambassador in Iran commented: '... the British
hope the USSR will obtain petroleum rights in Iran because the British
think that their own concession will be safer and that no future Iran
government will be likely to nationalise the oil of the country if the
[Russians] have a concession here too'.[85] Earlier, in 1940, the British
Secretary of State for India had questioned 'whether we should not
deliberately do a deal with Russia over Iran, as Grey did in 1907 (or
Ribbentrop over Poland in 1939), encouraging her to do what she likes in
the north, so long as she recognises our interests in the south'.[86]

As regards the United States, the State Department observed in 1946
that 'the US together with other countries of the non-Soviet world believes
that there is no objective reason why the so-called capitalist system and
Communist system cannot peacefully exist provided neither attempts to

extend the area of its system by aggressive and ultimately forcible means at the expense of the other'.[87] A joint meeting between the State Department and the Department of Defence in 1950, meanwhile, considered 'the suggestion that has been made before, and may be made again, that the USSR and the United States divide the world into spheres of influence'.[88] Similarly, a Policy Planning Staff paper of 1951 considered US foreign policy aims and possible geopolitical scenarios after a major war. Several dangers presented themselves, one of which was that:

... Western Europe might emerge as a separate entity of great potential power not allied to us in a dependable fashion. In this case we may wish to work toward arrangements with Latin America and the English-speaking members of the British Commonwealth; we might even wish to develop Russia as a natural counter-poise to a German dominated Western Europe so as to limit the burden of responsibility on us for keeping such a Western European power complex within safe bounds.[89]

By around 1950 the framework of the postwar system was apparent. Britain sought to maintain its great power status by firm support for basic US policy objectives, as the 'junior partner in an orbit of power predominantly under American aegis'. At the same time, Britain could still independently counter threats to the new system under construction and to its own specific interests, by proceeding to engage in various interventions in the colonies and elsewhere, ensuring that the correct form of economic and political 'development' was pursued (see Chapters 3 and 4). First-order goals of Anglo-American power were to harness the Third World's economic resources to the Western economies and the 'consolidation' of the West under US auspices. The control of the world economy was threatened above all by independent, nationalist forces in the Third World, especially in the Middle East where the crucial oil resources lay. The Soviet Union was a threat of a much lower order than this, though recourse to the 'Soviet threat' was useful in providing the ideological background to policy carried out for other purposes.

Control over respective spheres of influence could be maintained by referring to the threat of the other. Meanwhile, the real threats could be dealt with as required, with the support of other elements in the propaganda system. The threat of a wayward Western Europe – the world's most industrialized centre and the key to Western consolidation under US auspices – could similarly be reckoned with partly by the superpowers reaching a tacit understanding, whilst the US presented policy as based on the East–West struggle. Western European leaders participated since they could also benefit, to a large extent imitating the presentations of US leaders whilst presiding over economic and political 'stability' in their own countries. When the Soviet Union collapsed, the public justification for foreign policy was instantly removed and Western Europe and Japan could no longer be so easily disciplined. Other justifications for US aggression in the Third World needed to be created. In the present era, they are drugs, fanatical Arabs, international terrorism – whatever is handiest at the time – the foreign policy goals essentially remaining the same (see Chapters 7 and 8). Efforts by the USA to assert its hegemony within the industrialised world, however, currently present far more dilemmas for US leaders as the collapse of the Soviet Union removes the cohesive ideological glue and points towards a greater assertion of independence on the part of the two other elements in the Northern triad. The West–South and US–West conflicts therefore continue into the present.

In conclusion, then, three principles, established in the aftermath of the Second World War, guided US and British planners throughout the postwar period. The first was that the world's major economic resources were to be effectively controlled by the West and its allies, irrespective of the aspirations of the local populations. The second principle was that the West could overtly or covertly intervene in states or regions where these resources lay, but could not present policy with regard to the first principle, instead usually taking recourse in the presentation of the 'Soviet threat'. The third principle was that international capitalism had to be maintained and expanded so that the fruits of these endeavours would accrue to the ruling groups, business elites and those associated with them in their own states. Dissent had therefore to be controlled on both the domestic and international levels, with propaganda in relation to the former, often with violence in relation to the latter. These principles remain in place in their essentials after the disintegration of the Soviet Union.

Notes

1. Foreign Office, 'Russian strategic intentions and the threat to peace', 7 December 1950, *Documents on British Foreign Policy*, Calendar to Ser. II, Vol. IV, p. 9/57.

2. Chiefs of Staff, 'Korea: Effect on British interests in the Far East', 7 July 1950, *Documents on British Foreign Policy*, Calendar to Ser. II, Vol. IV, p. 2/65.

3. Memorandum by Richard Clarke, 11 May 1945, *Anglo-American economic collaboration*, pp. 111–12.

4. Cabinet Office, Summary of conclusions of report, 29 October 1945, *Documents on British Foreign Policy*, Ser. I, Vol. II, p. 574.

5. Referring to the importance of Southeast Asia. Record of tripartite meeting, undated [1950], *Documents on British Foreign Policy*, Calendar to Ser. II, Vol. II, p. 387.

6. Memorandum for the Permanent Under-Secretary's Committee, 27 April 1950, *Documents on British Foreign Policy*, Ser. II, Vol. II, pp. 164–5.

7. Report of the Special 'Ad Hoc' Committee of the State–War–Navy Coordinating Committee, 21 April 1947, *FRUS*, 1947, Vol. III, p. 209.

8. Summary of remarks by McGhee, 25 October 1950, *FRUS*, 1950, Vol. V, p. 1571; see also Memorandum by the CIA, 24 September 1951, *FRUS*, 1951, Vol. I, p. 206.

9. State Department memorandum, undated [1947], *FRUS*, 1947, Vol. V, p. 531.

10. Ibid., p. 532.

11. State Department policy statement on Indochina, 27 September 1948, *FRUS*, 1948, Vol. VI, pp. 44–5.

12. Minister in Saigon to Secretary of State, 24 February 1951, *FRUS*, 1951, Vol. VI, p. 385.

13. State Department policy statement on Indochina, 27 September 1948, *FRUS*, 1948, Vol. VI, p. 48.

14. Churchill to Eisenhower, 8 July 1954, *Churchill–Eisenhower correspondence*, p. 155.

15. Office of Near Eastern Affairs, 'Regional policy statement: Near East', 28 December 1950, *FRUS*, 1950, Vol. V, pp. 271–2.

16. For example, memorandum by the Chief of the Division of South Asian Affairs, 5 November 1947, *FRUS*, 1947, Vol. V, p. 580; Statement by the US and UK groups, undated [1947], *FRUS*, 1947, Vol. V, pp. 610–11; Memorandum by the CIA, 24 September 1951, *FRUS*, 1951, Vol. I, p. 205.

17. State Department memorandum, undated [1947], *FRUS*, 1947, Vol. V, p. 513.

18. Ibid., p. 511.

19. Bureau of Near Eastern, South Asian and African Affairs, 'Regional policy statement on Africa south of the Sahara', 29 December 1950, *FRUS*, 1950, Vol. V, p. 1587.

20. Memorandum by McGhee, 12 April 1950, *FRUS*, 1950, Vol. V, p. 1516; See also memorandum of conversation, 19 September 1950, *FRUS*, 1950, Vol. V, p. 1552; Memorandum of conversation, 25 September 1950, *FRUS*, 1950, Vol. V, p. 1559.

21. Summary of remarks by McGhee, 25 October 1950, *FRUS*, 1950, Vol. V, pp. 1570, 1572.

22. Diplomatic Agent in Tangier to Secretary of State, 30 January 1947, *FRUS*, 1947, Vol. V, p. 673.

23. Policy paper by McGhee, 'A new approach in Asia', 30 August 1950, *FRUS*, 1950, Vol. VI, p. 138.

24. Minutes of a Policy Planning Staff meeting, 11 October 1949, *FRUS*, 1949, Vol. I, p. 400.

25. Office of South Asian Affairs, 'Regional policy statement: South Asia', 9 October 1950, *FRUS*, 1950, Vol. V, pp. 246–7.

26. United States delegation at the tripartite meetings to Secretary of State, 4 May 1950, *FRUS*, 1950, Vol. III, p. 963.

27. Report of the Mutual Defence Assistance Programme Mission to Southeast Asia, 6 December 1950, *FRUS*, 1950, Vol. VI, p. 168.

28. Memorandum for the Permanent Under-Secretary's Committee, 27 April 1950, *Documents on British Foreign Policy*, Ser. II, Vol. II, p. 162.

29. Memorandum by R. Scott, 1 February 1951, *Documents on British Foreign Policy*, Ser. II, Vol. IV, p. 349.

30. Memorandum by the Secretary of State for Foreign Affairs, 20 April 1950, PRO, CAB 129/39 CP (50) 78.

31. Memorandum by Bevin, 20 April 1950, *Documents on British Foreign Policy*, Ser. II, Vol. II, pp. 67–8.

32. State Department memorandum, 1 December 1945, *FRUS*, 1946, Vol. I, p. 1137.

33. Ambassador to Iran to Secretary of State, 25 September 1945, *FRUS*, 1945, Vol. VIII, p. 419.

34. See, for example, with regard to Grenada and El Salvador, Blum, pp. 312–13, 327–30.

35. British academic Joseph Frankel has elucidated on this general point in his book on British foreign policy: 'It is one of the recurrent themes of political argument that politicians not only perceive what they wish to perceive, but that they hide their preferences in seemingly objective and generally unarticulated assumptions, either through ignorance, or in order to deceive others, or to spare themselves the trouble and often

the pain or shock of a more realistic appraisal. It is a fairly arbitrary task to choose for analysis the assumptions which are most relevant. In foreign policy, as in all other areas of social behaviour, the assumptions are legion; most of them remain hidden not only from those who analyse behaviour from the outside but also from the people directly involved. The human tendency is to remain consistent in one's thinking, to restrict adjustment to the minimum; this works for continuity and tradition and frequently blinds us to such evidence as disturbs the balance of our image. Only when discrepancies have become really blatant, and policy outcomes highly unsatisfactory and disturbing, are our assumptions fundamentally re-examined.' *British foreign policy 1945–1973,* Royal Institute of International Affairs/Oxford University Press, London, 1975, pp. 89–90.

36. Foreign Office, 'Russian strategic intentions and the threat to peace', 7 December 1950, *Documents on British Foreign Policy,* Calendar to Ser. II, Vol. IV, pp. 9/42–54.

37. Report to the President by the National Security Council, Appendix A, 8 August 1951, *FRUS,* 1951, Vol. I, p. 152; my emphasis.

38. Northedge, p. 187.

39. Lord Beloff, 'The end of the British Empire and the assumption of world-wide commitments by the United States', in W. Roger Louis and Hedley Bull (eds), *The 'special relationship': Anglo-American relations since 1945,* Clarendon, Oxford, 1986, p. 257.

40. David Watt, 'Introduction: the Anglo-American special relationship', in Louis and Bull (eds), p. 4.

41. See, for example, Frankel (p. 128), who writes that in the Middle East 'Soviet expansionism was clearly in evidence and the radical nationalist alternatives seemed unpromising [to Britain], not only for this reason but also because they seemed to threaten British economic interests and not be in the interests of the people concerned, as we interpret them'. No doubt Britain was gravely concerned with the interests of the people of the Middle East.

42. Frankel, p. 128.

43. David Reynolds, *Britannia overruled: British policy and world power in the twentieth century,* Longman, London, 1991, pp. 187–90.

44. International Institute for Strategic Studies (IISS), *Strategic survey 1988–1989,* IISS, London, 1989, p. 41.

45. Record of US and UK meeting, 24 April 1950, *Documents on British Foreign Policy,* Ser. II, Vol. II, p. 93.

46. Foreign Office brief, 19 April 1950, *Documents on British Foreign Policy,* Ser. II, Vol. II, p. 62.

47. Permanent Under-Secretary's Committee, 'The United Kingdom and the United Nations', 25 April 1950, *Documents on British Foreign Policy,* Calendar to Ser. II, Vol. II, p. 144.

48. Chiefs of Staff, 'Defence policy and global strategy', 7 June 1950, *Documents on British Foreign Policy,* Ser. II, Vol. IV, p. 414.

49. Foreign Office brief, 19 April 1950, *Documents on British Foreign Policy,* Ser. II, Vol. II, p. 62.

50. National Security Council report, 30 March 1948, *FRUS,* 1948, Vol. I, Part 2, p. 549.

51. Memorandum by Bevin and Hall, 25 August 1945, *Documents on British Foreign Policy,* Ser. I, Vol. II, p. 27.

52. Record of a Foreign Office meeting, 9 July 1945, *Documents on British Foreign Policy,* Ser. I, Vol. I, p. 112.

53. William Blum, *The CIA: A forgotten history,* Zed, London, 1986, pp. 23–31.

54. Memorandum by Far Eastern Department, 10 September 1945, *Documents on British Foreign Policy,* Ser. I, Vol. II, p. 98.

55. J. Anderson to Earl of Halifax, 18 July 1945, *Documents on British Foreign Policy,* Ser. I, Vol. I, p. 737.

56. Bruce Cumings, *The origins of the Korean War, Volume II: The roaring of the cataract, 1947–1950*, Princeton University Press, Princeton, 1990, pp. 50, 57, 168, 469–70.

57. Ibid., pp. 628, 635, 758, 760.

58. Record of US–UK meeting, 9 May 1950, *Documents on British Foreign Policy*, Ser. II, Vol. II, p. 273.

59. O. Franks to W. Strang, 28 April 1950, *Documents on British Foreign Policy*, Ser. II, Vol. II, p. 187.

60. Policy Planning Staff, 'Review of current trends: US foreign policy', 24 February 1948, *FRUS*, 1948, Vol. I, Part 2, p. 515.

61. Ann Deighton, 'Towards a "Western strategy": the making of British policy towards Germany, 1945–46', in Deighton (ed.), p. 58.

62. Record of tripartite meeting, 11 May 1950, *Documents on British Foreign Policy*, Ser. II, Vol. II, p. 306.

63. Matthias Peter, 'Britain, the cold war and the economics of German rearmament, 1949–51', in Deighton (ed.), p. 274.

64. Foreign Office brief, 24 April 1950, *Documents on British Foreign Policy*, Ser. II, Vol. II, pp. 100–101, 106.

65. R. Makins to E. Hall-Patch, 28 April 1950, *Documents on British Foreign Policy*, Ser. II, Vol. II, p. 183.

66. Report of the Special 'Ad Hoc' Committee of the State–War–Navy Coordinating Committee, Annex A to Appendix A, 21 April 1947, *FRUS*, 1947, Vol. III, p. 210.

67. Enclosure in Kennan to Acheson, 23 May 1947, *FRUS*, 1947, Vol. III, pp. 224–5.

68. Report of the Special 'Ad Hoc' Committee of the State–War–Navy Coordinating Committee, Appendix B, 21 April 1947, *FRUS*, 1947, Vol. III, p. 217.

69. Enclosure in Kennan to Acheson, 23 May 1947, *FRUS*, 1947, Vol. III, p. 229.

70. For the text of NSC68 and subsequent citations see *FRUS*, 1950, Vol. I, pp. 234–92.

71. Kennan to Secretary of State, 17 February 1950, *FRUS*, 1950, Vol. I, pp. 160–2.

72. Schaub to Lay, 8 May 1950, *FRUS*, 1950, Vol. I, p. 301.

73. Thorp to Secretary of State, 5 April 1950, *FRUS*, 1950, Vol. I, pp. 218–19.

74. Record of a meeting of the State–Defence Policy Review Group, 16 March 1950, *FRUS*, 1950, Vol. I, p. 198.

75. *FRUS*, 1950, Vol. I, p. 252; my emphasis.

76. Record of a meeting of the State–Defence Policy Review Group, 16 March 1950, *FRUS*, 1950, Vol. I, p. 199.

77. *FRUS*, 1950, Vol. I, pp. 258, 286; my emphasis.

78. Report to the President by the National Security Council, 8 August 1951, *FRUS*, 1951, Vol. I, pp. 139, 140.

79. *FRUS*, 1950, Vol. I, p. 265.

80. Hare to Webb, 5 April 1950, *FRUS*, 1950, Vol. I, pp. 220–1.

81. Barrett to Secretary of State, 6 April 1950, *FRUS*, 1950, Vol. I, p. 225.

82. See, for example, J. Garrison and P. Shivpuri, *The Russian threat: Its myths and realities*, Gateway, London, 1983.

83. Memorandum by Clark Kerr, 27 March 1945, *The Foreign Office and the Kremlin*, p. 198.

84. Minute by Viscount Hood, 3 September 1945, *Documents on British Foreign Policy*, Ser. I, Vol. II, p. 47.

85. Ambassador in Iran to Secretary of State, 11 January 1947, *FRUS*, 1947, Vol. V, p. 892.

86. Louise L'Estrange Fawcett, 'Invitations to cold war: British policy in Iran, 1941–47', in Deighton (ed.), p. 186.

87. Matthews to State–War–Navy Coordinating Committee, 1 April 1946, *FRUS*, 1946, Vol. I, p. 1169.

88. Record of a meeting of the State–Defence Policy Review Group, 16 March 1950, *FRUS*, 1950, Vol. I, p. 197.

89. Policy Planning Staff paper, 26 June 1951, *FRUS*, 1951, Vol. I, pp. 99–100.

PART TWO

THE COLONIAL IMPERATIVE

CHAPTER 3

COLONIALISM UNDER DECOLONISATION

Britain expended considerable effort to construct the postwar world according to its basic aims and priorities. Most obviously, this effort took the form of military interventions overseas, which were marked by brutality and violence, abuse of human rights, and disregard for international law and the United Nations. In this chapter three British interventions abroad are considered, on each one of the three Third World continents.

Restoring order: Malaya

Between 1948 and 1960 British military forces were deployed in the 'emergency' or 'counter-insurgency' campaign in Malaya, a British colony until independence in 1957. This was Britain's first major military campaign outside Europe since the end of the Second World War and has often been described as 'Britain's Asian Cold War'.[1] This description is correct if by 'Cold War' is meant not the conflict with the Soviet Union but the imperative – outlined in Part One – of ordering important areas of the world upon acceptable economic and political lines.

British documents make clear the importance of using Malayan economic resources for the benefit of the British economy. 'Malaya', the Colonial Office stated in 1950, 'possesses ... valuable minerals – coal, bauxite, tungsten, gold, iron ore, manganese, ilmenite and china clay.' However, its main riches were rubber and tin. 'Apart from rubber', the same report noted, 'the tin mining industry of Malaya is the biggest dollar earner in the British Commonwealth.'[2] Tin exports constituted around 12–15 per cent of the colony's revenue,[3] whilst 'on rubber sales depends 3/4 of the Federation's income'.[4] As a result of colonialism, Malaya was effectively owned by Europe, primarily Britain. The Colonial Office noted that 'British capital provides the backing for the bulk of the industrial enterprises in the Federation and in Singapore.'[5] A large number of the mining companies were also registered in Britain.[6] Most important, however, in the early 1950s 70 per cent of the acreage of rubber estates (and 42 per cent of total rubber acreage) was owned by European (primarily British) business interests. By contrast, the figures for Asian ownership were 29 per cent and 30 per cent respectively.[7]

These first-order interests in Malaya were clearly enunciated in a House of Lords debate in February 1952. Lord Ogmore noted:

> In economics, before the war, and to a large extent still, [Malaya's] eggs are, so to speak, in two baskets, the one tin and the other rubber. Very fortunate it is for this country that those baskets are there, because they have very largely supported the standard of living of the people of this country and the sterling area ever since the war ended; what we should do without Malaya, and its earnings in tin and rubber, I do not know.[8]

Lord Milverton cautioned their lordships 'not [to] forget ... that the prize in this contest is the richest country for its size and population in the world'. This was due to its 'rubber and tin, the coal and iron ore ... all the tropical produce of Malaya, from palm oil to pineapples – to say nothing of the oil of Brunei and Sarawak'. Malaya was the 'greatest material prize in South-East Asia'.[9]

The chief problem with the insurgency was that it threatened British control over this 'material prize', in particular by disrupting the dollar-earning exports of the rubber and tin industries. The Colonial Secretary remarked in 1948 that Malaya 'is by far the most important source of dollars in the colonial empire and it would gravely worsen the whole dollar balance of the Sterling Area if there were serious interference with Malayan exports'.[10] The *Economist* fully concurred, noting: '... if the rubber industry decays Malaya will decay too. Communism will find a fertile field in what should have been the Commonwealth's best dollar earner.'[11] In the above-mentioned House of Lords debate, the Earl of Listowel had stated, '... even if [the insurgents] do not score any military or political successes, they can wreck the economy of Malaya.' Existing deposits of tin were being 'quickly used up and, owing to Communist activities in the jungle and on the jungle fringe, no new areas are being prospected for future working'. Unless new prospecting were to be resumed over a large area, 'tin mining will cease abruptly' in around ten to twelve years. The situation as regards rubber was 'no less alarming', with the fall in output 'largely due to the direct and indirect effects of communist sabotage'.[12]

An influential big-business pressure group – Joint Malayan Interests – supported these assertions, warning the Colonial Office of 'soft-hearted doctrinaires, with emphasis on early self-government' for the colony, and imploring the government that 'until the fight against banditry has been won there can be no question of any further moves towards self-government'. 'The immediate effects' of the emergency, 'apart from serious loss of life, are economic – losses through direct damage, interruption of work by operations and intimidation, causing loss of manpower and falling outputs and the enormous cost which adds fuel to the fires of inflation'.[13]

Britain's military forces were dispatched to 'defend' Malaya from these threats to the 'stability' of the country. 'In its narrower context', the Foreign

Office observed, the 'war against bandits is very much a war in defence of [the] rubber industry'.[14] Richard Allen, in a study of the war in Malaya, is correct to observe that the insurgents 'brought the established order in Malaya for a time to the edge of disaster' – 'order' needing to be understood in the sense outlined in Chapter 2.[15]

This is not to say that the threat of communism represented by the Malayan insurgents was not perceived by British planners as real or that it was no element at all in British policy. Yet the term 'communism' needs to be understood. Britain's primary interest in Malaya was economic, and it wished to continue to use the resources of that country for the benefit of British business interests. Communism in Malaya simply posed the threat that Britain would lose control over these economic resources. There was never any question of military intervention in Malaya by either the USSR or China. Nor, indeed, was any material support ever proffered by either the USSR or China to the insurgents in Malaya; the emergency was a purely internal affair. 'No operational links have been established as existing,' the Colonial Office reported four years after the beginning of the emergency.[16] Rather, as the *Economist* described, the significance of the Chinese revolution of 1949 – which, the British feared, might be repeated in Malaya – and, one might add, the significance, of communism generally, was that the communists 'are moving towards an economy and a type of trade in which there will be no place for the foreign manufacturer, the foreign banker or the foreign trader'.[17]

British policy could not be presented as being based primarily on economic motives, even though they were often openly expressed. Rather, the propaganda system needed to state that Britain was in Malaya simply to defend the 'free world' from Russian and/or Chinese aggression and communist expansionism, as part of the Cold War. Subsequent works of scholarship reinforced this version of history with near-perfect discipline.

One of the most reputable analysts of early postwar British foreign policy, Ritchie Ovendale, for example, notes in one study that Malaya at the beginning of the emergency in 1948 was 'an area of imperial responsibility'. That is, Malaya was an area conquered and subjugated by Britain and which Britain was continuing to use for its own ends; in the same way, one might describe the former East Germany as 'an area of Soviet responsibility'. Ovendale continues by noting that Britain was 'fighting the communist terrorists to enable Malaya to become independent and help itself'. Later, quick mention is made of the fact that 'Britain was dependent on the area for rubber, tea and jute. Earnings from Malaya helped the sterling area's dollar pool. A combination of Western technology and Eastern manpower could be welded into a formidable partnership.' Then, 'the economic ties could not be severed without serious consequences'. In all, this is described as 'a peculiarly close relationship with those countries in South-East Asia within the sterling area'. These are the only mentions in the study of Britain's economic motives in Malaya.

Ovendale's language, too, is interesting: Britain is 'dependent' on some of these resources and the profits from British control of them are 'earnings'. If these do not accrue to Britain there will be 'serious consequences'. In other words, British control over Malayan resources is somewhat excused since the British need is so great and the stakes so momentous. ('Formidable partnership' and 'close relationship', meanwhile, might more properly be viewed as euphemisms for continued economic exploitation.) Ovendale often faithfully reports the deliberations of British planners without any dissenting comments. Thus he writes that Britain's 'long term objective' in Southeast Asia was 'to improve economic and social conditions' there, though how this is compatible with Britain's reaping the profits from Malayan rubber and tin exports at the expense of the poverty-stricken population is left unexplained. Overall, he contends, Britain's 'immediate intention' in the region, rather than deriving from economic motives, was to 'prevent the spread of communism and to resist Russian expansion'.[18].

A less subtle approach is adopted by Robert Jackson who, in a book-length study of the emergency, makes no mention at all of Britain's economic motives or the use of rubber and tin resources for British purposes. Rather, Britain was simply resisting communist expansion. 'Even by April 1950, the extent of the communist threat to Malaya was not fully appreciated by the British government,' Jackson comments. Things changed, he claimed, with the election of Churchill as Prime Minister in 1951: 'Churchill's shrewd instinct grasped the fact that if Malaya fell under communist domination, the rest of Asia would quickly follow.' This supposed fear often repeated in the documents is presented as a fact.[19]

Returning to real-life history, at the root of the emergency was the failure of the British colonial authorities to guarantee the rights of the Chinese in Malaya, who made up nearly 45 per cent of the population. Proposals for a new political structure to create a racial equilibrium between the Chinese and the Malay community and remove the latter's ascendancy over the former, which Britain had traditionally promoted, had been defeated by Malays and the ex-colonial Malayan lobby.[20] By 1948 Britain was promoting a new federal constitution that would confirm Malay privileges and resign the huge majority (about 90 per cent[21]) of Chinese to noncitizenship. At the same time, a series of strikes and general labour unrest, aided by an increasingly powerful trade union movement, resulted in a crackdown by the colonial authorities involving the banning of some trade unions, imprisonment of some of their members and harassment of the left-wing press. Thus the beginning of the emergency in 1948 created opportunities for the British colonial government in the labour field. Colonial officials observed that 'emergency conditions' – for example 'the enforcement of the curfew in some areas' – 'have tended to damp down the endeavours of keen trade unionists'.[22] Also, 'the emergency regulations and the police action under them have undoubtedly reduced the amount of active resistance to wage reductions and retrenchments', and in Singapore the number of unions 'has decreased since the emergency started'.[23] The Colonial Office in London declared in February 1949: '... it is now more than six months since a state of emergency was declared in Singapore and during this period the colony has been almost entirely free from labour troubles.'[24]

Thomas Kaplan comments that 'with the political and economic path to power effectively blocked' by Britain, the Malayan Communist Party – which was to provide the backbone of the insurgency – 'had two alternatives, either to accept that their role in the British succession would be limited, or to go to ground and hope to pressurise the British to leave'.[25] An insurgent movement was formed, out of one that had been trained and armed by Britain to resist the Japanese occupation of the country during the Second World War; the Chinese had offered the only active resistance to the Japanese occupiers. The insurgency was comprised almost entirely of disaffected Chinese and received considerable support from Chinese 'squatters', who numbered over half a million. The 'squatters' were described by the Foreign Office in 1952:

> The vast majority of the poorer Chinese were employed in the tin mines and on the rubber estates and they suffered most from the Japanese occupation of the country. ... During the Japanese occupation, they were deprived both of their normal employment and of the opportunity to return to their homeland. ... Large numbers of Chinese were forced out of useful employment and had no alternative but to follow the example of other distressed Chinese, who in small numbers had been obliged to scratch for a living in the jungle clearings even before the war.[26]

It was these 'squatters' who were to be the chief object of Britain's draconian measures in the colony.

In 1952 a memorandum by the British Defence Secretary stipulated that, from now on, the insurgents – previously usually referred to as 'bandits' – would be officially known as 'communist terrorists' or CTs.[27] Subsequent scholarship concurred. Richard Allen contrasts the 'CTs ... as they came to be known' with the Malay and British security forces, the 'defenders of Malaya', in his term. Allen comments that 'the eventually successful campaign' against them 'has been defined as the crafty use of a shoe-string'.[28] It is a view that accords little with reality. To combat an insurgent force that was usually around 3,000–6,000,[29] the 'defenders of Malaya' embarked upon an often brutal counterinsurgency war which involved large-scale bombing, dictatorial police measures and the wholesale 'resettlement' of hundreds of thousands of 'squatters', tactics that Allen describes as 'certain useful methods' to combat the insurgents.[30] The High Commissioner in Malaya, Gerald Templer, noted that 'the hard core of armed communists in this country are fanatics and must be, and will be, exterminated'.[31]

'During his two years in office,' Richard Clutterbuck, a former British official in Malaya, writes, 'two-thirds of the guerrillas were wiped out'; to the author, this fact is a testament to Templer's 'dynamism and leadership'.[32] Clutterbuck describes one plan effected by Britain in 1952. The first stage 'was to establish an outer ring of ambushes to prevent an exodus from the killing ground'. Then, after waiting for the insurgents to consume their stocks of food in the jungle, 'stage V – the killing stage – would come'. 'In the second month of the operation,' Clutterbuck notes, 'the kill rate rose and by the time the two months were up ... a total of twenty-five guerrillas had been eliminated.' 'These were,' the author states, 'by any standards, two highly successful months.'[33]

Another way of killing or subjugating the enemy was aerial bombardment – in which Britain could boast much expertise in pre-war days of 'policing' its empire, especially in the Middle East. Some 4,500 air strikes were conducted in the first five years of the Malayan war.[34] Robert Jackson writes:

> ... during 1956, some 545,000 lb. of bombs had been dropped on a supposed [guerrilla] encampment ... but a lack of accurate pinpoints had nullified the effect. The camp was again attacked at the beginning of May 1957 ... [dropping] a total of 94,000 lb. of bombs, but because of inaccurate target information this weight of explosive was 250 yards off target. Then, on 15 May ... 70,000 lb. of bombs were dropped.

'The attack was entirely successful', Jackson declares, since 'four terrorists were killed'. The author notes that 'the 500 lb. nose-fused bomb ... was employed from August 1948' and had 'a mean area of effectiveness of 15,000 square feet'. 'Another very viable weapon', meanwhile, was the 20lb. fragmentation bomb. 'Since a Sutherland could carry a load of 190, its effect on terrorist morale was considerable,' he states. 'Unfortunately, it was not used in great numbers, despite its excellent potential as a harassing weapon.' Perhaps equally unfortunate was a Lincoln bomber, once 'dropping its bombs 600 yards short ... killing twelve civilians and injuring twenty-six others'.[35]

A young British officer commented that – in combating the insurgents, who were themselves indulging in gross atrocities – 'we were shooting people. We were killing them. ... This was raw savage success. It was butchery. It was horror.' Jackson comments:

> but, like seasoned jungle veterans, they became accustomed to it. They coped, and coped very well, and boys of 19 emerged from the jungle as men with leadership experience that would carry them through any experience they might encounter on their return to civilian life.[36]

One Brigadier simply told his colonel: '... you have killed more Communist terrorists in my brigade than any other battalion and I am very sorry to lose you.' Running totals of kills were published and became a source of competition between army units. One British army conscript recalled: '... when we had an officer who did come out with us on patrol I realised that he was only interested in one thing: killing as many people as possible.'[37]

Brian Lapping observes in his study of the end of the British empire that there was 'some vicious conduct by the British forces, who routinely beat up Chinese squatters when they refused, or possibly were unable, to give information' about the insurgents.[38] At Batang Kali in December 1948 the British army slaughtered twenty-four Chinese villagers (referred to by Jackson as 'male terrorist suspects'[39]), before burning the village. The British government claimed initially that the villagers were guerrillas, and then that they were trying to escape, neither of which was true. A Scotland Yard inquiry into the massacre was called off by the Heath government in 1970 and the full details have never been officially investigated.[40] There were also cases of the bodies of dead guerrillas being exhibited in public.[41] This was good practice, according to the *Scotsman*, since 'simple-minded peasants are told and come to believe that the communist leaders are invulnerable'.[42] British soldiers had also forced women workers to strip in order to search them, allegedly on suspicion of smuggling supplies to the insurgents.[43]

Decapitation of insurgents was a little more unusual – intended as a way of identifying dead guerrillas when it was not possible to bring their corpses in from the jungle – and a photograph of a Marine Commando holding two insurgents' heads caused a public outcry in April 1952. The Colonial Office privately noted: '... there is no doubt that under international law a similar case in wartime would be a war crime.'[44] Dyak headhunters from Borneo worked alongside the 'security forces', High Commissioner Templer having suggested that Dyaks should be used not only for tracking 'but in their traditional role as head-hunters'.[45] Templer 'thinks it is essential that the practice [decapitation] should continue', although this would only be necessary 'in very rare cases', the Colonial Office observed.[46] It also noted that, because of the recent outcry over this issue, 'it would be well to delay any public statement on this matter for some months'.[47] The Colonial Office also warned that, in addition to decapitation, 'other practices may have grown up, particularly in units which employ Dyaks, which would provide ugly photographs'.[48] The *Daily Telegraph* commented: '... there is still some hesitancy about using that force in Malaya because of the Dyaks' reputation as headhunters', but 'the Dyaks ... would be superb fighters in the Malayan jungle, and it would be absurd if uninformed public opinion at home were to oppose their use'.[49]

Another British war measure was the infliction of temporary 'collective punishments' on villages in which it was deemed some villagers were aiding the insurgents. At Tanjong Malim in March 1952 Templer imposed a twenty-two-hour house curfew, banned everyone from leaving the village, closed the schools and stopped bus services and reduced the rice rations for 20,000 people.[50] The latter measure prompted a letter to the Colonial Office from the London School of Hygiene and Tropical Medicine, which noted that the 'chronically undernourished Malayan' might not be able to survive as a result. 'This measure is bound to result in an increase, not only of sickness but also of deaths, particularly amongst the mothers and very young children.'[51] 'Another class of sufferers', a press report noted, 'are families which share outside latrines. Already people have been fined for leaving their homes to use one.'[52]

In another instance of collective punishment – at Sengei Pelek the following month – measures included a house curfew, a reduction of 40 per cent in the rice ration and the construction of a 'chain-link fence 22 yards outside the existing barbed wire fence' around the town. The colonial government explained that these measures were being imposed upon the 4,000 villagers 'for their continually supplying food' to the insurgents and 'because they did not give information to the authorities'[53] (surely a far worse crime than decapitation). This was what the *Times* referred to as 'deal[ing] firmly' with those who were aiding the insurgents.[54]

Jackson comments: 'Templer's methods were certainly unorthodox but there was no doubt that they produced results.'[55] Allen concurs, noting that 'one obvious justification of the Templer methods and measures ... is that the course he set was maintained after his departure and achieved in the end virtually complete success'.[56]

The 'resettlement' programme was a further measure enacted by the 'defenders of Malaya' to secure the proper control of the country; this 'resettlement' involved the removal of over half a million Chinese squatters into 'new villages'. The Colonial Office referred to the policy as 'a great piece of social development'.[57] Lapping describes what the policy meant in reality:

> A community of squatters would be surrounded in their huts at dawn, when they were all asleep, forced into lorries and settled in a new village encircled by barbed wire with searchlights round the periphery to prevent movement at night. Before the 'new villagers' were let out in the mornings to go to work in the paddy fields, soldiers or police searched them for rice, clothes, weapons or messages. Many complained both that the new villages lacked essential facilities and that they were no more than concentration camps.[58]

In Jackson's view, however, the new villages were 'protected by barbed wire'.[59]

A further gain for the resettlement policy was 'a pool of cheap labour available for employers',[60] described by Clutterbuck as 'an unprecedented opportunity for work for the displaced squatters on the rubber estates'.[61]

'An essential aspect' of the resettlement policy, a newsletter of the Malayan government correctly stated, 'is to educate [the Chinese] into accepting the control of government'[62] – control over them, that is, by the British and Malays. 'We still have a long way to go in conditioning the [Chinese]', the colonial government declared, 'to accept policies which can easily be twisted by the opposition to appear as acts of colonial oppression.' But the task was made easier since 'it must always be emphasised that the Chinese mind is schizophrenic and ever subject to the twin stimuli of racialism and self-interest'.[63] The *Times* commented that the British policy of allowing some villagers to bear arms was 'an imaginative gesture' on the part of the High Commissioner, 'which, more than anything else, shows that the government is prepared to trust the Malayan Chinese'.[64]

There were various other measures designed to secure the compliance of the population in the British design for the country's future. The detention laws resulted in 34,000 people being held for varying periods throughout the first eight years of the emergency; another 15,000 were deported.[65] The Foreign Office explained that the purpose of the detention regulations was 'to cover the cases of persons who are a menace to public security but who cannot, because of insufficient evidence, be brought to trial'. By December 1950, 10,000 people were detained in camps. The laws that enabled the High Commissioner to deport detainees extended 'to certain categories of dependants of the person concerned'.[66] The High Commissioner's view was that 'the removal of all the detainees to China would contribute more than any other single factor to the disruption' of the insurgency.[67]

Many of the methods used by Britain in the Malayan war were later taken up with even more devastating effect by the United States in Vietnam, particularly resettlement, which became the 'strategic hamlet' programme. In the late 1960s, during the Vietnam War, Britain trained US, Vietnamese and Thai troops at its jungle warfare school in Malaya; one of Britain's leading counter-insurgency experts in Malaya later advised the Nixon regime on Vietnam policy for several years.[68] Anticipating US tactics in Vietnam, Britain had experimented with the use of chemicals as defoliants and crop destroyers from the early 1950s. From June to October 1952, for example, 1,250 acres of roadside vegetation at possible ambush points (an average of 23½ miles of one side of the road per month) were sprayed with defoliant.[69] This was described as a policy of 'national importance',[70] in which the chemicals giant ICI provided its services, seeing it, according to the Colonial Office, as 'a lucrative field for experiment'.[71]

Britain achieved all of its main aims in Malaya: the insurgents were defeated and, with independence in 1957, the country was set upon a course of political and economic development in which Britain's substantial economic interests were essentially preserved. The Imperial Affairs Committee of the British Conservative Party urged that Singapore, one part of the Malayan Federation, would 'remain autonomous as far ahead as one cares to look, under direct British control, held in trust for the military and economic defence of the Commonwealth and free [sic] world – like Gibraltar, or Panama by the USA'.[72] At independence, 85 per cent of Malayan export earnings still derived from tin and rubber. Chris Dixon has observed that 'some 70 per cent of the profits from registered companies were in foreign, mainly British, hands and were largely repatriated. Agency houses, largely European owned, controlled 70 per cent of foreign trade and 75 per cent of plantations.' Furthermore, 'independence brought no significant reduction in the degree of foreign control over the economy', which remained 'closely tied to foreign interests' into the 1960s and 1970s. By 1971, 80 per cent of mining, 62 per cent of manufacturing and 58 per cent of construction were foreign-owned, mainly by Britain.[73] The established order had been protected.

The good fight in Africa: Kenya

Similar concerns preoccupied British planners in another colony: Kenya. Here Britain declared a state of emergency in 1952 and military forces were sent to quell a rebellion by the Mau Mau movement, which consisted predominantly of Kikuyu, the largest Kenyan ethnic group. The Attorney-General in the Kenyan colonial government called Mau Mau 'a secret underground nationalistic organisation which is virulently anti-European'.[74] A government-sponsored report on the origins of Mau Mau noted that it was 'the violent manifestation of a limited revolutionary movement' and that 'it was no sudden uprising' but the result of 'a long period of political unrest among the Kikuyu people of Kenya, and was the evolutionary child of the first subversive Kikuyu political organisation – the Kikuyu association'.[75]

Mau Mau received no material or financial support from elsewhere. 'There is no evidence of any such assistance being given' to Mau Mau from 'territories outside Kenya', Kenya's Deputy Governor informed the Secretary of State for the Colonies in 1953.[76] It was 'a purely East African manifestation'[77] and decidedly not communist. 'There is no evidence that communism or communist agents have had any direct or indirect part in the organisation or direction of the Mau Mau itself, or its activities,' a Colonial Office report stated. Its activities were, rather, 'in an African idiom'.[78]

In short, Mau Mau was the violent, nationalist expression of revolt against British colonial repression. 'The causes of the revolt', David Maughan-Brown writes in an extensively documented study of Mau Mau, 'were ... socio-economic and political and amounted, to put it crudely, to the economic exploitation and administrative repression of the [K]ikuyu by the white settlers and the colonial state.'[79] Britain had established in

Kenya a system of institutionalised racism and exploitation of the indigenous population. The Governor of Kenya explained the racist policy to the Secretary of State in 1955:

> Up to 1923, the policy of segregation as between Europeans and other immigrant races followed as a measure of sanitation. The White Paper of 1923 recommended 'as a sanitation measure, [that] segregation of Europeans and Asiatics is not absolutely essential for the preservation of the health of community', but that for the present it was considered desirable to keep residential quarters of natives, so far as practicable, separate from those of immigrant races.[80]

These 'residential quarters' for the natives – who happened to make up the overwhelming majority of the population – were, the Governor explained, 'behind anything that I have seen elsewhere on the continent'.[81] Further, it was estimated that half of the urban workers in private industry and one quarter of those in public services received wages insufficient to provide for their basic needs.[82] As late as 1960 – three years before independence – Africans, who made up 90 per cent of the workforce, accounted for only 45 per cent of the total wage bill.[83] A crucial aspect of the colonial economy was the taxation system 'which increased poverty and dependence in the reserves [allocated to Africans] by a net transfer of resources out of them'.[84]

This was the situation that pertained at home for the nearly 100,000 Kenyan Africans who had fought on Britain's side in the Second World War. It was, the Governor explained, a result of Britain's 'determination to persevere in the task to which we have set our minds – to civilise a great mass of human beings who are in a very primitive moral and social state'.[85] In reality – as Maughan-Brown has pointed out – the ideology of the British settlers and the colonial state in Kenya as expressed in its institutions and regulations closely resembled that of the fascist movements of the years between the First and Second World Wars.[86]

The most significant indicator of enforced African subservience to colonial rule – and what lay at the root of the Mau Mau revolt – concerned land. Around 0.7 per cent of Kenya's population – the white settlers – owned 20 per cent of the best land in Kenya, the White Highlands. Put another way, fewer than 30,000 whites, of whom only 3,000 owned agricultural land in the White Highlands, owned more arable land than 1 million Kikuyu. By 1945 there were over 200,000 registered African squatters in the White Highlands, over half of whom were Kikuyu. Called '"resident native" labourers', they performed tasks as 'a cheap, malleable and readily accessible African labour force'.[87]

African nationalist opposition to this system had been expressed by the Kenya African Union (KAU) in 1947. 'The chief characteristic of all labour – skilled or not', it explained, 'is the low wages obtaining in Kenya.' 'The greatest problem which requires urgent consideration is that of the old man and woman who cannot perform hard manual labour. The settlers simply turn them off their land – rightly according to law.' The KAU referred to the squatter system of recent years as a 'new slavery' and explained that 'modern serfdom has come into being as cheap labour can be found everywhere in the colony'. 'The greater majority of the dying Africans and those suffering from malnutrition accrues as an upshot of the meagre allowances that our people earn. Due to this, ninety per cent of our people live in the most deplorable conditions ever afforded to a human being.'[88]

Britain was well aware of the situation, though its officials thought about things rather differently. In a 1945 report the colonial government noted that 'the principal item in the natural resources of Kenya is the land, and in this term we include the colony's mineral resources. It seems to us that our major objective must clearly be the preservation and the wise use of this most important asset.' The Deputy Governor explained:

> It is of greatest importance on all grounds of Imperial policy and for the future well being and prosperity of the native people that there should be a vigorous and well established British settlement in these highlands, for without it there is no hope of successfully overcoming the immense problems which confront us in this part of the world and of erecting here a permanent structure of enlightenment and civilisation.[89]

The following year, in an after-dinner speech, the Governor himself declared: '… the greater part of the wealth of the country is at present in our hands. … This land we have made is our land by right – by right of achievement'; this was not an 'exclusive right', he said, but rather a 'joint one'. Explaining to the Africans that 'their Africa has gone for ever', since they were now living in 'a world which we have made, under the humanitarian impulses of the late nineteenth and the twentieth century', the Governor declared: 'We appear to Africans as being immensely wealthy and nearly all of them are in fact very poor. … But these are social and economic differences and the problems of this country in that respect are social and economic and not political; nor are they to be solved by political devices.' Britain was in Kenya 'as of right, the product of historical events which reflect the greatest glory of our fathers and grandfathers'.[90] Actually, Britain had engaged in mass slaughter to subjugate Kenya colony. Churchill referred in 1908 to one expedition by stating that 'surely it cannot be necessary to go on killing these defenceless people on such an enormous scale'.[91] But let us put this aside.

Unfortunately for Britain, Africans were indeed engaging in politics. Conventionally, the declaration of the state of emergency in October 1952 has been seen as a response to Mau Mau terrorism which was getting increasingly out of control. In reality the declaration was a cause of (rather than a response to) the war. Moreover, the documents also confirm that it was precisely because nationalist Africans were becoming increasingly politically mobilised that the state of emergency was imposed. The subsequent war by the British was directed not only against the Mau Mau movement itself but also against unacceptable nationalist political organisation.

In the year previous to October 1952, there had actually been fewer murders and serious woundings than in previous years.[92] A few days before the declaration – on 15 October – the Governor cabled London that in the previous week 'there had been some falling off in crimes, both Mau Mau and otherwise'.[93] Yet two days later he confirmed that the declaration would take effect from 20 October.[94] The declaration itself prompted an increase in these crimes.

The real problem for the colonial government was that Jomo Kenyatta and other KAU leaders who were calling for widespread land reform and self-government were becoming increasingly popular and drawing ever-larger numbers of people to their public meetings. Radical trade unionists were taking control of the country's unions as the KAU gradually extended its influence throughout the country as a whole.[95] The Governor explained to London that the plans for the declaration of the emergency might appear 'excessive' but 'Kenyatta has succeeded in building up right under the nose of authority a powerful organisation affecting all sides of life among the Kikuyu'.[96] Two months prior to the declaration, a colonial official noted a 'worsening of the internal security situation': 'recent large KAU meetings' had been coupled with a 'serious increase of Mau Mau activities ... in each area where [Kenyatta] spoke'. One recent large KAU meeting had been 'attended by twenty to thirty thousand people, who were so excited and truculent that the preservation of law and order hung upon a thread'. 'We decided', the official noted, 'that we would be wrong to allow any further meetings of the KAU.'[97] Another official noted that the KAU and 'various satellite groups' were 'demanding ... the "return" of the White Highlands to the Kikuyu and self-government on the Gold Coast model'. At recent KAU meetings at which Kenyatta had been the key speaker, the official said, 'large crowds have attended and treated him and his utterances with enthusiastic respect'.[98]

The answer, the Governor stated a few days before the declaration, was that 'we must remove Kenyatta and several of his henchmen during the next few weeks'.[99] The Attorney-General explained: '... our main problem on the long term view is to ensure that Jomo Kenyatta and his immediate followers are not let out at the end of the emergency but are kept in custody for a very substantial period of years.'[100] He further declared that 'one of the principal reasons' for declaring a state of emergency 'would be to enable us to make detention orders against the leading African agitators'.[101] When the state of emergency was declared the authorities jailed dozens of KAU leaders and every branch chairman who was not already in jail.[102]

In seeking to justify the political repression of the nationalists, the British authorities needed to portray Kenyatta as the instigator of the Mau Mau movement. The only problem was that Kenyatta had consistently denounced it. At one meeting, the Attorney-General observed in a communication to the Colonial Office in London, Kenyatta publicly condemned Mau Mau and the 30,000 Kikuyu present at the meeting held up their hands to 'signify that they approved of his denunciation of Mau Mau'. The Attorney-General even stated: '... if this resistance movement gathers strength, then I think we should succeed in rolling back the Mau Mau movement before too long'.[103] At his subsequent trial, Kenyatta was sentenced to seven years' imprisonment as a result of what the defending counsel called 'the most childishly weak case made against any man in any important trial in the history of the British empire',[104] one that was patently trumped up to dispose of the country's leading nationalist.

Overall, the situation in Kenya was strikingly similar to that which had occurred four years earlier in Malaya: with the political road to reform blocked by the authorities, just grievances found their expression in increasing violence. The war that ensued resulted in atrocities being committed by both rebel and government forces, as in Malaya. The British similarly resorted to dictatorial police measures; 153,000 arrests, for example, were made in the first fourteen months of the war.[105] The sheer number of deaths at the hands of the government forces suggests that there was a deliberate shoot-to-kill policy. The Mau Mau killed 590 members of the security forces and 1,819 Africans, 32 European and 26 Asian civilians. This compares with around 10,000 killings by government forces.[106]

The methods used by the police were particularly vile and there was 'a constant stream of reports of brutalities by police, military and home guards'.[107] These brutalities included the slicing off of ears, the boring of holes in eardrums, flogging until death, the pouring of paraffin over suspects who were then set alight, and the burning of eardrums with lighted cigarettes.[108] A report by Canon Bewes, Africa Secretary of the Church Missionary Society, noted that a European policeman 'had picked up a man, had him laid on the ground with his legs apart and had him beaten on the private parts in an attempt to extract a confession'. 'Some of the people', Bewes noted, 'had been using castrating instruments and ... in one instance two men had died under castration.' A metal 'castrating instrument' 'had also been reported as being used to clamp onto the fingers of people who were unwilling to give information and ... if the information was not given the tips of the fingers were cut off'. Bewes stated that there were also a number of cases of rape perpetrated by the army.[109] A Kenyan police team sent to the neighbouring colony of Tanganyika to 'screen' Kikuyu there were found guilty by the Tanganyikan authorities of 'violence, in the form of whipping on the soles of the feet, burning with lighted cigarettes and tying leather thongs round the neck and dragging the victims along the ground'. Of the 170–200 interrogated, 'at least 32 were badly injured'.[110]

In Kenya itself, one army captain was quoted as informing a sergeant-major that 'he could shoot anybody he liked provided they were black'.[111] The British and Kenyan armies, meanwhile, indulged in 'indiscriminate shooting', with some battalions keeping scoreboards recording 'kills'. These practices included a £5 reward for the first subunit to kill an insurgent.[112] Frank Kitson, later to apply his counterinsurgency skills to Northern Ireland, once commented: '... three Africans appeared walking down the track towards us: a perfect target. Unfortunately they were policemen.'[113]

Between 1952 and 1956, 1,015 people were hanged, 297 for murder and 559 for unlawful possession of arms or administering the Mau Mau oath.[114] The Governor of Kenya even proposed that the death penalty should be applied to those who were 'helping' the insurgents, 'whether directly or indirectly',[115] and to those committing 'acts of sabotage'.[116] The latter was too much even for the Colonial Secretary, who noted that the scope of such a provision would be so broad that the death penalty 'would be applicable to deliberate obstruction by motorist of baker's van delivering bread to military unit or to intentional puncturing of sanitary inspector's bicycle'.[117] The threat of the death penalty also was used, and public gallows were once erected on a golf course and in a prison camp.[118]

Nevertheless, the British owed the success with which they defeated the Mau Mau primarily to a policy similar to that applied in Malaya: the confinement of tens of thousands of Kikuyu in detention camps and 'resettlement' ('repatriation') operations. Within a year of the declaration of the state of emergency some 80,000 Kikuyu – mainly squatters from the White Highlands – had been 'repatriated' to the so-called 'Native Land Unit'; a policy of 'villageisation' was implemented as a result of which their livestock was confiscated and many were subjected to forced labour within the confines of fortified camps. In the detention camps, the inmates were classified as 'blacks' if they were Mau Mau officials or supporters, 'greys' if they were suspected of being such with no evidence, and 'whites' if they had no Mau Mau connections; the latter were subsequently released. Diseases spread in the camps; one had over 400 typhoid cases, and around 90 people died as a result.[119] The colonial government reported:

> ... 'the sudden confinement of thousands of Africans behind barb wire has set very considerable and difficult medical problems. This has been aggravated by the fact that of necessity there has been little distinction between the fit and the unfit when the question of detention is being considered. Consequently, infectious disease has been introduced into the camps from the start.[120]

Four hundred and two people were to die in the camps by June 1954 alone.[121]

Brutality by the warders was systematic. Imperial historian V.G. Kiernan comments that 'the special prisons where those considered incorrigible were incarcerated ... were probably as bad as any similar Nazi or Japanese establishments'.[122] One former rehabilitation officer noted that 'Japanese methods of torture' were being practised by one camp commandant.[123]

> The plight of detainees in the detention camps in Rift Valley province during 1954 and 1955 [when he was an officer there] ... included short rations, overwork, brutality, humiliating and disgusting treatment and flogging – all in violation of the United Nations Universal Declaration on Human Rights.

In one camp, 'the detainees were being systematically ill-treated, underfed, overworked and flogged by the Security Officer'.

> The women and children, in conditions of severe overcrowding, were sleeping on the bare stone or wooden floors as the Commandant had forbidden them to construct beds. ... The lavatories were merely large pits in the ground ... with the excreta lapping over the top.

At another camp, where 'forced labour' was practised, 'one European officer made the detainees work at pointless hard labour tasks 12 hours a day'. The commandant was seen 'punching and kicking detainees' and, on the orders of a European officer, warders were 'sent into one of the compounds ... with orders to "beat up" the detainees. This they proceeded to do with sticks, lumps of wood and whips. Several European officers ... joined in the beating.' The order had been given 'for no apparent reason'. 'Some African detainees had been knocked unconscious and nearly 100 were treated in hospital.'[124] A well-publicised massacre occurred at Hola detention camp in March 1959, when warders killed eleven inmates.[125]

The issue of forced labour produced some interesting correspondence between the Kenya government and the Colonial Office and provide an insight into official British values. On 19 February 1953 the Deputy Governor telegrammed London stating: 'I shall not be surprised if the Governor shortly feels obliged to recommend that he be allowed to put people ... compulsorily to work in the reserves or areas being prepared for settlement by Kikuyu or other African tribes.'[126] The Governor then asked the Secretary of State for the Colonies whether 'there is any possibility of obtaining exemption from the provisions of the [United Nations] Forced Labour Convention [of] 1930 ... to be directed to paid work'.[127] The Colonial Office debated the issue and recognised that implementation of the proposal would be illegal. It was clearly noted that 'compulsory labour as proposed by Kenya would be a breach of the Forced Labour Convention' and 'there was no procedure for claiming exemption from its provisions'. It also noted that forced labour was on the agenda of the present session of the United Nations and that 'the UK delegation had been briefed to meet possible attacks on existing laws in Malaya and Kenya but any extension of the system in Kenya would inevitably give rise to further criticism'. But despite the participants' expressed understanding of the illegality of forced labour, the minutes of the meeting note that 'if the measures could be introduced without publicity, or delayed until after the session, the UK delegation's task would be easier'. Rather than dismissing the idea as a violation of international law, this Colonial Office meeting decided that 'Kenya should be asked to submit regulations in draft for consideration in consultation with the Foreign Secretary and Minister of Labour before a final decision was taken.'[128] The Colonial Secretary then wrote to the Governor explaining that 'if ... the proposal for compulsory employment is to be pursued it means facing up to the fact that we shall be breaking the Convention'. Even though, as noted earlier, 'there was no procedure for claiming exemption from its pro-visions', the Colonial Secretary declared:

> the only justification I can see for sustaining this breach would be (a) that we are dealing with very exceptional circumstances not contemplated by the Con-vention and (b) that we are not offending against the spirit of the Convention which was framed primarily to prevent the exploitation of labour.

He then stated: 'I should be grateful to know of any further considerations there may be to strengthen the case for compulsion.'[129] The Governor replied that he had 're-examined the position' and was 'very anxious not to embarrass you. I now think that by a combination of economic induce-ments and use of sanctions under existing law ... it may well be possible to attain our objective.'[130]

Britain's general objectives in Kenya were attained highly successfully with, as in Malaya, a combination of straightforward violence and social engineering. The transition to a friendly government at independence in 1963 could not have been achieved, however, without substantial efforts in the political and economic fields.

The cultivation of an African elite whose task would be to preside over Kenyan independence and who would preserve British economic and political interests in the country was not an easy one, given that many of the most popular nationalist leaders had been imprisoned in 1952 with the declaration of the state of emergency. Two months after this, the Colonial Office made the 'suggestion' of 'giving moderate and loyal Africans some positive part to play in the present crisis'. Of course, it noted, 'there can be no question, so long as the emergency lasts, of any constitutional change at the centre' since the declaration of the state of emergency had been intended precisely to prevent this. The Colonial Office's suggestion – that some interracial advisory committees should be established – would therefore have to be purely cosmetic. 'We are not so naïve as to think that advisory committees will bring much increase in wisdom to bear on immediate problems,' the Colonial Office noted. Their importance was that 'they can ... play a useful part in associating with the process of government persons who would otherwise be condemned to more sterile and therefore frequently dangerous activities'. This was 'of particular value in Kenya at the present when there is really so little that you can do to give moderate Africans a sense of purpose'.[131]

But the most significant schemes for ensuring that the correct type of political and economic 'development' would be pursued by Kenya after independence involved the British-planned land reforms for the White Highlands. According to Arthur Hazlewood's study of the Kenyan economy, the purpose of the Swynnerton Plan of the mid-1950s was that 'able, energetic or rich Africans would be able to acquire more land and bad or poor farmers less, creating a landed and a landless class.' Hazlewood continues by noting that there was 'a large and growing class of landless probably numbering more than 400,000 and on the other hand there is no doubt that men (and women) of wealth have been able to acquire land on a large scale'. This 'growth of inequalities in land holding' is a central feature of 'development' as understood in Western usage, with resources under the control of the wealthy who grow wealthier at the expense of the poor growing poorer.[132]

In the land transfer schemes of the years shortly before independence, new African 'settlers' were forced to pay for land that they regarded as rightfully theirs and that had been taken over by European settlers. 'The majority of landless people were unable to raise even the basic sums needed as a down payment for the purchase of land,'[133] so that over half the land was transferred almost intact to wealthy Africans in partnerships or limited liability companies.[134] Gary Wasserman comments in his analysis of the land issue in Kenya that the African middle classes who were rich enough to acquire land 'through land titles, loan repayments and some felt gratitude to the new government, were expected to acquire a vested interest against any radical transformation of the society'. The World Bank and the Commonwealth Development Corporation provided financial aid for these schemes, which 'reflected the European and colonial hopes of using foreign investment to bolster a moderate nationalist state and to preserve European economic (and political) interests'. These schemes helped to tie the independence leaders into a form of development closely aligned to British, and Western, interests. According to Wasserman:

> For starters, there was the obligation to repay the loans, hence to make the plots 'profitable'; to maintain an open economy favourable to private investment, hence to limit nationalisations; to maintain the chief export-earner, European-dominated capital agriculture (and an economic structure congenial to it), hence to refuse to expropriate Europeans or place limits on land holdings.

Overall, 'the decolonisation process aimed to preserve the colonial political economy and, beyond that, to integrate an indigenous elite into positions of authority where they could protect the important interests in the system'.[135]

The disenfranchisement of the poor therefore continued after independence. Political power now rested in the hands of the previously unreliable Kenyatta, who as President accepted the validity of the land transfers – 'the most hated part of colonialism', according to Wasserman.[136] Subsequent policy aimed to 'Africanise' the economy at the same time as accommodating the interests of the transnational corporations who held – and continue to hold – a significant stake in the country. In 1958, one third of privately owned assets in Kenya were owned by nonresidents, mainly transnational companies.[137] 'By 1978,' fifteen years after political independence, Kenya analysts Bethwell Ogot and Tiyambe Zeleza note, 'Kenya was still a dependent export economy, heavily penetrated by foreign capital from all the major capitalist countries, so that she was more firmly and broadly integrated into the world capitalist system than at independence.'[138]

A report produced in the same year by the International Labour Organisation enunciated the achievements of the British-based designs for Kenyan 'development' that were subsequently pursued in their essentials by independence leaders. Those 'who have benefited substantially from the rapid growth of the economy since independence' included the elites who replaced the British in 'the high level jobs', 'a much bigger group of persons' who 'benefited from the transfer of land from European farmers to African settlers', and the employees in the modern, urban sectors 'who have been able to secure increases of 6–8 per cent a year in their real incomes'. However, 'the group of persons who have failed to derive much benefit from the growth generated since independence includes the great majority of small holders, employees in the rural sector, the urban working poor and the urban and rural unemployed'.[139] By the middle 1970s, the richest 20 per cent of the population received 70 per cent of total income, so that the wealthy elites enjoyed standards of living often comparable with their richest counterparts in the West, whilst a substantial proportion of the population suffered from grinding poverty. Hazlewood comments: 'Disraeli wrote of England in the 1840s as Two Nations, and this is a useful characterisation of the developing countries today, including Kenya';[140] an interesting and apt parallel, given essential British and Western priorities, and those of the ruling Third World elites who follow their lead and guidance.

Countering democracy: British Guiana

In 1953 Britain sent a cruiser, two frigates and seven hundred troops to its South American colony of British Guiana, suspended the constitution there and overthrew the democratically elected government. In April 1953, the People's Progressive Party (PPP) under Cheddi Jagan had won 18 out of the 24 seats in the country's first elections carried out under universal adult suffrage. But Jagan's programme of social and economic reforms was the wrong type of democracy for Britain – since it threatened control over the territory's resources by Britain and allied transnational business interests – and he was overthrown by the Churchill government just 133 days after assuming office.

If Britain's key interests in Malaya were rubber and tin and in Kenya land, in British Guiana the key resources in British eyes were sugar and, to a lesser extent, bauxite. 28,000 people out of the country's total working population of 100,000 were employed in the sugar industry. About 20 per cent of the total population lived on the sugar estates, more than half of them in estate-owned houses.[141] Almost all the sugar cane was grown on seventeen large plantations owned by private companies. One of these – Booker Bros. McConnell – had a controlling interest in the majority of the plantations.[142] The colony's bauxite exports accounted for one fifth of total world production; 90 per cent of the colony's output was in the hands of a single company, the Demerara Bauxite Company, a subsidiary of the Aluminium Company of Canada (ALC).[143] Together, the sugar and bauxite concerns accounted for 90 per cent of the country's exports:[144] the country was therefore effectively owned and controlled by Britain in alliance with two transnational companies.

In 1953, Britain had great future plans for the colony. 'Until two or three years ago,' the Governor declared, 'exploration of [the] vast timber resources had been spasmodic, haphazard and by somewhat primitive methods. Now however the Colonial Development Corporation have entered the field with an investment of over £1 million and are extracting timber on an extensive scale.' According to the Governor, a 'great development is also taking place in the gold mining industry and quite recently there has been an upsurge of interest in the search for strategic minerals'.[145] However, to attract the foreign capital to develop these resources required 'that in the coming years conditions in British Guiana should continue to be such as will attract it – conditions political as well as otherwise. ... Nothing must be done which could sap confidence.'[146]

British Guiana's colonial function as a provider of cheap raw materials to the northern nations appeared to work remarkably well. Its bauxite provided 85 per cent of the supply for the Canadian aluminium industry, contributing to the large profits (Canadian $29 million in 1951) made by ALC. In turn, Britain was heavily dependent on Canadian exports for its aluminium supplies. Furthermore, according to ALC's 1952 company report, a 'substantial ... percentage' of its aluminium shipments went to the 'defence needs' of Britain and the United States.[147] Here, then, was an instructive example of how an elementary feature of the international system worked. Britain controlled the territory in which raw materials were mined in alliance with transnational companies. The companies (who benefited from the subjugation of the territory through the cheap labour and raw materials on offer) as well as the colonial government (which received the bulk of its revenues from the companies' operations and taxes) could therefore accrue large revenues from the exploitation of the country's resources and population. At the same time, the fruits of much of this labour were directed towards the military in the home countries. The system depended ultimately, however, on a crucial notion: the 'Soviet threat'. As discussed below, Britain's ability to overthrow democracy and eliminate the nationalist threat in British Guiana required a pretext: nationalist leader Cheddi Jagan was to be designated an agent of the international communist conspiracy. At the same time, in order to justify at home the direction of scarce resources towards the military, recourse could be made to global Soviet expansionism. At the two levels therefore – control over raw materials in the Third World on the one hand and the allocation of resources to the military at home on the other – the Cold War confrontation proved useful.

Those who were slightly less fortunate in this state of affairs included those upon whose backs the system functioned. The people of British Guiana endured 'squalor and poverty' in a society with a 'long glaring contrast between rich and poor', the *Manchester Guardian* commented in 1953.[148] A 1939 official report described the population as living 'closely crowded in ranges on the verge of collapse, lacking every amenity and frequently almost surrounded by stagnant water'. By 1949 there were 'dilapidated and obsolete ranges, long condemned from all quarters. ... The ranges which are the main target of attack were built by the sugar estates to house the indentured labourers.'[149] The Governor noted:

> The sugar estates are to a considerable extent the crux of the situation ... It is there that the extremist is so well supported. It is so easy for him to point to the dreadful housing and social conditions which exist (and to ignore the improvements) and compare them with the comfortable quarters and the neat compounds and the recreational facilities of the staff who are predominantly European. It is also easy for him to allege unfair profits being transferred to absentee landlords and to blame, as is done, the British government for the conditions which exist.[150]

A Colonial Office report in 1954 – one year after the British intervention – noted that 'the sugar companies in British Guiana may not in future be immune from criticism on the score that they are "big business", very efficiently run, but run for the sole benefit of their owners or shareholders'.[151] A government report of 1953 observed with some understatement that since 'the mining companies (mostly Demerara Bauxite Co.) have made profits of approximately £1m a year for the past four years and have distributed £600,000 a year in dividends', 'there may well, therefore, be scope for some increase in mining taxation in the territory'.[152]

It was mainly because Jagan's PPP sought to improve the 'dreadful housing and social conditions' that it was elected to office. The British government's Commonwealth Relations Office stated that the PPP 'was in fact elected to power on a mildly socialist programme, the implementation of which would have been in general of great value to the territory'.[153] The Secretary of State for the Colonies – who was to be instrumental in ordering the British intervention – noted a week after the PPP's electoral triumph that its programme was 'no more extreme' than that of the British Labour Party. 'It contains none of the usual communist aims and it advocates industrial development through the encouragement of foreign capital'. The Colonial Secretary then magnanimously suggested: '... we should ... accept the verdict of the electorate.' Nevertheless, Britain would 'take action without delay if [PPP leaders] seek to use their position to further the communist cause', whether elected or not.[154]

In practice Jagan's and the PPP's plans went beyond the acceptable. They called for redistribution of economic resources towards the welfare needs of the workforce, the strengthening of the position of the trade unions and the curbing of the exploitation and dominance of the sugar multinational Bookers.[155] An indicator of Jagan's outlook, is that the PPP leader had also (and correctly) noted that:

> Present British foreign policy has meant a crushing burden of rearmament and dependence on the dollar areas for food and raw materials, which can be paid for, not by the export of industrial goods to the dollar areas, but only by the continued exploitation of dollar earning raw material, food and mineral resources from Malaya, Africa, British Guiana and other parts of the Colonial Empire. All the so-called development plans for the colonial territories have been devised with this aim in view.[156]

According to the London-based Latin America Bureau, once in power Jagan:

> ... consistently exposed the social cost of the existing economic system to the mass of Guyanese in terms of their wages, working and health conditions and the unrepresentativeness of the local and central governments. He fought for increasing minimum wage levels and improvements in the health services and exposed the privileged position of the sugar companies in terms of access to public funds which bolstered the profits the industry generated and sent abroad.[157]

Equally important, at the end of August 1953, the PPP ministers called for a strike amongst the sugar workers who were fighting for the Sugar Producers' Association to recognise the Guianan Industrial Workers' Union. By 10 September, the Governor of British Guiana noted that the sugar industry was 'at complete standstill'.[158] All in all, this state of affairs contributed to what a British MP later referred to as the PPP's having 'overstepped the limits of what we regard as decent government'.[159]

On 8 September the sugar multinational Bookers had stated that the strike meant 'a loss of profits' and that 'the present situation can only be dealt with effectively by the Colonial Office'. Indeed, it was said, 'unless something drastic is done, Bookers will cease to exist as a large firm in 5 years'.[160] Whilst the sugar strike effectively ended, it was clear that the PPP retained the wrong priorities. On 9 October, the British Governor announced that the constitution was being suspended and the elected ministers were being removed from office. A few hundred British troops landed and three warships remained stationed off the Guianan coast. The Queen signed the order suspending the constitution and overthrowing the government.[161]

On the day the decision was finally taken to intervene with military force the Colonial Secretary noted that the PPP has 'completely destroyed the confidence of the business community and all moderate opinion'.[162] He later noted that 'a number of American or overseas firms ... were already abandoning their projects in British Guiana. Firms with British and Canadian capital ... [i.e. the sugar and bauxite transnationals] were already hanging back and were very apprehensive about the dangerous political climate.' The danger was that conditions were being created that were 'inimical to investment either domestic or overseas'; thus the PPP were 'threatening the order of the Colony ... and undermining ... its present economic stability'.[163] The PPP ministers' behaviour had the effect of 'destroying the confidence of the business community', but fortunately Britain 'took action before that further deterioration showed itself in the action of the business community'.[164] A few days after the troop deployments, the Governor noted that the 'interim government' was making efforts 'to restore normal conditions and economic stability in the Colony'.[165] In December the Colonial Secretary again warned of the threat of democracy, noting that if Britain had permitted new elections in British Guiana instead of suspending the constitution 'the same party would have been elected again'.[166]

Since overthrowing nationalist leaders who advocate improving social and economic conditions is not good public relations, a suitable pretext was necessary. Announcing the British intervention to the Guianan people on 9 October, the Governor stated that Britain had acted 'to prevent Communist subversion of the government' and that the elected ministers and the PPP were 'completely under the control of a communist clique ... their objective was to turn British Guiana into a totalitarian state subordinate to Moscow and a dangerous platform for extending communist influence in the Western hemisphere'.[167] The stance was repeated by the Colonial Secretary in the House of Commons: it was all 'part of the deadly design to turn British Guiana into a totalitarian state dominated by communist ideas', and Britain was 'faced with part of the international communist conspiracy'.[168] One internal British document at the time somewhat gave the game away, however. The UK delegation to the United Nations cabled the Colonial Secretary a week before the overthrow and stated:

> If our action can be presented as firm step taken to prevent attempt by communist elements to sabotage new and progressive constitution, it will be welcomed by American public and accepted by most United Nations opinion. If on the other hand it is allowed to appear as just another attempt by Britain to stifle a popular nationalist movement ... effect can only be bad. ... To secure desired result some preparation of public opinion seems to be essential.[169]

The United States supported the British attack on British Guiana; the State Department remarking that the US was 'gratified to note that the British government is taking firm action to meet the situation. ... the United States believes the British action justifiable.'[170] The British embassy in Washington declared that the State Department 'have worked in very well with us over this crisis ... if the Jagans wished to come to this country in order to publicise their case they would not be allowed visas. This goes for any of their buddies too.'[171]

The stance of the opposition Labour Party in Britain was particularly interesting. James Griffiths, the former Colonial Secretary, concurred in the House of Commons with the Governor's 9 October statement that the aim of the PPP leaders 'was to turn British Guiana into a totalitarian state subordinate to Moscow'. But, he stated, the Labour Party 'believe that a suspension of the constitution should be the last and not the first resort' – the question was whether other emergency powers 'ought to be used before the extreme power of suspension is used'. Labour leader Clement Attlee agreed, saying that 'the [Churchill] government brought in the last thing they should have done and ... they brought it in first'. The Labour Party, that is, accepted the principle of Britain's right to overthrow democracy but disputed its timing. Griffiths sympathised with his successor as Colonial Secretary, noting that 'the office is an interesting, exciting, hard and responsible one for we are dealing with 70 million people who are growing up. They are adolescents who are politically immature.'[172]

Now that the Guyanese had been treated to a dose of political maturity by one of the 'older, mellower and more advanced nations of the world' (see p. 18), the task was to ensure that business as usual would prevail under conditions of economic stability. The elected government was replaced by one nominated by the Governor and containing many members who had been defeated candidates in the April elections. Two of the PPP leaders – Cheddi and Janet Jagan – were sentenced to six months' hard labour for violating restriction orders; other leaders were detained without trial for three-month periods.[173] In the House of Commons debate two weeks after the overthrow of democracy, the Colonial Secretary observed, presumably with a straight face, that the British Government 'must steadily

... seek to build up a political system in British Guiana which will give the inhabitants a chance of developing democratic institutions'.[174] Britain would now foster 'some body representing Guianese opinion upon whose advice the Governor may rely' but 'upon whose advice he will not be bound to act in the interim period'.[175] Eighteen months after the overthrow of Jagan's government the Governor commented that it was impossible to 'assess future military needs until we have experienced renewed political activity, but my present view is that we will need one company of regular troops until representative government has been successfully restored'.[176] The presence of British troops would provide 'a short term insurance against disorders' since 'while political activity is at an enforced standstill it would be rash to dispense with all troops'.[177]

It took until 1964 before 'representative government' was restored. In the 1957 elections Britain attempted to rig a defeat for Jagan, who remained PPP leader, but unfortunately the wrong party won nine of the fourteen elected seats and Jagan became prime minister once more.[178] Still under Jagan's leadership, the PPP also won the 1961 elections. Beginning in the following year, however, the US Central Intelligence Agency (CIA), operating with British permission, helped finance a destabilization campaign against the Jagan government, which culminated in the 'centrepiece of the CIA's programme in British Guiana', a general strike beginning in April 1963. CIA agents gave 'advice to local union leaders on how to organise and sustain' the strike, and 'provided funds and food supplies to keep the strikers going', according to the *New York Times*. At least $1 million is thought to have been directed towards the toppling of the democratically elected government.[179] Former CIA agent Philip Agee wrote that the 1964 election victory of Jagan's opponent, Forbes Burnham, was 'largely due to CIA operations over the past five years to strengthen the anti-Jagan trade unions'.[180] In the 1964 elections, however, the PPP remained the largest party and won 24 out of 53 seats. But the constitution had again been amended by Britain, this time to a system of proportional representation, so that a rival coalition grouping under the more acceptable leadership of Forbes Burnham could take power. Britain had also refused to grant independence to British Guiana lest it should be presided over by Jagan's PPP.

'Once the PPP had been removed from office' after the 1964 elections, the Latin America Bureau comments, 'the main obstacle to independence had been overcome'.[181] Thus independence eventually proceeded in 1966, enabling the economic direction of British Guiana to be more easily geared to Western interests. The sugar transnational Bookers was assured of 'a remarkable degree of control over the economy, both through its dominant position in the sugar industry and through its interests in fisheries, cattle, timber, insurance, advertising and retail commerce'.[182]

Notes

1. For example, Thomas Kaplan, 'Britain's Asian Cold War: Malaya', in Deighton (ed.), p. 201.

2. Colonial Office report, 28 March 1950, PRO, CO 717/196/52821/20.

3. Lennox Mills, *Malaya: A political and economic appraisal*, University of Minnesota Press, Minneapolis, 1958, p. 206.

4. Colonial Office report on Malaya, 'Papers on the emergency in Malaya', January 1952, PRO, CO 1022/22/SEA 10/14/08.

5. Colonial Office Information Department, 'Malaya: Brief for Minister of State', undated [1952], PRO, CO 1022/267/SEA 192/469/01.

6. Mills, p. 206.

7. Lim Chong-Yah, *Economic development of modern Malaya*, Oxford University Press, Kuala Lumpur, pp. 117, 331.

8. House of Lords debate, 27 February 1952, Col. 302.

9. Ibid., Col. 333.

10. Kaplan, p. 204.

11. 'A plan for rubber', *Economist*, 9 October 1954.

12. House of Lords debate, 27 February 1952, Col. 346.

13. Memorandum submitted by the delegation of Joint Malayan Interests at a meeting at the Colonial Office, 15 November 1951, PRO, CO 1022/39/SEA 10/93/01.

14. Foreign Office to Washington, 26 October 1950, PRO, CO 717/203/52911.

15. Richard Allen, *Malaysia: Prospect and retrospect*, Oxford University Press, London, 1968, p. 95.

16. Colonial Office report on Malaya, 'Papers on the emergency in Malaya', January 1952, PRO, CO 1022/22/SEA 10/14/08.

17. Quoted in *Monthly review of Chinese affairs*, July 1949, CO 717/182/52928.

18. Ritchie Ovendale, *The English-speaking alliance: Britain, the United States, the Dominions and the cold war, 1945–1951*, George Allen and Unwin, London, 1985, pp. 151–63.

19. Robert Jackson, *The Malayan emergency: The Commonwealth's war 1948–1966*, Routledge, London, 1991, pp. 19, 39.

20. Kaplan, p. 205.

21. Memorandum by Tang Cheng Lock to Secretary of State for the Colonies and Secretary of State for War, 19 May 1950, PRO, CO 717/205/52934.

22. Unheaded, undated [1949], PRO, CO 717/163/52748.

23. Letter from the Governor of Singapore to the Secretary of State for the Colonies, 23 March 1949, PRO, CO 717/163/52748.

24. Draft letter from J. Higham to Sir Francis Gimson, 14 February 1949, PRO, CO 717/163/52748.

25. Kaplan, p. 207.

26. 'The squatter problem in Malaya', March 1952, PRO, CO 1022/29/SEA 10/72/01.

27. Memorandum from the Secretary of Defence, undated [1952], 'Official designation of the communist forces', PRO, CO 1022/48/SEA 10/172/01.

28. Allen, p. 94.

29. Foreign Office to various representatives abroad, 21 February 1952, PRO, CO 1022/2/SEA 10/03; Commonwealth Relations Office to various High Commissioners, 29 December 1953, PRO, CO 1022/2/SEA 10/03.

30. Allen, p. 91.

31. Broadcast speech to Australia, 12 October 1952, PRO, CO 1022/2/SEA 10/03.

32. Richard Clutterbuck, *Conflict and violence in Singapore and Malaysia, 1945–1983*, Graham Brash (Pte), Singapore, 1985, p. 186.

33. Clutterbuck, pp. 215–16.

34. V.G. Kiernan, *European empires from conquest to collapse, 1815–1960*, Fontana, 1982, p. 212.

35. Jackson, pp. 77, 82, 84.

36. Ibid., p. 45.

37. Cited in Charles Allen, *The savage wars of peace: Soldiers' voices 1945–1989*, Futura, 1990, pp. 12, 21–2, 26.

38. Brian Lapping, *End of empire*, Paladin, London, 1989, p. 219.

39. Jackson, p. 45.

40. Lapping, pp. 219–20; Inside Story, 'In cold blood', Channel Four TV (Britain), 9 September 1992.

41. See PRO, CO 1022/45/SEA 10/162/02.

42. J.W. Goodwin, 'Bodies of dead rebels on public view', *Scotsman*, 22 August 1952.

43. See PRO, CO 1030/33/FED 12/568/01.

44. Memorandum by T. Jerrom to J. Higham, 30 April 1952, PRO, CO 1022/45/SEA 10/162/02.

45. Memorandum by T. Jerrom to J. Higham, 19 May 1952, PRO, CO 1022/45/SEA 10/162/02.

46. Memorandum from J. Higham to Mr. Paskin, 6 May 1952, PRO, CO 1022/45/SEA 10/162/02.

47. Memorandum from T. Jerrom to J. Higham, 19 May 1952, PRO, CO 1022/45/SEA 10/162/02.

48. Memorandum from T. Jerrom to J. Higham, 12 May 1952, PRO, CO 1022/45/SEA 10/162/02.

49. Denis Warner, '500 sea Dyaks for Malaya', *Daily Telegraph*, 23 May 1952.

50. '20,000 punished for "cowardly silence"', *Daily Telegraph*, 28 March 1952.

51. Letter from M. Grant, London School of Hygiene and Tropical Medicine, to Mr. Tuner, Colonial Office, undated [1953], PRO, CO 1022/54/SEA 10/409/01.

52. Michael Davidson, 'Templer sends a letter to the people', *Observer*, 6 April 1952.

53. Selangor government press statement, D.INF 4/52/95 (Emerg), 10 April 1952, PRO, CO 1022/55/SEA 10/409/02.

54. 'Terrorists aided', *Times*, 12 April 1952.

55. Jackson, p. 26.

56. Allen, p. 101.

57. South East Asia Department, Brief for Selwyn Lloyd at the North Atlantic Council, 21 April 1953, PRO, CO 1022/2/SEA 10/03.

58. Lapping, p. 223.

59. Jackson, p. 20.

60. Kiernan, p. 212.

61. Clutterbuck, p. 176.

62. *Monthly review of Chinese affairs*, December 1949, PRO, CO 717/182/52928.

63. Memorandum from J. Biddulph, Secretary for Chinese Affairs, Singapore, 6 June 1951, PRO, CO 1022/148/SEA 75/167/01.

64. 'Role of the Malayan home guard', *Times*, 10 July 1953.

65. Clutterbuck, p. 169.

66. Foreign Office telegram to various HM representatives, 22 March 1951, PRO, CO 1022/2/SEA 10/03.

67. Memorandum by the Secretary of State for the Colonies, 'Chinese detainees in Malaya', CAB 21/1682, DO (50) 93, 15 November 1950.

68. Fred Halliday, *Arabia without Sultans*, Penguin, Harmondsworth, 1974, p. 359; Bloch and Fitzgerald, p. 74.

69. H. Kearns and E. Woodford, 'The chemical control of roadside vegetation: Report of a visit to the Federation of Malaya, 4–23 December 1952', 2 February 1953, PRO, CO 1022/26/SEA 10/45/01.

70. Ibid.

71. A. Humphrey, Federation of Malaya to J. Higham, 19 January 1953, PRO, CO 1022/26/SEA 10/45/01.

72. Letter from Mr Dodds Parker, Imperial Affairs Committee of the Conservative Party, to O. Lyttelton, Secretary of State for the Colonies, 22 January 1953, PRO, CO 1022/62/SEA 19/4/02.

73. Chris Dixon, *South East Asia in the world-economy*, CUP, Cambridge, 1991, pp. 183, 186.

74. J. Whyatt to P. Rogers, 2 September 1952, PRO, CO 822/437.

75. The Corfield Report, 'Historical survey of the origins and growth of Mau Mau', undated, Chapter II, p. 1., PRO, CO 822/1222.

76. Deputy Governor to Secretary of State for the Colonies, 13 July 1953, PRO, CO 822/495.

77. O. Lyttelton to Sir Waldron Smithers, 30 December 1952, PRO, CO 822/461.

78. Colonial Office report, Intel No. 228, 17 October 1952, PRO, CO 822/462; see also Colonial Office report, 'Is Mau Mau communist-inspired?', 7 July 1953, PRO, CO 822/461.

79. David Maughan-Brown, *Land, freedom and fiction: History and ideology in Kenya*, Zed, London, 1985, p. 49.

80. E. Baring to Secretary of State for the Colonies, 21 November 1955, PRO, CO 822/937.

81. E. Baring to W. Gorell Barnes, 27 October 1952, PRO, CO 822/450.

82. Maughan-Brown, p. 29.

83. Arthur Hazlewood, *The economy of Kenya: The Kenyatta era*, OUP, Oxford, 1979, p. 7.

84. Maughan-Brown, p. 185.

85. Quoted in the Corfield Report, op. cit, Chapter XVI, p. 1.

86. Maughan-Brown, pp. 93-7.

87. Tabitha Tanogo, *Squatters and the roots of Mau Mau 1905-63*, James Currey, London, 1987, pp. 150, 126, 2; Maughan-Brown, p. 24.

88. 'A memorandum on the economic, political, educational and social aspects of the African in Kenya Colony by the Kenya African Union', undated [1947], PRO, CO 533/557/1.

89. Deputy Governor to Secretary of State for the Colonies, 19 March 1945, PRO, CO 533/534/11.

90. 'His Excellency Sir Philip Mitchell's speech at the Caledonian Society of Kenya's dinner, Nairobi, 30 November 1946', PRO, CO 533/549/2.

91. Lapping, p. 469.

92. Maughan-Brown, p. 36.

93. E. Baring to Secretary of State for the Colonies, 15 October 1952, PRO, CO 822/444.

94. E. Baring to Secretary of State for the Colonies, 17 October 1952, PRO, CO 822/444.

95. Bethwell A. Ogot and Tiyambe Zeleza, 'Kenya: The road to independence and after', in Gifford and Louis (eds), *Decolonisation, 1960-80*, p. 405.

96. E. Baring to Secretary of State for the Colonies, 9 October 1952, PRO, CO 822/444.

97. Government of Kenya Secretariat [name illegible] to P. Rogers, 25 August 1952, PRO, CO 822/435.

98. H. Potter to P. Rogers, 17 August 1952, PRO, CO 822/436.

99. E. Baring to Secretary of State for the Colonies, 10 October 1952, PRO, CO 822/443.

100. J. Whyatt to K. Roberts-Wray, 19 October 1952, PRO, CO 822/728.

101. J. Whyatt to K. Roberts-Wray, 8 October 1952, PRO, CO 822/728.

102. John Spencer, *The Kenya African Union*, KPI, London, 1985, p. 232.

103. J. Whyatt to P. Rogers, 2 September 1952, PRO, CO 822/437.

104. Lapping, p. 491.

105. Deputy Governor to Secretary of State for the Colonies, 15 December 1953, PRO, CO 822/471.

106. A. Clayton, *Counter-insurgency in Kenya 1952–1960*, Transafrica, Nairobi, 1976, p. 54.

107. 'Extract from a letter to Canon Bewes from the Rev. Neville Langford-Smith', 9 February 1953, PRO, CO 822/471.

108. Maughan-Brown, pp. 40–41; Clayton, *Counter Insurgency*, p. 44.

109. Canon Bewes to the Governor, 28 January 1953, PRO, CO 822/471.

110. E. Twining to W. Gorell-Barnes, 25 November 1953, PRO, CO 822/499.

111. Clayton, p. 111.

112. Clayton, p. 38.

113. Maughan-Brown, p. 40.

114. Clayton, p. 54.

115. E. Baring to Secretary of State for the Colonies, 20 April 1953, PRO, CO 822/728.

116. E. Baring to Secretary of State for the Colonies, 13 October 1953, PRO, CO 822/729.

117. Secretary of State for the Colonies to E. Baring, 24 October 1953, PRO, CO 822/729.

118. Clayton, p. 15.

119. E. Baring to Secretary of State for the Colonies, 16 October 1954, PRO, CO 822/801.

120. 'Health in detention camps', report by H. Stott, 23 September 1954, PRO, CO 822/801.

121. Clayton, p. 54.

122. Kiernan, p. 221.

123. Kenneth Wanstall, 'I saw men tortured', *Reynold's News*, 13 January 1957.

124. Philip Meldon, 'My two years in Kenya', undated [January 1957], PRO, CO 822/1237; see also affidavit of Victor Shuter, 10 January 1959, PRO, CO, 822/1271 and Eileen Fletcher, 'My comments on the government memorandum concerning my charges about Kenya', 8 January 1957, PRO, CO 822/1236.

125. Clayton, *Counter Insurgency*, p. 56.

126. Deputy Governor to Secretary of State for the Colonies, 19 February 1953, PRO, CO 822/505.

127. E. Baring to Secretary of State for the Colonies, 28 September 1953, PRO, CO 822/505.

128. Notes of a Colonial Office meeting, 28 September 1953, PRO, CO 822/505.

129. Secretary of State for the Colonies to E. Baring, 7 October 1953, PRO, CO 822/505.

130. E. Baring to Secretary of State for the Colonies, 15 October 1953, PRO, CO 822/505.

131. W. Gorell-Barnes to E. Baring, 1 December 1952, PRO, CO 822/450.

132. Hazlewood, pp. 34, 10.

133. Tanogo, p. 172.

134. Ogot and Zeleza, p. 413.

135. Gary Wasserman, *Politics of Decolonisation: Kenya, Europeans and the land issue 1960–1965*, Cambridge University Press, Cambridge, 1976, pp. 172–4.

136. Wasserman, p. 175.

137. Nicola Swainson, *The development of corporate capitalism in Kenya 1918–77*, University of California Press, Los Angeles, 1980, p. 130.

138. Ogot and Zeleza, p. 426.

139. Eric Crawford and Erik Thorbecke, 'Employment, income distribution, poverty alleviation and basic needs in Kenya', Report of an International Labour Organisation Consulting Mission, Cornell University, 1978, p. 96.

140. Hazlewood, p. 193.

141. N. Mayle to the Governor, 12 April 1952, PRO, CO 1031/995.

142. *Report of the British Guiana Constitution Commission*, Cmnd. 9274, London, HMSO, 1954, p. 10.

143. Ibid., p. 12.

144. 'Editorial form the "Daily Chronicle"' (British Guiana), 6 December 1953, PRO, CO 1031/235; *Report of the British Guiana ...* , p. 12.

145. Speech by the Governor, C. Woolley, undated [1953], PRO, CO 1031/1003.

146. 'Farewell address by His Excellency the Governor, Sir Charles Campbell Woolley, to the Legislative Council, British Guiana, on Wednesday, the 27th August, 1952', PRO, CO 1031/287.

147. Aluminium Company of Canada Ltd, *25th Annual Report: 1952*, PRO, CO 1031/1103; UK High Commissioner in Canada to Commonwealth Relations Office, 10 November 1953, PRO, CO 1031/1189.

148. *Manchester Guardian* editorial, quoted in K. Martin to J. Campbell, 26 October 1953, PRO, CO 1031/61.

149. Colonial Office, 'British Guiana: Housing', undated [1953], PRO, CO 1031/235.

150. Note by Governor, undated [September 1953], PRO, CO 1031/121.

151. Colonial Office report, 'The economic production of sugar cane by individual farmers', 8 January 1954, PRO, CO 1031/1444.

152. 'British Guiana: The economic consequences of the PPP', undated [1953], unsigned [British Guiana government], PRO, CO 1031/298.

153. CRO to various UK High Commissioners, 30 September 1953, PRO, PREM 11/827.

154. Secretary of State for the Colonies (O. Lyttelton) to Prime Minister, 5 May 1953, PRO, PREM 11/827.

155. Latin America Bureau (LAB), *Guyana: Fraudulent revolution*, LAB, London, 1984, p. 32.

156. 'Press statement by Hon. Dr. Cheddi Jagan', 1 November 1951, PRO, CO 1031/776.

157. LAB, *Guyana*, p. 31.

158. Governor to Secretary of State for the Colonies, 10 September 1953, PRO, CO 1031/60.

159. Nigel Nicolson MP, House of Commons debates, 22 October 1953, Col. 2259.

160. H. Seaford to J. Campbell, 8 September 1953, PRO, CO 1031/121.

161. Thomas Spinner, *A political and social history of Guyana, 1945–1983*, Westview Press, London, 1984, p. 44.

162. Secretary of State for the Colonies, 'Cabinet: British Guiana', 25 September 1953, PRO, PREM 11/827.

163. Secretary of State for the Colonies, House of Commons debates, 22 October 1953, Cols. 2179, 2166.

164. 'British Guiana: The economic consequences of the PPP', undated [1953], unsigned [British Guiana government], PRO, CO 1031/298.

165. Governor to Secretary of State for the Colonies, 23 October 1953, PRO, CO 1031/1171.

166. House of Commons debates, 7 December 1953, cited in Spinner, p. 55.

167. 'Statement by Her Majesty's government', 9 October 1953, PRO, CO 1031/1003.

168. Secretary of State for the Colonies, House of Commons debates, 22 October 1953, Cols. 2166, 2173.

169. UK delegation to the United Nations to Secretary of State for the Colonies, 30 September 1953, PRO, PREM 11/827.

170. State Department Policy Information, 'Situation in British Guiana (2)', EUR-42, 9 October 1953, PRO, CO 1031/1189.

171. A. Campbell to J. Vernon, 16 October 1953, PRO, CO 1031/1189.

172. House of Commons debates, 22 October 1953, Cols. 2190, 2195, 2196, 2198.

173. LAB, *Guyana*, pp. 33–5.

174. House of Commons debates, 22 October 1953, Col. 2183.

175. Secretary of State for the Colonies, House of Commons debates, 22 October 1953, Col. 2183.

176. Governor to Secretary of State for the Colonies, 23 May 1955, PRO, CO 1031/1437.

177. Officer Administrating the Government of British Guiana to Secretary of State for the Colonies, 5 September 1955, PRO, CO 1031/1437.

178. Spinner, p. 71.

179. Blum, pp. 118–23; Spinner, pp. 91–101.

180. Philip Agee, *Inside the company: CIA diary*, London, 1975, p. 406.

181. LAB, *Guyana*, p. 46.

182. LAB, *Guyana*, p. 47.

CHAPTER 4

CONTROLLING THE MIDDLE EAST:
THE EARLY YEARS

As we have seen in Chapter 1, the construction of a world order under the guidelines laid out in the years immediately following the Second World War required control over the Middle East and in particular its oil reserves, that 'vital prize for any power interested in world influence or domination', as Britain had put it. The first major effort to this end – essentially a joint Anglo-American operation – was the overthrow of the government of Iran in the 1953 coup. Over the next two decades various further means were employed to secure primary goals in the Middle East. For Britain this involved outright invasion of another country (Egypt in 1956, the only one of these later actions that the USA refused to support strongly), the fighting of colonial wars (Oman in 1957–59 and 1964–76 and Aden in 1964–67), the organisation of more coups (in three Gulf emirates between 1965 and 1970) and military intervention in support of favoured clients in the region (Jordan in 1958 and Kuwait in 1961). The evidence suggests that, in the last two operations, Britain fabricated military threats to the regimes as a pretext for intervention. We turn to Iran first.

A 'great venture': overthrowing the government of Iran

In August 1953 a coup overthrew Iran's nationalist government of Moham-med Musaddiq and installed the Shah in power. The Shah subsequently used widespread repression and torture to institute a dictatorship that lasted until the 1979 Islamic revolution. The 1953 coup is conventionally regarded primarily as a CIA operation, yet the planning record reveals not only that Britain was the prime mover in the initial project to overthrow the government but also that British resources contributed significantly to the eventual success of the operation. Two first-hand accounts of the Anglo-American sponsorship of the coup – by the MI6 and CIA agents primarily responsible for it – are useful in reconstructing events.[1] Many of the secret planning documents that reveal the British role have been removed from public access and some of them remain closed until the next century – for reasons of 'national security'. Nevertheless, a fairly clear picture still emerges. Churchill once told the CIA agent responsible for the operation that he 'would have loved nothing better than to have served under your command in this great venture'.[2]

We have already, in Chapter 3, encountered the basic plot of the coup. A nationalist government seeks to remove neocolonial control of the country's resources with the aim of using them for national development purposes, thus incurring Western wrath, the allegation of a 'communist threat' to the country, and finally action to help bring about the removal of the heretical government; the main difference between the intervention in Iran and that in British Guiana in the same year was that the former operation was covert.

In the early 1950s the Anglo-Iranian Oil Company (AIOC) – later renamed British Petroleum – which was managed from London and owned by the British government and British private citizens, controlled Iran's main source of income: oil. According to one British official, the AIOC 'has become in effect an imperium in imperio in Persia'. Iranian nationalists objected to the fact that the AIOC not only made revenues from Iranian oil 'greatly in excess of the revenues of the Persian government but [it] dominates the whole economic life of Persia, and therefore impairs her independence'. The AIOC was recognised as 'a great foreign organisation controlling Persia's economic life and destiny'.[3] The British oil business fared well from this state of affairs; the AIOC made £170 million in profits in 1950 alone.[4]

Iranians could also point to the AIOC's effectively autonomous rule in the parts of the country where the oilfields lay, its low wage rates, and the fact that the Iranian government was being paid royalties of 10 per cent or 12 per cent of the company's net proceeds, whilst the British government received as much as 30 per cent of these in taxes alone.[5] Shown the overcrowded housing afforded to some of the AIOC workers, a British official commented, '... well, this is just the way all Iranians live.'[6]

Britain's ambassador in Tehran commented: '... it is so important to prevent the Persians from destroying their main source of revenue ... by trying to run it themselves ... the need for Persia is not to run the oil industry for herself (which she cannot do) but to profit from the technical ability of the West.'[7] The British Minister of Fuel and Power explained that 'in the case of a mineral like oil [the Iranians] are of course morally entitled to a royalty' but to say 'that morally they are entitled to 50%, or ... even more of the profits of enterprises to which they have made no contribution whatever, is bunk, and ought to be shown to be bunk'.[8]

The British priority was to support political 'stability' in the country, in effect by aiding Iranian parliamentarians and prime ministers 'to preserve the existing social order from which they profit so greatly'[9] – as did, it might be added, British oil interests. One difference with the National Front (of which Musaddiq was leader) was that, according to the ambassador in Iran, its members were 'comparatively free from the taint of having amassed wealth and influence through the improper use of official positions; they can therefore attack the majority deputies, few of whom are in the same happy condition, without fear of dangerous counter attacks'.[10] According to British foreign policy analyst William Roger Louis, Musaddiq:

> managed to wrench control of the affairs of Iran from the hands of the large landowners, who as a class were allied with the wealthy merchants and members of the professional community, including the army and the civil service. Musaddiq had the support of the younger and 'westernised' nationalists against the rich and corrupt.[11]

The origin of British planning to aid the overthrow of Musaddiq lay in his decision to nationalise oil operations in Iran, which was passed into law in May 1951, the month after he became prime minister. In the dispute that followed, Musaddiq offered to compensate the AIOC but Britain demanded either a new oil concession or a settlement that would include compensation for loss of future profits. 'In other words', according to Iranian scholar Homa Katouzian, 'the Iranians would have had either to give up the spirit of the nationalisation or to compensate the AIOC not just for its investment but for all the oil which it would have produced in the next 40 years.'[12] Nationalisation and the offer of compensation were perfectly legitimate in international law though this did not appear to be relevant in guiding subsequent British actions. 'If Musaddiq seemed to be inflexible', Katouzian comments further, 'it was because he insisted on basic principles which would have been observed if the dispute had been between two equal nations.'[13] It was a fatal misunderstanding, for which he – and ultimately the Iranians – paid dearly. 'Persian public opinion', the British ambassador commented, 'is unanimous in rejecting the [British] offer.'[14] But Britain did 'not consider that a deal on acceptable terms can ever be made with' Musaddiq.[15] According to the Foreign Office's description of the US State Department's view, 'a reasonable solution with Musaddiq is impossible'; nevertheless, it added ominously, 'there is hope of a change which would bring moderate elements into control'.[16]

A number of options were available for removing the threat posed to British oil interests. First, the Chiefs of Staff observed that 'the simplest method of bringing the Persians to heel might well be simply to stop the production and export of oil'. This the AIOC subsequently did, depriving Iran of its main source of income until the 1953 coup, even though, as the Chiefs of Staff had noted, 'the effect might be to bankrupt Persia thus possibly leading to revolution'.[17] Other, mainly US oil companies aided the policy by refusing to handle Iranian oil, 'principally to prevent other oil-exporting countries … from learning a "bad" lesson from Iran's example', Katouzian comments;[18] an early example of the 'domino theory'.

The second dimension of British policy was to exert pressure, and

begin covert planning, to install 'a more reasonable government', as Foreign
Secretary Anthony Eden put it.[19] 'It has been our objective for some time
to get Sayyid Zia appointed Prime Minister,' the Foreign Office noted in
September 1951.[20] This was a man who had 'no popular support' and
whose appointment 'was likely to provoke a strong public reaction',
according to Iranian academic Fakhreddin Azimi.[21] But Zia had the quality
of being 'the one man who would be able, and anxious, to get a reasonable
oil settlement with us' and adopt a long-term policy of 'development and
reform which is essential for Persia's future stability', one Foreign Office
memorandum noted.[22]

The third option was direct military intervention. The military occupation and holding of the area around Abadan – the site of the world's
largest oil refinery and the centre of the AIOC's operations – 'would
demonstrate once and for all to the Persians British determination not to
allow the ... AIOC to be evicted from Persia and might well result in the
downfall of the Mussadiq regime and its replacement by more reasonable
elements prepared to negotiate a settlement'. Also, 'it might be expected
to produce a salutary effect throughout the Middle East and elsewhere,
as evidence that United Kingdom interests could not be recklessly
molested with impunity'.[23] Plans were thus laid for war against Iran. It
was recognised, for instance, that 'on Abadan island the Persians now
had four infantry battalions, a naval and marine garrison of some 1,200
men, and a dozen or so modern American tanks'.[24] This option was
viewed by the Foreign Office, however, as 'quite impracticable' because
of 'the risk that the Persians could effectively resist the comparatively
small number of troops which could be brought in quickly'.[25] The Foreign
Secretary and the Defence Minister of the then Labour government both
favoured the use of military force to seize the oil installations. The option
of military intervention was kept open until September 1951, when the
British government finally decided on the evacuation of British personnel
instead.[26]

Upon coming into office the following month, Churchill berated his
predecessors 'who had scuttled and run from Abadan when a splutter of
musketry would have ended the matter'.[27] 'If we had fired the volley you
were responsible for at Ismaila at Abadan,' Churchill explained to his
Foreign Secretary, Eden, 'none of these difficulties ... would have occurred.'[28] (The reference was to the British action at the town of Ismaila,
in Egypt, in January 1952. After an assault by Egyptian rebels on a British
military base, Britain occupied the town of Ismaila, surrounded the police
headquarters, and then proceeded to engage in a turkey shoot, killing fifty
people and wounding a hundred before the surrender.[29]) In Iran, however,
despite Labour's inaction, Churchill noted a few months into his term
that 'by sitting still on the safety valve and showing no weariness we are
gradually getting them into submission'.[30]

'Our policy', a British official explained, 'was to get rid of Mossadeq as soon as possible.'[31] Thus the Labour government initiated the plan to organise the overthrow of the Iranian Prime Minister. In June 1951, shortly after Musaddiq's oil nationalisation decree, Ann Lambton, a lecturer at the School of Oriental and African Studies in London, had suggested in a conversation with a Foreign Office official 'covert means ... to undermine the position of Mr Moussadek' and that the 'ideal man to do it would be Dr Zaehner', an Oxford lecturer who had been 'extremely successful in covert propaganda in 1944' in Iran.[32] Zaehner was swiftly despatched to Iran by the Labour government to aid the fall of Musaddiq, for which he was provided with considerable sums of money.[33]

After the failure of the oil negotiations the main British negotiator advised the Shah that the 'only solution' was 'a strong government under martial law and the bad boys in prison for two years or so'.[34] The ambassador in Tehran concurred, noting that 'if only the Shah can be induced to take a strong line there is a good chance that Musaddiq may be got rid of'. 'Any new government that is worth its salt' would then 'have to take drastic action against individual extremists'.[35] A fortnight later, in September 1951, the embassy was noting its preference 'for a change of government to be engineered'.[36] An adviser at the British embassy, Colonel Wheeler, explained on 29 September that 'combined Anglo-American action could, of course, have removed [Musaddiq] at any time during the past six months. ... Given a united Anglo-American front, a change of government could almost certainly be effected without difficulty or disturbance.'[37] In November, the Foreign Office official who had discussed 'covert means' with Lambton reported that 'our ... unofficial efforts to undermine Dr Mussadiq are making good progress'.[38]

With 1952 came the British preference for 'a non-communist coup d'etat preferably in the name of the Shah. This would mean an authoritarian regime,'[39] the embassy in Tehran noted. On 28 January the Foreign Office declared that 'the only hope of getting rid of Dr Mussadiq lies in a coup d'état, provided always a strong man can be found equal to the task.' It also observed that the ambassador in Iran believed that this 'strong man' would 'rule in the name of the Shah'. 'Such a dictator', the Foreign Office continued, expressing the ambassador's preference, 'would carry out the necessary administrative and economic reforms and settle the oil question on reasonable terms.' In fact, the Foreign Office noted, the ambassador 'seems to favour the authoritarian coup d'état'. 'An oil settlement to have any chance of acceptance by Dr Mussadiq would no doubt mean an appreciable departure from our principles', the Foreign Office memorandum stated. It then stated who such a reasonable new leader might be: General Zahidi, who was to become Prime Minister after the coup.[40]

By March 1952, the British embassy was observing that, unfortunately, the army was 'unlikely to take overt action against Musadiq' but that its attitude might become 'more positive'.[41] The following month, the Shah was reported to be 'proud' of resisting British pressures for 'precipitory action,'[42] since Britain had 'made it abundantly clear that we desire the fall of Musaddiq as soon as possible'.[43] In July and August the embassy continued to note that General Zahidi 'might well be adequate' for presiding over a coup;[44] in fact, as an alternative to Musaddiq, Zahidi was 'the only one immediately in sight'.[45] On 4 August embassy official Sam Falle suggested that 'we propose to the Americans that another member of the National Front be brought into power', before noting that 'this proposal has recently been made by the State Department'. The memorandum continues: 'We should leave the name-suggesting to the Americans. ... It should not be difficult to bring the Americans' candidate ... to power.' Then, the minute states, in order to secure an acceptable oil agreement this candidate would in turn be removed 'in favour of someone more prepared to reach agreement with us'. This strategy 'should be easier than the removal of Mussadiq who is, unfortunately, regarded by many of the ignorant as a messiah'.[46] Falle met Zahidi on 6 August and recorded that 'he is increasing his activity and has the courage to put himself up as a candidate for the premiership in these dangerous times. ... I understand that he has contacts, probably indirect, with the Americans and I suggested to him that there would be no harm in making his claims further known to the Americans.' Zahidi, Falle concluded, 'does seem to offer some alternative to Mussadiq'.[47] The ambassador then confirmed that Zahidi 'will make his own contacts with [the] American embassy and does not wish to appear to be our candidate'.[48]

In October 1952, the Iranian government closed down the British embassy (claiming – correctly – that certain intrigues were taking place there), thus removing Britain's cover for its covert activities. An MI6 and Foreign Office team met with the CIA in November and proposed the joint overthrow of the Iranian government based on Britain's already well-laid plans.[49] Agents of the British in Iran had been provided with a radio transmitter with which to maintain contact with MI6, and the head of the MI6 operation put the CIA in touch with other useful allies in the country.[50] British pay-offs had already secured the cooperation of 'senior officers of the army and police, deputies and senators, mullahs, merchants, newspaper editors and elder statesmen, as well as mob leaders'. 'These forces', the MI6 agent in charge of the British end of the operation explained, 'were to seize control of Tehran, preferably with the support of the Shah but if necessary without it, and to arrest Musaddiq and his ministers'.[51]

On 3 February 1953 a British delegation met with the CIA director and the US Secretary of State and decided to send the head of the CIA's operation to investigate the situation in Iran.[52] On 18 March 'the CIA was

ready to discuss tactics in detail with us for the overthrow of Musaddiq'
and it was formally agreed in April that General Zahidi was the acceptable
candidate to replace him.[53] By then, destabilisation other than by bribery
was taking place and British and US agents were also involved in plans to
kidnap key officials and political personalities. In one incident the Chief
of Police was abducted, tortured and murdered.[54] The go-ahead for the
coup was finally given by the USA in late June – Britain by then already
having presented a 'complete plan' to the CIA[55] – and Churchill's authorisation soon followed, the date being set for mid-August.[56] That month,
the head of the CIA operation met with the Shah, the CIA director
visited some members of the Shah's family in Switzerland, whilst a US
army general arrived in Tehran to meet 'old friends', among whom numbered the Shah and General Zahidi.[57]

When the coup scenario finally began, huge demonstrations proceeded
in the streets of Tehran, funded by CIA and MI6 money, $1 million of
which was in a safe in the US embassy[58] and £1.5 million of which had
been delivered by Britain to its agents in Iran, according to the MI6
officer responsible for delivering it.[59] According to then CIA agent Richard
Cottam, '... that mob that came into north Tehran and was decisive in
the overthrow was a mercenary mob. It had no ideology. That mob was
paid for by American dollars and the amount of money that was used has
to have been very large.'[60] One key aspect of the plot was to portray the
demonstrating mobs as supporters of the Communist Party – Tudeh – in
order to provide a suitable pretext for the coup and the assumption of
control by the Shah. Cottam observes that agents working on behalf of
the British 'saw the opportunity and sent the people we had under our
control into the streets to act as if they were Tudeh. They were more than
just provocateurs, they were shock troops, who acted as if they were
Tudeh people throwing rocks at mosques and priests.'[61] 'The purpose',
Brian Lapping explains, 'was to frighten the majority of Iranians into
believing that a victory for Mussadeq would be a victory for the Tudeh,
the Soviet Union and irreligion.'[62]

The head of the CIA operation sent envoys to the commanders of
some provincial armies, encouraging them to move on to Tehran.[63] In the
fighting in the capital, three hundred people were killed before Musaddiq's
supporters were defeated by the Shah's forces. A US general later testified
that 'the guns they had in their hands, the trucks they rode in, the
armoured cars that they drove through the streets, and the radio communications that permitted their control, were all furnished through the
[US] military defence assistance program'.[64]

'All in all,' US Iran analyst Barry Rubin comments, 'only five Americans
with a half-dozen Iranian contacts had organised the entire uprising.'[65]
The British input, however, had clearly been significant. One Iranian agent
of the British – Shahpour Reporter, who subsequently served as adviser

to the Shah – was rewarded with a knighthood, before becoming a chief middleman for British arms sales to Iran, in particular for the manufacturers of Chieftain tanks and Rapier missiles.[66] Two years after the coup, the head of the MI6 end of the operation became director of the Royal Institute of International Affairs, one of Britain's leading 'independent' academic research institutes.[67]

The customary explanation of the coup asserts that it occurred in response to an impending takeover by the Communist Party – Tudeh, which had close contacts with the Soviet Union – and therefore prevented the establishment of a Soviet-backed regime. A slight variation of the 'communist threat' scenario deems Musaddiq's government to have been increasingly reliant on the Tudeh to the extent that the latter were gaining ascendancy.[68] Neither of these two explanations can be properly substantiated.

In September 1952 the UK ambassador had noted that 'the communists have been opportunist rather than far-sighted [and] they have played a largely passive role, content to let matters take their course with only general encouragement from the sidelines ... they have not been a major factor in the development of the Mussadiq brand of nationalism'.[69] In March 1953, a few months before the coup, the US embassy stated that 'there was little evidence that in recent months the Tudeh had gained in popular strength, although its steady infiltration of the Iranian government and other institutions [had] continued'.[70] As for the Tudeh's attempting a coup, a State Department intelligence report of January 1953 noted that 'an open Tudeh move for power ... would probably unite independents and non-communists of all political leanings and would result ... in energetic efforts to destroy the Tudeh by force'.[71] Iranian scholar Fakhreddin Azimi concurs with this reasoning, noting:

> although the Tudeh had been successful in enlisting a number of officers, the military authorities were not unaware of this. ... The seizure of power by means of a coup was not part of Tudeh strategy, and it was also unlikely that the Russians ... would endorse such a move. In any case, the state ... and the army ... not to mention the religious establishment, were still capable of countering a Tudeh coup.

Musaddiq himself did not fear a communist coup 'but rather a right-wing royalist coup', like that which did occur, with important Anglo-American sponsorship.[72]

The alleged communist threat was, however, used to great effect. The Foreign Office stated: '... it is essential at all costs that His Majesty's Government should avoid getting into a position where they could be represented as a capitalist power attacking a Nationalist Persia.'[73] In fact, the British consistently used this 'communist threat' scenario to promote US interest in taking action against Musaddiq, since it had been US policy, much to Britain's consternation, previously to support Musaddiq as a counter to communist influence in the country.[74] The British embassy in Tehran noted in August 1952 that, in proposing the overthrow of Musaddiq to the Americans, 'we could say that, although we naturally wish to reach an oil settlement eventually, we appreciate that the first and most important objective is to prevent Persia going communist'.[75] The MI6 agent believed 'the Americans would be more likely to work with us if they saw the problem as one of containing communism rather than restoring the position of the AIOC'.[76] The deliberate funding of demonstrators posing as Tudeh supporters also gives the game away as to the degree of seriousness with which the communist threat was actually feared.[77]

'I owe my throne to God, my people, my army – and to you,' the Shah told the head of the CIA operation responsible for installing him; by 'you' he meant the USA and Britain.[78] Now that a 'dictator' had been installed in line with Foreign Office wishes, 'stability' could be restored, initially under the auspices of the favoured candidate for prime minister, General Zahidi. Thus the British understanding, outlined in 1951, that the Shah 'does not sufficiently check the members of his family and their entourage from interference in politics and their profitable incursions into business' and that 'the chief complaint of his political critics [is] that he wishes to monopolise power for himself' became harsh reality.[79] An agreement was signed the year following the coup establishing a new oil consortium in which Britain and the US both had a 40 per cent interest, and which controlled the production, pricing and export of Iranian oil. Britain's share was thus reduced from the complete control it had prior to Musaddiq but was nevertheless more than the latter's nationalisation plan had envisaged. The USA, meanwhile, had gained a significant stake in Iranian oil. Continued Western exploitation of Iranian oil could therefore resume, though now with the USA having achieved a substantial economic stake and political influence in the country, a change of fortune that symbolised the relative power of the partners in the 'special relationship'.

The Shah proceeded to 'monopolise power for himself' by instituting a dictatorship, ending representative government and assuming almost complete power, in a regime that lasted for a quarter of a century. 'The more dictatorial his regime became,' US Iran specialist Eric Hooglund comments, 'the closer the US–Iran relationship became.'[80] The Shah's regime killed around 10,000 people, about half of these during the revolution in 1978. In 1975, Amnesty International observed that Iran had the 'highest rate of death penalties in the world, no valid system of civilian courts and a history of torture which is beyond belief. No country in the world has a worse record in human rights than Iran.'[81] Rubin notes that 'prisoners were subjected to horrendous torture, equal to the worst ever devised', in a system in which 'the entire population was subjected to a constant, all-pervasive terror'.[82] For the USA the Shah was 'that rarest of

leaders, an unconditional ally' (Henry Kissinger).[83] The secret police responsible for these atrocities – SAVAK – had been created by the USA
and trained by Israel; a former CIA analyst stated that the CIA instructed
SAVAK in torture techniques.[84] According to Hassan Sana, a former
coordinator of SAVAK, Britain also trained some of SAVAK's officers
when it was set up in 1957. In exchange for providing information on
Arab countries, Sana claimed, SAVAK was given a free hand in intelligence
gathering in Britain. The SAS, meanwhile, trained the Shah's Special Forces
for operations against Kurdish guerrillas in northern Iran and was entrusted
with the protection of a British GCHQ monitoring station on the Iran–
Soviet border.[85]

The Shah had an appropriate understanding of economic priorities,
and the economic fruits of political repression accrued primarily to a
minority elite. Twenty years after the coup, the top 20 per cent of households accounted for nearly half of all consumption expenditure, whilst the
bottom 40 per cent accounted for 15 per cent of consumption expenditure
and less than 12 per cent of total income.[86] Some of those who failed to
benefit from the 'extreme concentration of wealth' in Iran[87] – for example,
the poor migrants and squatters in Tehran – were forced to engage
regularly in a 'desperate contest for shelter and land';[88] in a system that
was in large part the result of the considered actions and priorities of
Anglo-American power.

More interventions: Egypt, Oman, Aden and the Gulf

The British invasion of Egypt in 1956, three years after the overthrow of
Musaddiq, was another result of the threat posed to fundamental British
interests in the Middle East. As the leader of Arab nationalism, the
Egyptian president, Gamal Abdel Nasser, offered an alternative to British
power in the Middle East, in particular by opposing a British-sponsored
defence treaty – the Baghdad Pact – and the alliances Britain had developed
with Turkey, Iraq and Jordan, as well as the neocolonial control Britain
then exercised over the Gulf states and their oil resources. The Foreign
Office recognised in January 1956 that Nasser was 'avowedly anti-Com-
munist' but was 'unfortunately ... strongly neutralist'. 'He will not only
seek to get help without strings from both the West and the Soviet bloc,
but to the extent that he succeeds he will encourage other Arab countries
to do the same.' 'At the worst', this would mean that 'our traditional
friends may start to wonder whether enmity or at least neutrality is not
more profitable than friendship'.[89]

The Egyptian government's decision in July 1956 to nationalize the
Suez Canal Company – in which the British government held around 40
per cent of the shares and from which it reaped millions of pounds in

profits for the Treasury – was the final straw in deciding Britain to act. Before this, in March 1956, the Foreign Secretary had already told the Cabinet that 'instead of seeking to conciliate or support Colonel Nasser, we should do our utmost to counter Egyptian policy and to uphold our friends in the Middle East'.[90] Prime minister Anthony Eden concluded at the same time that Nasser 'must be got rid of'.[91] 'I want him destroyed ... I want him removed,' Eden told his Foreign Office Minister, Anthony Nutting, according to the latter's memoirs. (Later, Nutting admitted that the word Eden had actually used was 'murdered'.)[92] The Foreign Office Minister replied that the alternative to Nasser would be anarchy in Egypt, to which the Prime Minister countered, 'I don't give a damn if there's anarchy and chaos in Egypt'.[93] The option of reliance on the United Nations to solve the dispute over nationalisation of the Suez Canal Company was dismissed since 'neither the Security Council nor the General Assembly could give us what we wanted', the Foreign Office Minister noted.[94]

In invading Egypt, Britain resorted to a conspiracy with France and Israel. Thus Israel attacked Egypt first, Britain and France then vetoed a United Nations resolution calling for Israeli withdrawal and began bombing Egyptian airfields. Five days later Britain and France dropped paratroopers into Egypt, ostensibly – as had been agreed in the secret plan with Israel – to separate the warring Israelis and Egyptians, though they had already stopped fighting. The invasion of Port Said and the neighbouring area is thought to have cost at least 750 Egyptian lives. British troops later described how 'several Wogs appeared running down the street immediately in front of us' and how 'we kept shooting all the time, half the time not at anyone in particular'. French troops, meanwhile, at one point emptied their magazines on a dozen surrendering fishermen.[95] Finally, on 6 November, and under US pressure, Britain was forced to agree to a UN call for a ceasefire.

The Prime Minister subsequently stated in the House of Commons that 'there was no foreknowledge that Israel would attack Egypt – there was not'[96]. This complemented the word of Foreign Secretary Selwyn Lloyd before the invasion, who had declared that 'it is quite wrong to state that Israel was incited to this action' by the British government and that 'there was no prior agreement between us about it'.[97] After playing a key role in organising and justifying the invasion of Egypt, Selwyn Lloyd remained Foreign Secretary in the subsequent Macmillan government, turning his hand to other interventions. Meanwhile, after the failed invasion, Britain reactivated a plot that, with Saudi money, aimed to assassinate the Egyptian president and his leading colleagues.[98]

It was understood, even by those Cabinet members dissenting from the immediate use of force against Egypt, that force could always be used as a last resort. Thus the Minister of Defence, who had been the chief dissenter in the Cabinet decision to intervene militarily, wrote to Eden before the invasion that 'as long as we do everything we can to get a satisfactory settlement by other means first, I have never excluded the use of force in the last resort'.[99] At the Cabinet meeting, on 28 August, military intervention was decided upon unanimously, the reservation being that Eden had to recognise that 'the possibilities of a peaceful settlement must be fully explored'.[100] Many leading figures were entirely supportive of the British resort to violence. For example, Gerald Templer (who, partly in recognition of his efforts in Malaya, had become Chief of the Imperial General Staff) stated that the invasion had 'checked a drift' in the Middle East. 'With a bit of luck we've not only stopped quite a big war in the Middle East' – presumably Templer was referring to that between Israel and Egypt, planned by Britain – 'but we've halted the march of Russia through the Middle East and on into the African continent'; Templer thus drew on the policy pretext that had been applied with such useful effect in Malaya.[101]

The following July (1957) British military forces were again called upon when the Sultan of Oman 'requested' British intervention to quell a revolt in the north of the country. In fact, Oman was a *de facto* client state, as closely controlled by Britain as any formal colony, and the war in Oman was in reality a British one: Oman's armed forces were commanded by British officers under the overall control of a British general; two British expatriates served as Secretaries for Financial Affairs and Petroleum Affairs in the government; the Military Secretary – another Briton – controlled the Sultan's internal intelligence and communications network; and the Director of Intelligence was also British. Foreign relations were also handled by Britain and Britons occupied the post of Minister of Foreign Affairs. A British bank had held a monopoly in Oman since 1948 and the management of Oman's oil company – Petroleum Development (Oman) Ltd (PDO) – was British, the managing director being 'the most powerful man in the country after the Sultan', according to Oman analyst John Townsend.[102]

The Omani regime was highly repressive and existed for the benefit of the Sultan – in power with British support since 1932 – his immediate entourage and Britain. The infant mortality rate in 1970 was 75 per cent, torture was commonplace in Omani prisons and the population was kept in a state of utterly impoverished subservience to the Sultan. Fred Halliday, in his study of the West's client regimes in Arabia, comments that 'the appalling misery of the Omani people, and the sadism, murder and torture of Said's regime were the responsibility of the British'.[103] With not even a pretence of political representation in the country, John Townsend observes, 'there was no way for the Omani people to make their voice heard by the Sultan unless it was to be quoted to him by spies'.[104] Another analyst, F.A. Clements, notes: 'In terms of social and economic progress no development had taken place.'[105] The main city – in Dhofar province – did not even have a public electricity supply until 1971 when a small power station began to function. Before 1970 there was only one school to serve the province. This had a total of 140 pupils, all chosen by the Sultan, with the intake limited to 25 a year.[106] The Sultan also had several thousand slaves, used as bodyguards, who were forbidden all contact with the native population.[107]

Resources were thus kept firmly in the correct hands. Oil, which had been the subject of much exploration throughout the 1950s, was finally discovered in commercial quantities in the early 1960s and the first exports began in 1967. The PDO was managed by Shell, which had an 85 per cent interest in Omani oil. With almost all Oman's income deriving from this source, 'the oil revenues were paid into the Sultan's account, and he in turn released a proportion to the exchequer', Townsend notes. Executive control of the country's finances, meanwhile, was in the hands of a Briton until 1975, when the Sultan appointed an Omani to the position.[108]

It was this regime to whose defence Britain came in 1957, eventually defeating the rebels in 1959. The British intervention included the bombing of rebel villages and strongholds by the Royal Air Force (RAF), and a guerrilla war fought principally by the SAS. At the beginning of the operations in 1957, Britain's Political Resident in Bahrain recommended bombing in support of the Sultan 'to show the population the power of weapons at our disposal'. This would help 'to inflict the maximum inconvenience on the population so that out of discomfort and boredom they will turn against the rebel minority'. There would be no ground troops at this stage so the rebels would be 'impotent against aircraft'; they could be bombed free of reprisal.[109] After the rebels had been pushed back to three villages on the Jebel mountain the Foreign Office noted that 'the Political Resident has recommended that the three villages concerned ... should be warned that unless they surrender the ringleaders of the revolt they will be destroyed one by one by bombing'.[110] In January 1959 the British Air Ministry stated that there had been 'continuous RAF activity' in the Jebel area and 'the aim of these operations has been to reduce the rebels' ability to hold out in the mountains by attacking their defensive positions and their means of existence, including the cultivation, animals and water supply of the local population assisting them'. Between July and December this 'air activity' involved 1,635 sorties, some 2,203 1,000lb bombs, 448 500lb bombs, 1,310 20lb fragmentation bombs and 924 rockets.[111]

A United Nations committee was formed in the early 1960s to investigate the situation in Oman; its report concluded that 'a serious international problem' arose from 'imperialistic policies and foreign intervention' in Oman.

Had it not been for the possibility of oil being discovered in the interior, the action taken by the United Kingdom might well have been less drastic and much damage, destruction, human suffering and loss of human life might have been avoided.

In December 1965 the UN General Assembly passed a resolution recognising Oman's right to self-determination, stating that this was being prevented by Britain's colonial presence, and calling upon Britain to withdraw.[112]

But in 1964 Britain had already become engaged again in Oman, however, in countering yet another revolt – the Dhofar Rebellion. The rebels' proclamation of June 1965 – calling for the liberation of Dhofar province – was, according to Townsend, 'the product of an economic and social frustration inflamed by a mindless political repression'.[113] Even by 1970 it was still forbidden to smoke in public, to play football, to wear glasses, shoes or trousers, to have electricity or to import medicine, to eat in public or to talk to anyone for more than fifteen minutes.[114] The Sultan's response to the rebel proclamation 'was not an alternative programme with proposals for reform or economic assistance ... but simply the use of even greater force'.[115] In this he was given crucial military support by Britain – in turn backed by the firm political support of the United States – and by the late 1960s Britain had around 700 troops, including an SAS contingent, RAF personnel and private mercenaries, in the country.[116] Customary methods were used in countering the rebels. A British army officer stated, that '... we ... burnt down rebel villages and shot their goats and cows. Any enemy corpses that we recovered were propped up in a corner of the [main city's market] as a salutary lesson to any would-be freedom fighters',[117] a tactic reminiscent of Malaya. A military contingent was also later sent by the Shah of Iran, taking time off from terrorising his own population to help out with necessary Western duties. Jordan – its pro-Western orientation reaffirmed by the 1958 British intervention (see below) – also sent military advisers to Oman whilst the US provided counterinsurgency aid routed through its key client in the region, Saudi Arabia.[118]

Similar British policies were pursued in the colony of Aden (later South Yemen) from 1964 to 1967, as Britain sought to counter a national liberation movement in favour of the continued rule of friendly despots; this time, however, British troops eventually withdrew in failure. A UN call in 1963 for Britain to withdraw from Aden and permit self-determination was rejected. Attacking the civilian population, RAF bombing destroyed rebel villages and crops, causing tens of thousands of people to flee. An official British investigation in 1971 observed that the British army had engaged in the torture of detainees, using methods including 'wall-standing, hooding, noise, bread and water diet and deprivation of sleep'. These techniques, the investigation found, 'have played an important part in counter-insurgency operations in Palestine, Malaya, Kenya and

Cyprus and more recently in the British Cameroons (1960–61), Brunei (1963), British Guiana (1964), Aden (1964–7), Borneo/Malaysia (1965–6), the Persian Gulf (1970–71) and in Northern Ireland (1971)'. Another official investigation concluded that pierced eardrums had been observed on detainees coming from an interrogation centre in Aden. The Red Cross and Amnesty International, meanwhile, were refused permission to interview detainees in one notorious prison.[119]

Britain and the United States struggled to enact further measures to maintain effective control over the Middle East, sometimes in competition with each other, as Britain had increasingly to accept its role as junior partner. Thus Nasser had originally assumed power in Egypt in 1952 in a coup aided by the CIA.[120] The CIA also provided funds to, and plotted with, a group of military officers in order to stage a coup in Syria in 1956–7, but the coup scenario was delayed initially by Israel's invasion of Egypt in 1956 and then by being exposed before it got off the ground. MI6 was similarly engaged in covert operations to overthrow the Syrian government and also interested in hastening the fall of Saudi Arabia's King Saud by exploiting splits in the Saudi ruling family. Wilbur Eveland, a former CIA officer in the Middle East, explained how George Young, MI6's deputy director, described British plans in the region at this time – which were not apparently put into practice:

> Young said that Egypt, Saudi Arabia and Syria threatened Britain's survival. Their governments would have to be subverted or overthrown. ... Priority must be given to Syria, which was about to become a Soviet satellite. Because adverse Saudi reaction to what would be done in Syria was sure to follow, the overthrow of King Saud would have to come next. Then, before Nasser could use Soviet bombers to eradicate Israel, he would have to be eliminated.[121]

As for the plan for Syria:

> Turkey would create border incidents; the Iraqis would stir up the desert tribes and the Parti Populaire Syrien in Lebanon would infiltrate the borders until mass confusion justified the use of invading Iraqi troops.[122]

Britain was successful, however, in overthrowing governments in its own Gulf preserve. One success occurred in 1965 when Britain deposed the ruler of the Gulf emirate of Sharjah. Another occurred in Abu Dhabi in 1966 when the ruler was replaced by his younger brother, thus ensuring the family regime's continuity. Yet another took place in Oman itself in July 1970 when the Sultan was replaced by his son, a Sandhurst graduate who had spent some time with a British regiment in Germany; the old Sultan was flown out of the country by the RAF. British officers and advisers, in particular the Chief Intelligence Officer of the South Arabian Forces, organised the coup and took part in the successful attack on the Sultan's palace. Immediately afterwards, government was in the hands of an interim advisory council which installed the new prime minister. This was chaired by one of the old Sultan's advisers and an organiser of the coup, a retired British colonel.[123] Threats to another Gulf regime – that of Bahrain – were successfully overcome when Britain helped to put down opposition demonstrations in 1956 and 1965. The *Economist* noted correctly that 'the British have no sympathy with the notion of political organisations in Bahrain'; or indeed, one might add, anywhere else in the Gulf.[124]

Preserving the family dictatorships in the Gulf was (and remains) of key importance to British planners. A 1957 Foreign Office memorandum noted that 'the United Kingdom position [in the Gulf] depends' upon 'its individual relation with' the rulers of the Gulf states. It identified a danger of them 'losing their authority to reformist or revolutionary movements which might reject the connexion with the United Kingdom'. 'Such reform movements', it was recognised, 'are throughout the Gulf heavily influenced by Egyptian propaganda' under Nasser; there was a danger of Gulf rulers and governments 'succumbing to the xenophobic influences of Arab nationalism'.[125]

The need to maintain in power friendly rulers who would do the West's bidding also took on significant proportions in Lebanon and Jordan in 1958 and Kuwait in 1961. At the same time that Britain intervened in Jordan, the United States did the same in Lebanon, propping up Lebanese leader Chamille Chamoun, who had been helped to power by the CIA in 1952.[126] In the British operations, the rulers invited military intervention ostensibly to avert an impending coup in the case of Jordan and an Iraqi invasion in the case of Kuwait. The evidence suggests, however, that the story is not so simple.

Fabricating a threat? I: Jordan 1958

The background to the British intervention in Jordan was that a July 1958 coup had overthrown the pro-British regime in Iraq – which formed a central pillar of British policy in the Middle East – and replaced it with a nationalist regime. Jordan's ruler, King Hussein – another bastion of the British position in the region, as well as a recipient of annual funding from the CIA[127]– formally requested British intervention on the evening of 16 July 1958.[128] Ostensibly, the reason for this request was that a coup would be attempted in Jordan on 17 July sponsored by the then United Arab Republic (comprising Syria and Egypt). Syria was also alleged to be moving troops towards its border with Jordan and infiltrating arms to dissident elements across it. Hussein requested the landing of British troops to bolster the Jordanian regime and forestall a coup on the pattern of that which had just occurred in Iraq. Britain formally accepted the invitation to deploy military forces on the following morning, 17 July,[129] and the first troops, eventually numbering 2,000, landed at 8.15 a.m.[130]

A brief reconstruction of events using recently declassified British documents reveals some interesting inconsistencies in the conventional interpretation of these events. First, on 14 July the Jordanian prime minister told the British ambassador that 'he was confident in the army's loyalty and that there would be no internal trouble in Jordan'.[131] On the morning of 16 July – in the evening of which day Hussein requested intervention – the British embassy in Amman reported to the Foreign Office that there was 'generally little change'[132] since its previous communications, which had reported 'all quiet in Amman'.[133] Also, there had been 'no noticeable reaction to United States entry into Lebanon'.[134] Up until the request for intervention there had been no reports from the embassy in Amman – at least none that could be found in the Public Records Office (PRO) – that suggested any unrest sufficient for a coup attempt, or indeed any unrest at all.

Second, the Jordanian army had informed the British embassy on 16 July that 'all commanders have been ordered to suppress any hostile demonstration ruthlessly'. Most important, the embassy was informed that 'Headquarters Jordan Arab Army are confident that the army can deal effectively with any internal security situation which may arise'.[135] The loyalty of the army had also been affirmed to the British consulate in Jerusalem, where the coup was also supposed to take place.[136]

Third, there is no evidence in any of the PRO files to support the allegation that a coup was about to be attempted. An internal minute of 18 July stated without further information that the British government 'have themselves a great deal of information from secret sources ... which confirms that the fears of the Jordanian government were well founded and that the overthrow of the government ... was planned for July 17'.[137] According to the embassy in Amman, Jordan's 'apprehensions' about the coup were 'based on information from British and American as well as their own sources'.[138] When British Prime Minister, Harold Macmillan, addressed the House of Commons on 17 July he likewise provided no evidence to support the allegation that there was 'precise information of a definite plot whose foreign authors had ordered it into operation today'. In fact, Macmillan was reduced to quoting from a Baghdad radio report stating that 'a revolution has started in Iraq and one in the Lebanon and tomorrow another revolution will start in Jordan', propaganda which was daily currency amongst the vying Middle Eastern regimes and thus could hardly constitute evidence.[139]

Thus it was with no reported unrest in Jordan, with the stated ability of the Jordanian army to cope even if there were unrest, and with no presented evidence of an impending coup, that Britain received an invitation to intervene. It is at least possible, therefore – and the evidence below on Kuwait shows that it appeared to be British practice – that the 'intelligence' about a coup on which Hussein based his request for intervention derived from sources who were seeking a pretext for military intervention. As noted above, the Amman embassy had stated that Jordan's intelligence was based partly on British and American sources. Macmillan also declared in the House of Commons that intelligence about a coup had been received 'from our own sources' and it was because of this that Jordan's apprehensions were 'well-founded'.[140]

If this were the case and if the intelligence did derive from sources with an ulterior motive, the 'request' for intervention was effectively forced on Hussein. Certainly, there is no doubt that Britain was intent on intervening, and as quickly as possible. Macmillan wrote to US President Eisenhower on 15 July – a day before the Jordanian request – '... we ought ... to urge the King to make his request at once' since 'it would be to our advantage not to let the situation drift'.[141] The Foreign Office even cabled to Amman on 16 July a proposed 'precise form of wording which the King should use if he decides' to request intervention. This wording was 'important in terms of public opinion and the United Nations' and it would have to be 'the most satisfactory from the legal and political points of view'.[142] The request, the Foreign Office stressed, should point out 'efforts made by or on behalf of a foreign power' to stage a coup and the 'imminent threat to the territorial integrity and political independence of Jordan',[143] phrases which were indeed later used to justify the intervention.

Whether or not Hussein was effectively duped into believing that a coup was about to take place does not detract from the underlying reason why Britain seized upon the opportunity for intervention. It was unfortunate that 'political support for King Hussein' in Jordan was 'extremely meagre'[144] and that his position was 'entirely dependent on such military strength as he can muster'.[145] And that, as the US State Department put it, it was not 'practicable to maintain the regime against the wishes of probably 90 per cent of the country's inhabitants'.[146] The Jordan operation of 1958 was intended as a clear message to anti-Western elements in the Middle East that Britain would prop up its friends in times of crisis.

Thus the British Prime Minister stated that the motive for prompt intervention in Jordan was to have a 'real impact upon the situation in the Middle East' generally.[147] Equally, the Foreign Office noted the day before Hussein requested intervention that 'if we had Western forces in both Lebanon and Jordan we should have some cards in our hands in working towards a restoration of the Western position in the Arab world', which the Iraqi coup and the continued rule of Egypt's Nasser were threatening.[148] As the Prime Minister stated a day after the intervention, 'it is not really Jordan but Iraq which is the real problem'.[149] Macmillan wrote to Eisenhower: '... no doubt you will justify' the US intervention in Lebanon 'as action against interference both from Egypt and from Syria against the independence of another state'. But privately it was understood that the

US intervention in Lebanon was inspired by 'what has happened in Iraq', the fear that the pro-Western regime there might be similarly overthrown from within by nationalist elements.[150] The evidence – limited though it is – suggests that there was no imminent coup threat in Jordan but that British planners feared that such a coup might eventually have occurred. Immediate intervention would help to forestall this possibility at the same time as reassuring British clients elsewhere in the Middle East.

There was optimism, too, that British intervention in Jordan might have another salutary effect, that of inciting a countercoup in Iraq: 'strengthen[ing] the morale of those elements in the Iraqi army that still remain loyal to the legitimate regime', as the Foreign Office put it.[151] The 'legitimate' regime was the previous one favoured by Britain; thus the Jordan operation would be embarked upon 'with the hope of restoring the situation in Iraq'.[152]

The documentary record also shows that an invasion of Iraq from Jordanian territory was considered by British planners but decided against. On 14 July the British embassy in Amman noted, 'King Hussein spoke of assembling loyal units of the Jordan Arab Army and marching into Iraq to restore order' and that the 'Army has been brought to a state of alert'.[153] The following day both the embassy in Washington and the Foreign Office in London were stating that the despatch of troops to Jordan was necessary 'not only to prevent the situation in Jordan from crumbling but also to establish a bridgehead from which action might be taken against Iraq'.[154] The embassy in Amman described Jordanian thinking as 'sending in a Jordanian force of one or two brigades' to Iraq 'supported by Western air cover'. 'An essential element in their thinking', the embassy noted, 'seems to be the presence in Jordan of British land forces as well as the RAF.'[155] By the day of intervention, however, it would appear from the documentary record that Jordan had dropped the invasion plan and that Britain had concurred.[156]

Fabricating a threat? II: Kuwait 1961

The above interpretation of British motives regarding Jordan is supported by consideration of the motives behind Britain's intervention in Kuwait in July 1961. Whilst there is no categorical proof, the evidence suggests that an Iraqi threat to Kuwait was deliberately fabricated by Britain as a pretext for military intervention. The stakes were perhaps even greater than in the case of Jordan. Intervention was intended to secure both the Kuwaiti emir's firm reliance on Britain for protection and favoured treatment for the huge British economic stake in the country.

Kuwait was then the world's third-largest oil-producing country, with around one quarter of the world's known reserves. British Petroleum (BP) had a 50 per cent interest in the Kuwait Oil Company and Shell, in which

Britain had a 40 per cent interest, had been granted a concession in Kuwait's offshore area in January 1961. Britain was the largest state investor in Kuwaiti oil, which provided around 40 per cent of Britain's oil supplies. Furthermore, Kuwait's sterling reserves accounted for about one third of total British sterling reserves and by 1961 Kuwait had invested around £300 million in British banks, providing a very significant lever over the British economy.[157]

British planners recognised the 'vital importance of Kuwait to our Middle East oil interests' and 'the advantages to this country, both in supplies and in the balance of payments, which flow from the operations of the British companies in an independent, affluent and friendly Kuwait and from Kuwait's readiness to accept and hold sterling'.[158] Indeed, according to 1958 US documents, the UK's 'financial stability would be seriously threatened' if Kuwaiti and Gulf oil were not available to Britain 'on reasonable terms', if Britain were 'deprived of the large investments made by that area in the UK' and if sterling were 'deprived of the support provided by Persian Gulf oil'.[159]

On 20 June 1961, Kuwait achieved nominal independence from Britain but with the agreement that the two governments would 'consult together on matters which concern them both' and a commitment by Britain to come to Kuwait's defence if the latter requested it. The continuation of this defence commitment after independence had been a significant success for the British government. A year earlier, under pressure of a growing Arab nationalism throughout the Middle East, the Emir had indicated his wish to end completely British protection of Kuwait; and also during the independence negotiations leading Kuwaiti figures had expressed opposition to continuing British guarantees after independence.[160] Moreover, soon after the Iraqi coup in 1958, Britain had advised the Emir to request military assistance, but the 'offer' had been rejected.[161] With independence, therefore, Britain had secured a formal protection agreement but its real solidity was questionable.

Two months before independence, British planners had expressed their fears. According to one memorandum: 'It is clear that, as the international personality of Kuwait grows, she will wish in various ways to show that she is no longer dependent upon us. But,' it went on 'we must continue to use the opportunities which our protective role will afford to ensure so far as we can that Kuwait does not materially upset the existing financial arrangements or cease to be a good holder of sterling.'[162]

Events then proceeded as follows. On 25 June, five days after the announcement of Kuwait's independence, Iraqi leader Abdul Karim Qasim publicly claimed Kuwait as part of Iraqi territory. Five days after this, at 8 a.m. on 30 June, after receiving information that Iraq might invade Kuwait, the Emir formally requested British military intervention.[163] At midday Britain acceded to the request and on the morning of 1 July

British forces – eventually numbering around 7,000 – landed. The alleged Iraqi threat never materialised.

First, it is interesting to consider the secret record assessing the Iraqi threat. On 26 June – one day after Iraq's publicly stated claim to Kuwait – the Foreign Office noted that 'Qasim's decision appears to have been taken on the spur of the moment' and 'on present indicators it seems on the whole unlikely that Qasim will resort to military action'.[164] The following day the British embassy in Washington reported that, in the view of the US State Department, Qasim's claim to Kuwait was a 'postural move'. 'They do not (repeat not) believe that he intends further action.'[165] On 28 June, the British embassy in Kuwait discounted 'the possibility of an Iraqi engineered internal coup in Kuwait'[166] whilst the consulate in Basra near the Kuwait border noted that 'no (repeat no) reliable informant has seen or heard any unusual troop movements'.[167]

Then, also on 28 June, the ambassador in Baghdad, who previously had not reported any unusual troop movements or war preparations, cabled London '… my most recent information reveals Qasim's intention to build up in Basra a striking force suitable for an attack on Kuwait'.[168] On 29 June the Foreign Office noted that 'there are now indications, still somewhat tenuous but pointing unmistakeably at preparations by Qasim to reinforce his troops near Basra with a tank regiment'.[169] Shortly afterwards the Foreign Office stated that 'the latest information shows Qasim to be making preparations which would enable him to make a very early military attack'.[170] The communiqué from Baghdad did not state what the source of the 'most recent information' was and neither did it elaborate on it. Its wording is also interesting: the Foreign Office had merely 'indications' which were 'somewhat tenuous'; how these could point to 'unmistakeable' war preparations is an open question.

It is important to note that it appears that the information signalling an Iraqi military threat to Kuwait came exclusively from the British embassy in Baghdad and that this assessment was based on the alleged movement of a tank regiment from Baghdad to Basra. However, the PRO files contain reports from the British consulate in Basra. Earlier on the same day that the Foreign Office reported the movement of a tank regiment towards Basra, the consulate there stated that 'in the last 48 hours there have been no (repeat no) further clear indications of intended aggressive action', that security patrols were normal and that Iraqi civilian aircraft were continuing to fly to Kuwait.[171] Furthermore, at 1 a.m. on 1 July – that is, after the Kuwaiti request for intervention and the British decision to intervene – the Basra consulate reported that 'evidence so far available in Basra area does not (repeat not) indicate that an attack on Kuwait has been under preparation'. It did note that a surprise attack could be mounted from Basra 'owing to the proximity of [the] Kuwait frontier' but this would always have been the case since there was an Iraqi military base there normally.[172] In fact, eleven days after the British intervention a Ministry of Defence report stated that it was 'unlikely' that any tanks had been moved to Basra between 29 June and 4 July.[173]

The British perception of an Iraqi threat might simply be put down to an intelligence failure, but this appears infeasible. At the time, RAF photoreconnaissance squadrons based in Bahrain could have provided detailed analysis of troop movements, and British assessments of Iraqi troop deployments in the Basra area had taken place on an almost regular basis before.[174] There is also evidence that the nature of the instructions to commanders who led the British intervention did not cover contingencies that would have arisen if there really were likely to be Iraqi aggression. Third, the size of the initial British intervention force was also unlikely to have been able to defend Kuwait from any Iraqi attack.[175]

The Emir's information on the Iraqi threat came almost exclusively from British sources. Therefore, the Emir's 'request' to the British may – as in the case of Jordan – have been a mere formality given the pressure from the intelligence reports. Again, Britain was eager to intervene. The Foreign Office noted on 29 June that 'we are taking a number of preparatory measures to place ourselves at the highest state of readiness in case it becomes necessary for us to introduce forces, at the Ruler's request, into Kuwait'.[176] On the same day, it instructed the embassy in Kuwait to inform the Emir of the 'preparations' against an Iraqi attack and that 'in order to enable our forces to move quickly enough if and when the danger appears imminent we need to have a formal request from the government of Kuwait'.[177] 'The moment has come' for the Emir to request our assistance, the Foreign Secretary stated.[178] 'We think the ruler should make this request forthwith,' the Foreign Office informed the Kuwait embassy.[179] By the morning of 30 June, the Foreign Office declared that it needed the request 'as soon as possible'.[180]

All in all, the evidence strongly suggests that Britain had already decided to move troops into the area[181] and that the alleged Iraqi threat was deliberately fabricated to achieve this end. Such a display of force could further reassure those friendly Middle Eastern regimes that were pivotal to the maintenance of British power in the world's most important region. In addition to effectively acting in collusion with Britain in Lebanon and Jordan, the USA also strongly supported the British action in Kuwait. Most important, the Kuwait intervention served to reaffirm the reliance of the Kuwaiti ruling family on British protection and to preserve the close relationship deemed so vital to London by virtue of Kuwait's enormous financial investments in the British economy. The intervention occurred at a time when the West's Middle Eastern client regimes were faced with increasing political pressure from Arab nationalist forces to renounce their close links with the West.

Notes

1. C.M. Woodhouse, *Something ventured*, Granada, London, 1982; Kermit Roosevelt, *Countercoup: The struggle for the control of Iran*, McGraw Hill, London, 1979.
2. Roosevelt, p. 207.
3. D. Fergusson to R. Stokes, 3 October 1951, PRO, FO 371/91599.
4. W. Roger Louis, *The British empire in the Middle East, 1945–1951: Arab nationalism, the United States and postwar imperialism*, Clarendon, Oxford, 1984, p. 682.
5. Homa Katouzian, *Musaddiq and the struggle for power in Iran*, I.B. Tauris & Co., London, 1990, p. 139.
6. Barry Rubin, *Paved with good intentions: The American experience and Iran*, Oxford University Press, Oxford, 1980, p. 67.
7. F. Shepherd to O. Franks, 2 October 1951, PRO, FO 371/91464.
8. D. Fergusson to R. Stokes, 3 October 1951, PRO, FO 371/91599.
9. G. Middleton to A. Eden, 25 February 1952, PRO, FO 248/1531.
10. F. Shepherd to H. Morrison, 15 March 1951, PRO, FO 371/91454.
11. Louis, p. 653.
12. Katouzian, p. 144.
13. Ibid., p. 145.
14. G. Middleton to A. Eden, 23 September 1952, PRO, FO 248/1531.
15. F. Shepherd to Foreign Office, 26 January 1952, PRO, FO 248/1531.
16. Foreign Office memorandum, 'Persia: the State Department's views', 16 April 1952, PRO, FO 371/98688.
17. Chiefs of Staff Committee, Confidential Annex to COS (51) 81st meeting, 16 May 1951, PRO, FO 371/91460.
18. Katouzian, p. 145.
19. A. Eden, 'Persia: Memorandum by the Secretary of State for Foreign Affairs', 5 August 1952, PRO, CAB 129/54/CP (52) 276.
20. R. Bowker to Prime Minister, 2 September 1951, PRO, FO 371/91463.
21. Cited in Fakhreddin Azimi, *Iran: The crisis of democracy 1941–1953*, I.B. Tauris & Co., London, 1989, p. 251.
22. R. Bowker to Prime Minister, 2 September 1951, PRO, FO 371/91463.
23. H. Morrison, 'Persia: Memorandum by the Secretary of State for Foreign Affairs', 20 July 1951, PRO, CAB 129/46/CP (51) 212.
24. Chiefs of Staff Committee meeting minutes, 4 May 1951, PRO, FO 371/91458.
25. Memorandum by G. Furlonge, 24 May 1951, PRO, FO 371/91460.
26. Louis, p. 676.
27. Lapping, p. 264.
28. Prime Minister to Foreign Secretary, 17 June 1952, PRO, FO 371/98600.
29. Lapping, p. 303.
30. Prime Minister to Foreign Secretary, 17 June 1952, PRO, FO 371/98600.
31. Lapping, p. 266.
32. E. Berthoud to R. Bowker, 15 June 1951, PRO, FO 371/91548.
33. Azimi, pp. 264–5; Lapping, p. 265.
34. Cited in Azimi, p. 262.
35. F. Shepherd to W. Strang, 11 September 1951, PRO, FO 371/91463.
36. Tehran to Foreign Office, 26 September 1951, PRO, FO 371/91464.
37. G. Wheeler to R. Bowker, 29 October 1951, PRO, FO 371/91464.
38. Memorandum by E. Berthoud, 2 November 1951, PRO, FO 371/91609.
39. Tehran to Foreign Office, 26 January 1952, PRO, FO 371/98684.
40. Foreign Office memorandum, 'Sir F. Shepherd's analysis of the Persian situation', 28 January 1952, PRO, FO 371/98684.
41. G. Middleton to Foreign Office, 5 March 1952, PRO, FO 248/1531.

42. Memorandum by Dr Zaehner, 17 May 1952, PRO, FO 248/1531.
43. Memorandum by Pyman, 17 April 1952, PRO, FO 248/1531.
44. Tehran to Foreign Office, 28 July 1952, CAB 129/54/CP (52) 275.
45. Memorandum by S. Falle, 2 August 1952, PRO, FO 248/1531.
46. Memorandum by S. Falle, 4 August 1952, PRO, FO 248/1531.
47. Memorandum by S. Falle, 7 August 1952, PRO, FO 248/1531.
48. G. Middleton to Foreign Office, 7 August 1952, PRO, FO 248/1531.
49. Lapping, p. 270; Rubin, p. 77.
50. Lapping, p. 269.
51. Woodhouse, p. 118.
52. Rubin, p. 78.
53. Woodhouse, p. 124.
54. Katouzian, pp. 183–4; Azimi, p. 320.
55. Roosevelt, p. 1.
56. Lapping, p. 271.
57. Roosevelt, pp. 146–55; Sephehr Zabih, *The Mossadeq era: Roots of the Iranian revolution*, Lake View Press, Chicago, 1982, pp. 124–5.
58. Blum, p. 72; Rubin, p. 82.
59. Lapping, p. 268.
60. Ibid., p. 274.
61. Ibid., pp. 273–4; see also Azimi, p. 331.
62. Ibid., p. 274.
63. Katouzian, p. 190.
64. Blum, p. 73.
65. Rubin, p. 84.
66. Sephehr Zabih, *The Mossadegh era: Roots of the Iranian revolution*, Lake View Press, Chicago, 1982, pp. 140–42.
67. Woodhouse, p. 138.
68. See, for example, Brian Holden Reid, 'The "Northern tier" and the Baghdad pact', in John Young (ed.), *The foreign policy of Churchill's peacetime administration, 1951–1955*, Leicester University Press, Leicester, 1988, pp. 165–6, 168.
69. G. Middleton to A. Eden, 23 September 1952, PRO, FO 248/1531.
70. US embassy Tehran dispatch, 19 May 1953, PRO, FO 371/104566.
71. Blum, p. 70.
72. See Azimi, p. 331–41.
73. Foreign Office to Washington, 8 June 1951, PRO, FO 371/91459.
74. Lapping, p. 270; Katouzian, p. 177.
75. Memorandum by S. Falle, 4 August 1952, FO 248/1531.
76. Woodhouse, p. 110.
77. AIOC documents discovered in June 1951 revealed that the company had actually been aiding the Tudeh press to render the latter's opposition to Musaddiq more effective. Katouzian, p. 115.
78. Roosevelt, p. ix.
79. F. Shepherd to H. Morrison, 21 May 1951, PRO, FO 371/91459.
80. Eric Hooglund, 'Iran', in Schraeder (ed.), p. 219.
81. Blum, p. 76.
82. Rubin, pp. 177–8.
83. Gabriel Kolko, *Confronting the Third World: United States foreign policy, 1945–1980*, Pantheon, New York, 1988, p. 265.
84. Blum, p. 76.
85. Jonathan Bloch and Patrick Fitzgerald, *British intelligence and covert action: Africa, Middle East and Europe since 1945*, Junction, London, 1983, pp. 44, 113.
86. Farhad Kazemi, *Poverty and revolution in Iran: The migrant poor, urban marginality and politics*, New York University Press, New York, 1980, p. 90.

87. Robert Looney, *The economic development of Iran: A recent survey with projections to 1981*, Praeger, New York, 1973, p. 31.

88. Charles Abrams, *Man's struggle for shelter in an urbanising world*, Cambridge, MIT Press, 1964, cited in Kazemi, p. 51.

89. Foreign Office brief, 11 January 1956, FO 371/118861/JE1053/1.

90. Cited in W. Scott Lucas, 'The path to Suez: Britain and the struggle for the Middle East, 1953–56', in Deighton (ed.), p. 268.

91. Cited in Anthony Adamthwaite, 'Suez revisited', in Dockrill and Young (eds), p. 229.

92. Keith Kyle, *Suez*, St Martin's Press, New York, 1991, p. 99.

93. Anthony Nutting, *No end of a lesson: The story of Suez*, Constable, London, 1967, pp. 34–5.

94. Nutting, p. 58.

95. Kyle, pp. 461–2.

96. House of Commons debates, 5th Series, Vol. 562, 1955–56, Col. 1518, 20 December 1956.

97. House of Commons debates, 5th Series, Vol. 558, 1955–56, Col. 1569, 31 October 1956.

98. Kyle, p. 149.

99. Cited in Adamthwaite, p. 238.

100. Ibid., p. 240.

101. Ibid., p. 235.

102. John Townsend, *Oman: The making of a modern state*, Croom Helm, London, 1977, pp. 63–71; J.E. Peterson, *Oman in the twentieth century: Political foundations of an emerging state*, Croom Helm, London, 1978, p. 81.

103. Fred Halliday, *Arabia*, pp. 274, 280.

104. Townsend, p. 73.

105. F.A. Clements, *Oman: The reborn land*, Longman, London, 1980, p. 102.

106. Ibid., p. 103.

107. Fred Halliday, 'Britain and the hidden war', *Sunday Times*, 22 March 1970.

108. Townsend, pp. 81–2.

109. Bahrain to Foreign Office, 21 July 1957, PRO, FO 371/126876/EA1015/59.

110. Foreign Office memorandum, 29 October 1957, PRO, FO 371/126890/EA1015/440.

111. Air Ministry memorandum, 13 January 1959, PRO, FO 371/140167/BA1195/7.

112. John Wilkinson, *The imamate tradition of Oman*, Cambridge University Press, Cambridge, 1987, p. 326.

113. Townsend, p. 98.

114. Fred Halliday, 'Britain and the hidden war', *Sunday Times*, 22 March 1970.

115. Townsend, p. 98.

116. Peterson, p. 191.

117. Cited in Gulf Committee, *Dhofar: Britain's colonial war in the Gulf*, Gulf Committee, London, January 1972, p. 58.

118. Halliday, *Arabia*, p. 297.

119. Ibid., pp. 205–6.

120. Kolko, p. 71.

121. Blum, pp. 91–5; Wilbur Crane Eveland, *Ropes of sand: America's failure in the Middle East*, Norton, 1980, pp. 169, 229.

122. Eveland, p. 170.

123. See Townsend, pp. 73–9; Peterson, pp. 202–3; J.B. Kelly, *Arabia, the Gulf and the West*, Weidenfeld and Nicolson, London, 1980, pp. 142, 202; Bloch and Fitzgerald, pp. 130, 136–7.

124. *Economist*, 14 May 1966, cited in Halliday, *Arabia*, p. 447.

125. Foreign Office memorandum, 'The Persian Gulf', undated [1957], PRO, FO371/126915/EA1051/1.
126. Blum, p. 103.
127. Ibid., p. 98.
128. Amman to Foreign Office, 16 July 1958, PRO, FO 371/134038, VJ 1091/1.
129. Foreign Office to Amman, 17 July 1958, PRO, FO 371/134038, VJ 1091/1.
130. Amman to Foreign Office, 17 July 1958, PRO, FO 371/134008, VJ015/35.
131. Amman to Foreign Office, 14 July 1958, PRO, FO 371/134008, VJ1015/36.
132. Amman to Foreign Office, 16 July 1958, PRO, FO 371/134008, VJ1015/35.
133. Amman to Foreign Office, 14 July 1958, PRO, FO 371/134008, VJ1015/35.
134. Amman to Foreign Office, 16 July 1958, PRO, FO 371/134008, VJ1015/35.
135. Ibid.
136. Jerusalem to Foreign Office, 17 July 1958, PRO, FO 371/134009, VJ1015/38.
137. Minute by the Chancellor of the Duchy of Lancaster, 18 July 1958, PRO, PREM 11/2380.
138. Amman to Foreign Office, 16 July 1958, PRO, FO 371/134038, VJ1091/1.
139. House of Commons debates, 5th series, Vol. 591, 1957–58, 17 July 1958, Cols. 1507–8.
140. Ibid., Col. 1438.
141. Foreign Office to Washington, 15 July 1958, PRO, FO 371/134009, VJ1015/37.
142. Foreign Office to Amman, 16 July 1958, PRO, FO 371/134009, VJ1015/47.
143. Ibid.
144. Minute by P. de Zulueta, 5 August 1958, PRO, PREM 11/2381.
145. Foreign Office to Washington, 15 July 1958, PRO, FO 371/134009, VJ1015/37.
146. Washington to Foreign Office, 5 August 1958, PRO, PREM 11/2381.
147. Foreign Office to Washington, 15 July 1958, PRO, FO 371/134009, VJ1015/37.
148. Ibid.
149. Foreign Office to Washington, 18 July 1958, PRO, FO 371/134038, VJ1091/10.
150. Foreign Office to Washington, 15 July 1958, PRO, PREM 11/2380.
151. Foreign Office minute, 16 July 1958, PRO, FO 371/134038/ VJ1091/3.
152. Foreign Office to Washington, 15 July 1958, PRO, PREM 11/2380.
153. Amman to Foreign Office, 14 July 1958, PRO, FO 371/134008/VJ1015/36.
154. Washington to Foreign Office, 15 July 1958, PRO, FO 371/134009/VJ1015/37; See also Foreign Office to Washington, 15 July 1958, ibid.
155. Amman to Foreign Office, 15 July 1958, PRO, FO 371/134009/VJ1015/40.
156. Amman to Foreign Office, 16 July 1958, PRO, FO 371/134038/VJ1091/1.
157. Mustafa Alani, Operation Vantage: British military intervention in Kuwait 1961, LAAM, Surbiton, 1990, pp. 72–3.
158. Memorandum by the Lord Privy Seal, 2 October 1961, in PRO, CAB 129, C(61)140.
159. Cited in Noam Chomsky, Deterring democracy, Vintage, London, 1992, p. 184.
160. Alani, pp. 54, 57–8, 251.
161. Ibid., p. 199.
162. Memorandum by the Lord Privy Seal, 6 April 1961, in PRO, CAB 129, C(61) 49.
163. Kuwait to Foreign Office, 30 June 1961, PRO, FO 371/156874/BK1193/25.
164. Foreign Office to Kuwait, 26 June 1961, PRO, FO 371/156845/BK1083/3.
165. Washington to Foreign Office, 27 June 1961, PRO, FO 371/156845/BK1083/9.
166. J. Richmond to Foreign Office, 28 June 1961, PRO, FO 371/156873/BK1193/9.
167. Basra to Foreign Office, 28 June 1961, PRO, FO 371/156873/BK1193/9.
168. Baghdad to Foreign Office, 28 June 1961, PRO, FO 371/156873/BK1193/14.
169. Foreign Office to Washington, 29 June 1961, PRO, FO 371/156874/BK1193/16.
170. Foreign Office to Kuwait, 29 June 1961, PRO, FO 371/156874/BK1193/24.
171. What the 'further' referred to is unclear: I could find no indications of 'intended

aggressive action' in the PRO files before this memorandum. Basra to Foreign Office, 29 June 1961, PRO, FO 371/156874/BK1193/26.

172. Basra to Foreign Office, 1 July 1961, PRO, FO 371/156874/BK1193/26.
173. Alani, p. 103.
174. Ibid., pp. 108–9.
175. Ibid., pp. 160-61.
176. Foreign Office to Ankara, 29 June 1961, PRO, FO 371/156874/BK1193/23.
177. Foreign Office to Kuwait, 29 June 1961, PRO, FO 371/156874/BK1193/24.
178. Foreign Office to Washington, 29 June 1961, PRO, FO 371/156874/BK1193/16.
179. Foreign Office to Kuwait, 29 June 1961, PRO, FO 371/156874/BK1193/24.
180. Foreign Office to Kuwait, 30 June 1961, PRO, FO 371/156874/BK1193/24.
181. See Alani, pp. 118, 253.

PART THREE

THE IRRELEVANCE OF HUMAN RIGHTS

CHAPTER 5

UNPEOPLE

Useful to an understanding of British foreign policy since the Second World War is the concept of *unpeople*: human beings who impede the pursuit of high policy and whose rights, often lives, therefore become irrelevant. In the real world, Britain has made significant contributions to many of the postwar era's horrors. These contributions have been made consistently – by both Labour and Conservative governments – not through any desire on the part of state leaders purposely to contribute to misery for its own sake, nor because individuals making policy are evil, but as the consequence of pursuing other, higher priorities than the avoidance of misery, in accordance with 'national interests'. Four contributions are considered in this chapter, though the irrelevance of human rights to British planners necessarily runs like a leitmotif throughout this study.

The irrelevance of human rights is intrinsically related to another theme of this study: the fact that British policy has been consistently opposed to the promotion of meaningful economic development in the Third World. Three out of the four case studies in this chapter – South Africa, Chile and Uganda – bear witness to the fact that the primary significance of the Third World to British leaders remains the same as was clearly outlined in the planning documents in the years immediately following the Second World War. The Third World acts primarily as a market for investments and exports and, therefore, a key policy aim is to offer support to the local elements who provide favourable conditions for this market, irrespective of how repressive they are. The fruits of the economic policies pursued under Western-style 'development' are, therefore, typically restricted to a small elite, whilst large sections of the population see few gains, or find that their condition worsens.

The victims number in the millions but if they are permitted to be heard in the information system the link between their suffering and British policy is regularly overlooked, or suppressed. In the media, reporting on human rights violations in faraway states often freely takes place, providing some important data. Of the five daily broadsheet newspapers in Britain – the *Daily Telegraph*, *Times*, *Financial Times*, *Independent* and *Guardian* – this is particularly true of the latter two. As I will attempt to show in this and subsequent chapters, the first three – which account for around 70 per cent of broadsheet readership[1] – systematically fail to elucidate the specific link between British policy and human rights abuses. The *Independent* also regularly portrays the reality of British foreign policy in an inaccurately benevolent light. These newspapers are firmly entrenched within a propaganda system and their reporting implicitly serves to promote the concept of Britain's basic benevolence outlined in the Introduction to this book. Of the five newspapers, only the *Guardian* – with around 17 per cent of broadsheet readership – tends to report on British foreign policy in a more independent manner. The other four newspapers are therefore the objects of analysis in this, and later, chapters in relation to press misrepresentation. Not all areas of British policy in the Third World are analysed here in this context, and fuller case studies of press reporting will be found in chapters 6 and 7.

Cases in which Britain appears to depart from an assumed general devotion to the protection of human rights are occasionally reported even in the newspapers under analysis here, but effectively as one-offs or with heavy qualifications attached to them, therefore involving no requirement to question Britain's basic foreign policy priorities. The main argument in this study is that the *systematic* link between the basic priorities and goals of British policy on the one hand and the horrors of large-scale human rights violations on the other is unmentionable in the propaganda system, even though that link is clearly recognisable in an analysis of the historical and contemporary record. It is, rather, an article of faith that Britain's general role in the world accords with the promotion of human rights abroad as a matter of course; only occasionally, it is sometimes conceded, does it go astray.

Removing the population: Diego Garcia

I turn first to the case of the Ilois people, the indigenous inhabitants of the Indian Ocean island of Diego Garcia.

In 1965 Mauritius was granted independence by the UK, on the barely concealed condition that London be allowed to buy from it the Chagos archipelago, which includes Diego Garcia. Britain during the decolonisation process thus actually created a new colony: the British Indian Ocean Territories (BIOT), which included Chagos, detached from Mauritius, and other islands detached from the Seychelles. In 1966 Britain signed a defence deal with the USA leasing the BIOT to it for fifty years with the option of a further twenty years' lease. Britain thus had ignored UN Resolution 2066XX passed by the General Assembly in December 1965 which called on London 'to take no action which would dismember the territory of Mauritius and to violate its territorial integrity'.[2] Higher matters were at stake: Diego Garcia was well situated as a military outpost for intervention in the Middle East. (It later acted as a US nuclear base and was used as a refuelling point for US bombers during the 1991 war against Iraq, for example.) It remains British sovereign territory and, despite Mauritian demands for its return, this sovereignty is 'not negotiable', Britain pointed out in 1991.[3]

The militarisation of the island required the removal of its 1,800 indigenous inhabitants, and this occurred between 1965 and 1973. In effecting their removal Britain violated articles 9 and 13 of the UN Declaration of Human Rights, which stated that 'no one should be subjected to arbitrary ... exile' and 'everybody has the right to return to his country'.[4] Britain expelled the Ilois people to Mauritius, John Madeley comments in a Minority Rights Group report, 'without any workable resettlement scheme; left them in abject poverty, gave them a tiny amount of compensation and later offered more on condition that the islanders renounced their rights ever to return home'. The expellees were allowed to take with them 'a minimum of personal possessions, packed into a small crate' and by 1975 most of them were living in the slums of the Mauritian capital in 'gross poverty; many were housed in shacks, most of them lacked enough food', and some had died of starvation and disease. A report commissioned by the Mauritian government in the early 1980s found that only 65 of the 942 Ilois householders were owners of land and houses; and 40 per cent of adults had no job.[5]

By 1972 the US Defense Department could tell Congress that 'the islands are virtually uninhabited and the erection of the base would thus cause no indigenous political problems'. In December 1974 a joint UK–US memorandum in question-and-answer form asked 'Is there any native population on the islands?'; its reply was 'no'. A British Ministry of Defence spokesman denied this was a deliberate misrepresentation of the situation by saying 'there is nothing in our files about inhabitants or about an evacuation', thus confirming that the former inhabitants of Diego Garcia had been officially designated by the state as unpeople.[6] Madeley comments further:

> Britain's treatment of the Ilois people stands in eloquent and stark contrast with the way the people of the Falkland islands were treated in the Spring of 1982. The invasion of the Falklands was furiously resisted by British forces travelling 8,000 miles at a cost of over a thousand million pounds and many British and Argentinian lives. Diego Garcia was handed over without its inhabitants – far from being defended – even being consulted before being removed.[7]

The Falklands parallel is also apt since five days before Argentina invaded the islands – and seventeen years after the first removals from Diego Garcia began – a final deal was initialled between Britain and the Ilois for compensation of £4 million. The Argentinian action elicited in the British press several noteworthy professions of principle with regard to international law and the rights of British subjects, professions that were somewhat lacking in the case of the Ilois. The editors of the *Financial*

Times, for example, noted that the invasion of the Falklands was an 'outrage' and 'an illegal and immoral means to make good territorial claims'. A solution to this particular action 'should not pass over the wishes of the Falkland Islanders who wish to preserve their traditions', the editors commented further.[8] 'If such bare-faced attacks were allowed to achieve their ends', *Financial Times* editors comment elsewhere, 'then the consequences would be grave not just in one or two remaining British outposts, but for peace in many areas.'[9]

The *Daily Telegraph* also supported the principled British government stance being taken following the Argentinian invasion. The editors noted, for example, that 'we are pledged to consider the wishes of the Falklanders "paramount", as Mrs Thatcher repeated last night' (in an emergency debate in the House of Commons).[10] They stated elsewhere that 'principle dictates' that the USA should support Britain over the Falklands since the USA cannot 'be indifferent to the imposition of foreign rule on people who have no desire for it'.[11] Britain's decision to send a task force 'was taken quite simply because it was the only alternative to a humiliating betrayal of the Falkland Islands';[12] and the invasion 'was clearly as illegal an act as can be imagined and has been so proclaimed by the United Nations Security Council'.[13] No such voices spoke similarly over the plight of the Ilois, and neither did they entertain the notion of ridiculing a principled stance taken in support of subject peoples who were so far away.

One might further imagine the international furore that would have been created if it had been the Soviet Union that in Diego Garcia had removed an entire population from its own land. It is a reasonable assumption that Western leaders would have denounced the action as grossly immoral, as the action of an evil state, whilst professing their own inviolable commitment to the United Nations charter, human rights and international law. The story would also surely have received widespread publicity rather than being consigned to virtual oblivion, in fact invariably unmentioned in histories of British foreign policy.

The efficacy of the system is evident in even grander examples of human rights violations. The removal of the Ilois – comparatively few in number – was a relatively easy touch. Britain's national priorities have contributed to still greater violations, however, involving millions of people. We turn, then, to the case of South Africa.

A country not hostile to our interests: South Africa

In February 1990 Frank Chikane, leader of the South African Council of Churches, appealed to churches in Britain 'to put pressure on their government to be on the side of the victims of apartheid, rather than on the side of the oppressors'.[14] Chikane had correctly interpreted history.

The basic fact is that since the Second World War Britain had been a consistent supporter – the world's most significant, though in close competition with the USA – of the South African apartheid regimes, and thus bore some responsibility for the miseries they inflicted both on their own people and on those of neighbouring states.

The extent of the horrors perpetrated by the South African regimes – both internally and externally – are well known. In 1990, Oxfam and the Catholic Institute for International Relations (CIIR) provided some gruesome details on the reality of apartheid: 2 million children were growing up stunted for lack of sufficient calories; the average infant mortality rate was 95 per thousand, one of the world's highest, and the rate was even higher in rural areas; per capita spending on health care was R597 for whites, R138 for urban blacks and R88 for rural blacks; life expectancy for whites was 72 years, for blacks 59; 1.6 per cent of whites lived below the poverty line, compared with 53 per cent of blacks; whites, comprising one sixth of the population, accounted for two thirds of all incomes; blacks, comprising three quarters of the population, accounted for one quarter of all incomes.[15]

The results of South African foreign policy were no less monumental. South Africa's persistent invasions of Angola and support for UNITA rebels there (in collaboration with the major UNITA sponsor, the USA) and the sponsorship of RENAMO rebels in Mozambique resulted in over 1.3 million lives being lost, half of them of children under five, in the decade after 1980. A further 500,000 children were orphaned and unknown thousands of people were disabled by war. Another 12 million people were directly affected by war, of whom 1.9 million were refugees in neighbouring states, 6.1 million were displaced in their own country and 4 million were reduced to 'abject poverty' by the economic destruction caused by war. Between 1980 and 1988 the economic costs of these wars was $62 billion, over three times the combined gross domestic product (GDP) of the countries of Southern Africa.[16] It is in this context that British policy towards South Africa must be viewed.

In the economic sphere, Britain was by far South Africa's most important international supporter. Between 1956 and 1970 Britain accounted for over half South Africa's foreign liabilities (though the proportion declined from 62 per cent in 1956 to 54 per cent in 1970).[17] As apartheid was further enforced in the 1950s and 1960s and black opposition was progressively crushed with violence, British capital invested in the country correspondingly rose, doubling between 1956 and 1970. According to South Africa specialist Geoff Berridge, 'South Africa was squarely on a par with the United States as a host to British capital and was only regularly outstripped in importance in this regard by Australia and Canada' during these years. 'No major sector of British capitalism', Berridge comments further, 'was without substantial representation in these investments.'[18]

These interests remained unmoved following the Sharpeville massacre of 1960, which focused world condemnation on South Africa as its 'security' forces killed sixty-nine people, most of them shot in the back, and wounded hundreds of others demonstrating against the pass laws. 'The bitter truth', Agrippah Mugomba comments in a study of arms sales to South Africa, is that this was 'performed with the aid of weapons supplied by Britain for use by the South African Police Force'.[19] In the decade following Sharpeville, foreign investment poured into the country as it was clear that conditions for profits were ripe and the population was being progressively disciplined and marginalised even further from the political process. South Africa's foreign liabilities almost doubled over the period, contributing to a prodigious boom in the apartheid economy.[20] By 1964, British investment accounted for 61 per cent of South Africa's foreign liabilities, a rise of 2 per cent over the year following the Sharpeville massacre.[21]

Western support for South Africa continued throughout the 1970s; in the two years following South Africa's invasion of Angola in 1975, IMF assistance to South Africa was greater than that provided to all other African states combined.[22] By the 1980s, as South Africa stepped up its regional terrorism in Angola and Mozambique, Britain remained the largest single investor in South Africa, with around 40 per cent of the total, accounting for about 10 per cent of all British overseas investments and providing around 16 per cent of total investment profits.[23] By the end of that decade of terror, in 1990, the United Kingdom–South Africa Trade Association estimated that British investment in South Africa accounted for as much as 50 per cent of total foreign investment in the country, involving £10 billion.[24] The chairman of the British Overseas Trade Board, meanwhile, noted that 'the UK has been a reliable – probably the most reliable – trading partner of South Africa'.[25]

Huge profits were to be made. In the eight years following Sharpeville, whilst the annual rate of return on British direct investments averaged just over 8 per cent throughout the world as a whole, the return on investments in South Africa was over 12 per cent. In the thirteen years between 1958 and 1970, South Africa was the highest earner on British direct investments overseas in four of these years and the second highest in six of them.[26] US companies also benefited. In 1960 the profit rate on US investments in South Africa was 17.5 per cent compared to 10.9 per cent worldwide; it rose, in 1962, to twice the worldwide average. 'So long as United States banks and business back us, we can go ahead,' a South African politician noted in 1963.[27]

Britain also profited from South Africa's occupation of Namibia, and from South Africa's export to it of the apartheid system and the repression it practised at home. In 1966 the UN General Assembly terminated South Africa's mandate over Namibia and called for its complete withdrawal from the territory. Security Council resolutions in 1970 proclaimed the illegality of the occupation, as did a 1971 ruling of the International Court of Justice, which also declared that other states were to refrain from 'any dealings with the Government of South Africa implying recognition of, or the legality of, such presence and administration'.[28] United Nations Decree No. 1 of 1974 further declared that any exploitation of Namibia's natural resources was illegal. Nevertheless, the British government signed a contract in 1968 with a British mining transnational – RTZ Corporation – for the supply of Namibian uranium from its Rossing mine, in which the largest equity holders were RTZ itself and a company owned wholly by the South African government. These dealings continued throughout the 1970s and the early 1980s, under both Labour and Conservative governments, violating international law and effectively upholding the illegal South African occupation of the country. A Foreign Office official, speaking in 1979, stated that, with regard to the illegal uranium contracts, 'the government does not consider that there is any international obligation for it to interfere'.[29]

At the Rossing mine itself, according to the former UN Commissioner for Namibia, 'workers are subjected twenty-four hours a day to low-level cancer-causing radiation. They are paid grossly discriminatory wages and suffer appalling working conditions and living standards.'[30] Colonial-style exploitation was visited upon the territory, with 30 per cent of Namibia's GDP leaving the country in the 1960s and 1970s as profits for the large transnational firms operating there. From the late 1950s to the late 1970s, meanwhile, a further one third of Namibia's GDP left for South Africa.[31] In 1977 Namibian church leaders signed a statement asserting that electric shocks, burning with cigarettes, and sleep deprivation were standard procedures of the operators of apartheid, helping – along with sheer violence, such as the massacre by South African troops of 750 people, mainly children and students, at a refugee camp in 1978 – to make the country safe for foreign investment.[32]

Let us turn to the level of political support provided by Britain to South Africa over the decades: there is little doubt that this corresponds to the level of economic backing, especially at the United Nations where Britain applied its veto on several occasions against resolutions hostile to South Africa. During 1965–74 Britain cast seven Security Council vetoes (six on Southern Rhodesia, one on South Africa); during 1975–84 it cast ten vetoes (nine on southern Africa, one on the Falklands); and during 1985–89 it cast nine vetoes (seven on southern Africa). 'The more recent vetoes', the former British Permanent Representative at the UN, Anthony Parsons, explained, were directed towards 'defending South Africa against United Nations attempts to take coercive action in regard to South African military activity in Angola and elsewhere' and towards preventing the imposition of mandatory economic sanctions.[33] Collective, international action against South Africa was consistently blocked by Britain and its allies, chiefly the United States and France.

The system of apartheid further entrenched by the South African

Nationalist Party government that assumed power in 1948 was little more than a continuation of the old, racist system previously established in the territory by Britain. In 1945, before the formalisation of postwar apartheid in 1948, Britain's High Commissioner in South Africa argued 'that the Natives should live apart from the European' and 'that it would be necessary to build a number of suitable Native townships' for this purpose, a central feature of formal apartheid which was soon implemented.[34]

US concerns on this matter are revealed in documents dating from 1950. The US representative in Johannesburg informed the State Department of the 'extremely unsatisfactory living conditions of the natives in the Johannesburg native townships'. He continued: 'to a large extent, the natives' living quarters consist of tin shacks, shanties and miserable slums. ... Tens of thousands of natives are crowded together in slums unsuitable for human habitation.'[35] The following month the US Assistant Secretary of State was informed by the South African Prime Minister that 'in order to ensure white survival, segregation measures were an absolute necessity' and that 'the Government was endeavouring to separate the whites and non-whites into individual residential areas'. The South African Prime Minister noted that 'all whites' were 'in favour of white supremacy'. Thus informed about the enforcement of apartheid, the Assistant Secretary of State declared that the United States 'viewed with tolerance' the steps the government was taking 'to handle its problems', and he wished the Prime Minister 'success in their solution'.[36]

In 1946, Britain and the US had voted against a UN resolution calling on Pretoria to conform 'with international obligations' on the treatment of Indians resident in South Africa. Two years after this, Britain abstained on a resolution simply requesting a conference between India and South Africa to resolve their differences. 'Throughout the 1950s,' US academic William Minter comments, 'Britain backed the South African contention that such discussion was excluded by Article 2(7) of the UN Charter, which forbids interference in domestic affairs'. Similarly in 1950 the US opposed a UN resolution asserting that racial segregation was based on discrimination and urging South Africa not to implement the Group Areas Act.[37]

A secret US Department of State policy statement, drawn up just after the Nationalist Party government assumed power in May 1948, revealed that the US government was aware that the new South African regime 'can be expected to promote a harsher administrative application of existing laws' such as native residence, pass laws and the colour bar in industry. Despite this, 'we welcome friendly relations with South Africa', the State Department noted, because of 'strategic considerations and also because South Africa represents an increasingly good market for our products'.[38]

Britain's signing of an agreement with South Africa in 1955 to use a military base at Simonstown revealed Britain's complicity with South Africa's domestic repression. South Africa violated the Simonstown agreement by mass removals of the 'non-white' population from the base area and then implemented the Native Urban Areas Act and the Group Areas Act which declared Simonstown 'an area for occupation and ownership by the white group'. Britain did not break off the agreement, however, thereby apparently acquiescing in the implementation of institutionalised racism. In 1962 Edward Heath reaffirmed the special relationship in defence with South Africa and told the House of Commons that future relations between Britain and South Africa would be the same as those with 'other friendly countries'.[39]

Berridge notes that after the Sharpeville massacre in 1960, the Macmillan government:

> ... refused to condemn the shootings and displayed a pronounced reluctance to say anything at all about what had happened. When ... the government finally brought itself to comment (three days after the event) ... its posture was revealed to be one of studied neutrality.

As Britain abstained in the subsequent UN vote condemning South Africa, Macmillan, according to his own memoirs, 'kept [Prime Minister] Dr. Verwoerd closely informed of our tactics and the reasons for them'. 'In the subsequent discussion in the Security Council', Berridge continues, 'the British government [took] a very conciliatory line towards' South Africa. The British representative's speech on the substance of the issue was 'little more than a pale reflection of that made earlier by South Africa's representative'.[40] When South Africa became a republic the following year, Britain ousted it neither from the Sterling Area nor from the Preference Area and continued arms sales to the regime.[41]

In November 1962, Britain (along with the US) voted against a UN resolution calling for the international isolation of South Africa; the following year it refused to support a total arms ban on the country. At a UN Security Council meeting in August 1963 – when Britain abstained on a resolution proposing a total arms ban – Britain's UN representative remained 'South Africa's best friend, though it is true that exceedingly strong competition for this role was offered by the French delegation', Berridge notes. Britain did agree in 1963 to impose a partial ban on arms 'which would enable the policy of apartheid to be enforced'. 'It is clear, however', Berridge comments, that this 'was nothing more than a public relations exercise' since 'many of the weapons which [Britain] insisted on continuing to sell which were ostensibly for external defence could equally well be turned to counter-insurgency purposes'.[42] This was the traditional position: British arms were sold to South Africa in the 1950s, for example, in the knowledge that they might be used for internal repression and the enforcement of apartheid.[43]

In November 1964, the Labour government agreed to a total arms embargo, but it refused to contemplate full economic sanctions and

maintained an abstentionist posture on UN resolutions condemning Western support for apartheid. This was the case even as the racist Rhodesian
regime sought to entrench white minority rule after the Unilateral Declaration of Independence of 1965 and as Pretoria kept the Rhodesian regime
afloat with economic links. 'It is evident that Britain under Labour was
almost as anxious to avoid giving unnecessary offence to the Nationalist
Party regime as Britain under the Conservatives,' Berridge observes.[44]

Four days after Heath's election victory in 1970, meanwhile, the new
British government announced its long-standing desire to resume arms
sales to South Africa, provoking a diplomatic crisis within the Commonwealth; the government approved a sale of military helicopters in February
1971.[45] As opposition leader, Heath had urged the resumption of arms
sales since 'this is not a case of supplying arms to a country hostile to our
own interests'. This view was seconded in March 1970, when the chairman
of the Conservative Party, Anthony Barber, noted that 'South Africa is
our ally and we shall treat it as such'.[46]

In the 1980s the then Prime Minister, Margaret Thatcher, took on the
traditional British mantle of South Africa's leading external supporter. Her
government rejected international calls for the implementation of full
economic sanctions that were supported by virtually the entire world apart
from the leading Western nations. While the official British line asserted
that dialogue with South African leaders and the avoidance of full sanctions
would force an end to apartheid, the Commonwealth Eminent Persons
Group reported, in 1986, that 'at present there is no genuine intention on
the part of the South African government to dismantle apartheid'.[47] In
1987, by which time Pretoria had virtually destroyed Angola and Mozambique through its sponsorship of terrorism, Thatcher solemnly denounced
terrorism – by branding the African National Congress (ANC) a 'typical
terrorist organisation'.[48] She thus betrayed similar loyalties as her US
counterpart, Ronald Reagan, one of whose officials noted that 'all he
knows about southern Africa is that he is on the side of the whites'.[49]

By the time President De Klerk delivered his speech of 2 February
1990 announcing several reforms and the proposed release of Nelson
Mandela, Britain was positively aching to resume business as normal.
Thatcher immediately invited De Klerk to visit Britain, and a few days
later Foreign Secretary Hurd announced his government's desire to lift
the voluntary ban on investment (formally at least, since Britain had
encouraged its violation anyway), at the same time as mentioning that 'we
are a long way from seeing the end of apartheid'.[50] Nine days after the De
Klerk speech the British Prime Minister announced that all sanctions not
subject to binding international agreements would be lifted.[51] Then, on 14
February, Hurd stated that his advice to British companies on making
new investments in South Africa would be 'make your own judgment on
straightforward commercial grounds in either direction, free from politically

motivated pressures'.[52] On 23 February Britain officially lifted the voluntary ban on new investment and promotion of tourism.

While Britain moved comprehensively to welcome South Africa firmly back into the family of nations, the old regime remained in place and continued the war against its own citizenry with the pillars of apartheid still entrenched. De Klerk himself, two months after his February speech, stated that 'majority rule is not suitable for a country like South Africa'; he preferred the watered-down alternative of 'power sharing', so that whites could maintain a privileged position.[53] The day after De Klerk's February speech Archbishop Trevor Huddleston wrote '... none of the measures [announced by De Klerk] is in fact the end of apartheid. Apartheid remains firmly in place; all the legislation which over the years imposed it upon the majority population remains in place.'[54] Four months after the speech the Secretary General of the Commonwealth concluded similarly that 'not one of the fundamental pillars of apartheid has yet been dismantled'.[55] Both the state of emergency and the Group Areas Act remained in force. A week before the speech South African police had opened fire on a crowd, killing two people; this was followed by an incident in which 'demonstrators in Cape Town protesting against segregated education were forced on to a razor wire when the police opened fire with water cannons and rubber bullets'.[56] A fortnight after the speech, the *Guardian* revealed the existence of an army 'death squad' which, according to the head of police investigations, had been responsible for 'various incidents of murder, arson, bomb explosions at buildings and intimidation'.[57] In March, the police opened fire on demonstrators, killing eight people and injuring three hundred.[58] In April the police shot four people dead and wounded twenty at a demonstration.[59] The following month, South African police killed a further three people.[60]

As the British Foreign Secretary urged British business to consider 'straightforward commercial grounds' for investing in South Africa free from 'politically motivated pressures', one could also read about the exploits of South Africa's client terrorists in Mozambique: RENAMO. A fortnight after the De Klerk speech RENAMO massacred forty-seven civilians in an attack on a passenger train, blew the train up, looted it and kidnapped several of the survivors.[61] Two days later, RENAMO killed a further sixty-six people in an ambush.[62] Six days after this, a further eleven civilians were murdered.[63] In March one could read about forced labour zones run by RENAMO:

> ... torture and deaths due to exhaustion are common. Imprisoned like slaves at night, [the inmates] are brutalised by their guards and forced to work all day. Women are raped and beaten to death, children are kidnapped and turned into bloodthirsty guerillas.[64]

Then, in May, the press reported that three thousand refugees who had escaped the fighting in Mozambique and fled into South Africa had been forced back into Mozambique, the same day as a further eighteen were killed in yet another massacre by RENAMO.[65] In June the *Guardian* reported on how the clandestine services of the South African military establishment were continuing to supply arms to RENAMO.[66] Finally, one could consult the testimony of Christian Aid's project officer on southern Africa to the House of Commons Foreign Affairs Committee in July, who noted:

> There is a lot of evidence that support [for RENAMO] is still coming through South Africa, much less evidence to say that it is directly sanctioned by the South African government but quite a lot of evidence that elements within South Africa and within the South African security forces are at least turning a blind eye, if not actually assisting with delivery of arms etc.[67]

Britain's early reactions to De Klerk's proposed reforms – when atrocities were still continuing at South Africa's behest – revealed the continuing priority of the special relationship with Pretoria over concerns about the horrors inflicted on the local populations. De Klerk subsequently moved to enact revolutionary changes in South Africa, dismantling apartheid and scheduling free elections which led to black majority rule. There was some justification, therefore, in offering carrots at the appropriate time to encourage these moves. Britain angered other European Union (EU) countries, however, in lifting the voluntary ban on investment eight months before the EU finally agreed to do so, and it appeared that, overall, Britain was motivated by its own specific need to maintain what Foreign Secretary Hurd called its 'special position' in South Africa.[68]

The basic priority given to economic interests is a common factor of all the industrialised states. Currently, their intention is to ensure that the new economic and political system being established in South Africa will continue to guarantee Western business interests profitable access to the country's considerable economic resources (especially minerals and an abundance of cheap labour); it amounts to a continuation, therefore, of their traditional postwar policy in South Africa, as elsewhere in the Third World. Western leaders often refer to this as helping South Africa to 're-enter the world economy'.[69] 'Japanese investors', according to *Africa Confidential*, 'are hoping for a special economic zone in southern Africa with South Africa as the infrastructural hub and with special tax incentives for investors', and are 'awaiting the economic policies of an ANC-dominated government', particularly regarding 'the repatriation of profits'.[70] Similarly, a General Agreement on Tariffs and Trade (GATT) report calls for 'a reorientation of production away from emphasis on satisfying limited domestic demand and more along the lines of South Africa's comparative advantage', essentially, therefore, a policy emphasising exports rather than devoting production specifically to the needs of the population.[71]

The United Kingdom–South Africa Trade Association, representing one hundred companies with business links with South Africa, has expressed its preference for the future:

> ... a non-racial democratic South Africa with a mixed but essentially free market economy enjoying normal business links with the world would be able to generate and sustain growth and bring to Southern Africa the sort of economic miracle that is needed and that we have witnessed in South East Asia.

According to the Southern African Association, also representing British companies with trading interests in Southern Africa, the southern Africa region may be 'the most promising area in Sub-Saharan Africa' for 'development'. 'Its mineral resources, with the exception of copper, have yet to be fully exploited.' One part of British government policy should therefore, according to the Association, be 'to persuade governments in the region to adopt more favourable investment climates'.[72]

The *Independent* newspaper also has enunciated current priorities, noting the West's concern for 'firm evidence from an ANC-led government' as to a 'firm commitment to a liberal market economy' and 'the prospects for profits and an expanding market'. If South Africa can create 'political stability', the paper adds correctly, 'there will be no lack of Britons ready to take a stake in the country's future'.[73] The *Guardian's* Martin Woollacott similarly notes:

> The main obstacles to reinvestment are not ideological. Above all, bankers say, South Africa needs to abandon capital controls which penalise both South Africans and foreigners moving capital out of the country. Once investors are assured that capital can be pulled out quickly and without penalty if things go wrong, then capital will move in readily or return.[74]

By May 1993 the ANC appeared to have succumbed – unsurprisingly given the international environment – to the pressures; the ANC leader Nelson Mandela announced a future investment code that would guarantee no expropriation of property or investments and the ability to repatriate profits and dividends.[75]

The lesson is that Britain and the leading Western nations will support whoever can provide these conditions, even an ANC-led government. Formerly, the ANC were seen as completely unreliable, espousing nationalisation of the main industries and an economic strategy geared primarily to recognising the interests of the population. Successive British governments refused even to meet ANC officials until 1990 (when the first official contact took place since 1919), even though the ANC was widely recognised as being the legitimate representative of the South African people.

Britain and the West had little interest in supporting apartheid in itself; it was rather the case that the economic and political conditions provided by South African governments under apartheid could guarantee substantial profitable investments. Had South Africa failed to provide this favourable economic climate, the historical record of Western policy towards other Third World states suggests that Britain would have denounced the evils of apartheid and aided its international isolation whilst expressing a commitment to support human rights and the freedom of the oppressed population; such a policy would have been similar to its stance towards communist states. The political system that developed in South Africa was noticeably similar to that in other Western-backed Third World states where ruling elites also preside over economic systems in which master and servant are assigned their place and wealth is distributed accordingly. The main difference in the case of South Africa is that the oppressors happened to be of a different colour, yet there is no guarantee in the current international environment that the struggle for the Souh African population's freedom from oppression by ruling elites will automatically end with the demise of apartheid.

Making striking political gestures: Chile

Conducting business with brutal regimes whose very priorities are systematically to oppress their populations is a traditional theme of British foreign policy. The customary explanation (or excuse) has been that these regimes have been on the right side in the Cold War and therefore deserving of, even necessitating, Western support. It was invariably the case, however, that these regimes provided favourable economic climates for Western business interests, the East–West conflict often having been a minor or even nonexistent factor. Such was the case in two further examples of British unconcern for human rights, Chile and Uganda.

The 1973 military coup that overthrew Chile's elected president Salvador Allende and instituted a dictatorship under General Pinochet was the culmination of three years of government destabilisation aided by the United States. As CIA director William Colby later put it, the CIA campaign in Chile was a 'prototype laboratory experiment to test the techniques of heavy financial investment in an effort to discredit and bring down a government'.[76] The CIA 'experiment' (which in fact had already been tried and trusted in Italy, Iran and elsewhere) involved an assortment of tactics: funding strikes and media propaganda to discredit the Allende government and give credibility to allegations of communist plots; financial support to extreme right-wing organisations which engaged in acts of violence; and the establishment of intelligence links with the Chilean armed forces. These measures were combined with economic pressure on Chile: the Nixon administration vetoed proposed loans from, for example, the World Bank and applied pressure on US banks not to loan capital to the country. The Chilean military finally acted in September 1973, whilst the

US navy patrolled off the Chilean coast and US military aircraft cruised in Chilean airspace or touched down at a US airbase near the Chilean border in Argentina.[77] The coup occurred six months after democratic elections in which Allende's party had increased its share of the vote over the 1970 figure.

The broadly socialist programme of Allende's coalition government had followed a welfare state model of economic development involving improved health care, education and housing facilities and the raising of wages to benefit the impoverished, often malnourished population. Also of particular concern to the US was that the Allende government nationalised the US copper companies and subtracted 'excess profits' earned in previous years from the compensation.[78] The United States feared that the elected government would instigate real improvements in the lot of the impoverished and encourage others elsewhere to pursue a similar course. Aides to Secretary of State Kissinger recall, for example, that the USA was concerned with the Chilean government since 'Allende was a living example of democratic social reform in Latin America'. Kissinger stated that the 'contagious example' of Chile would 'infect' not only Latin America but also southern Europe. This view reflected earlier US concerns over Castro's Cuba, such as that expressed in the CIA warning of 1964 that 'Cuba's experiment with almost total state socialism is being watched closely by other nations in the hemisphere and any appearance of success there would have an extensive impact on the statist trend elsewhere in the area'.[79]

In Chile after the September coup, sports stadia were turned into detention and torture centres, and opposition to the new regime was suppressed or simply eliminated in an orgy of terror: 11,000 people were killed in three months. In the following three years – 1974 to 1977 – a further 2,400 people 'disappeared' as the regime turned the media into a government propaganda machine, banned or circumscribed political parties and suppressed trade unions and other popular forces that were impeding the restoration of the traditional order. According to the CIIR:

> ... the single-minded ferocity of the coup and the subsequent deliberate use of torture, 'disappearances' and murder had at that time no parallel in the history of Chile or Latin America, a continent with a long experience of dictatorship and military brutality.

By the late 1970s the systematic use of disappearances had been abandoned by the regime. Instead, in the 1980s:

> ... opposition activists are murdered in so-called 'confrontations', that is, gun battles between the police and alleged terrorists. Some of these incidents are known to have been elaborately staged as a way of disposing of people who had already been detained. At other times, it is an excuse given for shooting someone in the course of a raid.

All in all, the CIIR observes, the Pinochet regime instigated a 'policy of permanent terror'.[80]

This terror was accompanied by an economic strategy that closely followed monetarist doctrine, espousing 'free market' capitalism and providing favourable conditions for foreign investment.[81] The economic programme resulted in a substantial redistribution of income away from the poor towards the already wealthy, in a context in which Chile was lent large sums of capital by international lending agencies. The real incomes of the poorest 20 per cent of Chilean families fell by 30 per cent between 1969 and 1978, whilst those of the richest 20 per cent increased by 15 per cent. By 1978, the top 20 per cent of households accounted for over half of all consumption (having risen from 43 per cent in 1969), with the bottom 40 per cent accounting for a mere 14 per cent (down from 20 per cent in 1969). In the first half of the 1980s, average wages declined by 20 per cent and the value of the minimum legal wage was halved.[82]

Political repression and economic strategy went hand in hand. Chile analyst Heraldo Munoz comments that the success of the economic strategy

> ... relied heavily on the absence of local trade union pressure for higher wages and, more generally, on the lack of organised political opposition. The role of the repression that followed the military coup became critical in terms of ensuring the stability of the new order.[83]

The dictatorship's economic strategy impressed the Thatcher government and indeed bore striking similarities to that pursued in Britain. Britain's Trade Minister Cecil Parkinson noted in 1980 that 'the Chilean economic experience is very similar to what we are developing here'.[84] Within a year of taking office in 1979, the Thatcher government had lifted the arms embargo against Chile imposed by the previous Labour government, resumed full diplomatic relations, and restored the full cover of the Export Credit Guarantee Department for trading with Chile.

To justify these measures the British government argued that the human rights situation in Chile had substantially improved. The *Daily Telegraph* followed this line, noting 'considerable recent improvements' in Chile's human rights record.[85] 'While the British government does not claim that all violations of human rights have ceased in Chile it is satisfied that there has been a considerable improvement,' the *Daily Telegraph*'s David Adamson reported. 'In any case', he continued, 'the situation is certainly no worse than in some other countries where Britain does not exercise an arms embargo, such as Argentina'; there thousands of people had been killed by the regime that took power in the 1976 coup.[86] Gordon Brook-Shepherd, writing in the *Sunday Telegraph*, noted that, since 120 of the world's states were either dictatorships or authoritarian, Britain could not halt arms sales to all of them.

For better or worse, arms have become a major component in the trade balance of the industrialised countries, as Mrs Thatcher recently underlined when she called publicly on Britain's armament manufacturers to produce less sophisticated weapons which would find readier markets in the Third World. ... If you try to trade only with genteel customers, you will soon be out of business; and let us note that, traditionally, John Bull has never even tried.[87]

The government's argument that the Chilean regime's human rights record had substantially improved was incorrect. A UN report published shortly before the British announcement of restored diplomatic relations noted that 'the regime was more tyrannical than before' and that torture was still widely used by the Chilean secret police.[88] Sheila Cassidy, a British missionary whose torture had led Britain to break off diplomatic relations in the first place, observed that the condemnation of Chile's human rights record at the UN a month before Britain's announcement was 'based upon violations such as arbitrary arrest, interrogation with torture, the recent finding of a mass grave containing 3,000 bodies and an economic policy leading to widespread malnutrition'. She further noted that the UN report included the statement that 'the persistence of unemployment and the entrenchment of a situation in which large sectors of the population are forced to exist on incomes which are insufficient to enable them to obtain food has resulted in a deterioration in the nutrition of the Chilean people'.[89] In fact, Britain's decision to resume arms sales to the Chilean dictatorship in July 1980 coincided with a period in which, according to Amnesty International:

There has been a steady increase in the abuse of human rights in Chile. This year alone 2,000 people have been arrested in a series of systematic house raids and many are said to have been tortured. ... There is concern that people will again start 'disappearing' as they did before 1978 and that the increase in cases of torture reported to Amnesty International in recent months marks a return to brutal repression.[90]

Two months after Britain's resumption of arms sales Amnesty declared:

A consistent picture emerges: of people seized by agents of the security service ... and taken blindfold on the floors of vans or cars to torture centres in barracks or secret locations. There, interrogation is accompanied by torture for days at a time; the *parilla*, a metal grid to which the victim is tied while electric shocks are administered, recurs again and again in the reports. ... Reports of arrests and torture were increasing as early as May and have leapt dramatically since the assassination of the director of the army intelligence school on 15 July. ... Since then ... dozens of torture reports have filtered out.[91]

Two further aspects of the situation merit attention. First, the British government temporarily tried to claim that Sheila Cassidy had not been tortured by the secret police after all but had rather been 'maltreated', a new formulation obviously intended to placate the Chilean regime as diplomatic relations were restored. 'Maybe she is wrong' about her torture, Foreign Office Minister Nicholas Ridley claimed. The *Daily Telegraph*'s Tony Allen-Mills subsequently noted that 'doubts about [Cassidy's] version first arose because of reports that she was associated with the Chilean revolutionary Left through contacts with Left-wing Roman Catholic nuns and priests'! 'The use of torture', he continued, 'has always been emphatically denied by Chilean authorities who admitted, however, that Dr Cassidy was "maltreated".'[92] The following day the *Daily Telegraph*'s Frank Taylor, who interviewed Cassidy on the plane taking her out of Chile, added to the story:

> Given Dr Cassidy's known political persuasions [she was a missionary, now training to be a nun] there was always the possibility that she exaggerated when recounting what her captors had done to her. But there was not any doubt in my mind that she was ill-treated.[93]

The following day, the Foreign Office retracted and accepted the fact that Cassidy had indeed been 'tortured'.

Second, six days before Britain lifted the arms embargo a British student was arrested by the Chilean police, tortured, threatened with sexual harassment and pressed to give up British citizenship. Claire Wilson recounted: 'I spent four days seated on a chair, blindfolded. In spite of the fact that I was pregnant, I was stripped and subjected to a simulated shooting. They put iron rods under my nails and gave me electric shocks.'[94] One press report claimed that the British government was informed of this four days before resuming arms sales, but went ahead anyway.[95] The government then claimed it knew only of Wilson's arrest and not her torture before deciding to resume arms sales, a fine dividing line given that torture of arrestees was widespread, if not routine, in Chile. The government was therefore informed of the torture of a British citizen at least one day after the announcement of resumed arms sales (and possibly before) but decided to go ahead as planned. The following month the British Trade Minister led a trade mission to the country.

A correct appreciation of British priorities was provided by Lord Montgomery, who noted that the restoration of diplomatic relations 'will be widely welcomed by British industry, commerce and banking'. But 'the reestablishment of harmonious relations will be a difficult task', he said, since whilst the Chilean economy had recently made a 'spectacular recovery', Britain had lost 'much goodwill' in the country.[96]

In the early 1980s, as Britain refused to condemn Chilean human rights violations in UN votes, according to Jon Barnes, former National Secretary of the Chilean Committee for Human Rights:

> Britain was indifferent when it came to concrete action and encouragement for those in Chile defending human rights, or intervention in individual cases of

repression. Human rights leaders in Chile complained that, unlike other embassies ... the British embassy maintained irregular contact, would not make enquiries when serious human rights cases arose and would not comment on reports.[97]

After the Falklands war in 1982, during which Chile had aided Britain militarily against its regional rival, Argentina, the relationship between London and the dictatorship in Santiago became even closer. The CIIR commented in 1986:

> Since 1982 the [Chilean] government has deployed an arsenal of repressive techniques to combat mounting protests: mass arrests in poor districts, internal exile, individual detention, torture and murder. The growing numbers of people affected are a barometer of opposition to the government and an indication of its political bankruptcy.[98]

In 1982, Britain sold fighter jets and bombers to Chile, held talks in London with the commander of Chile's navy – who had been in charge of it since the 1973 coup – and invited the head of Chile's air force to the Farnborough air show.[99] The following year Britain was reported to be negotiating the sale of a destroyer, fighter–interceptor aircraft and surface-to-air missiles and was preparing to ship enriched uranium to Chile.[100] Arms sales involving cruisers and destroyers followed and it was reported that Britain was continuing to use military facilities in Chile and was also training Chilean naval and air force personnel, both in Britain and Chile.[101] In 1985 Britain issued an export licence for a demonstration model of the Centaur multi-role vehicle, with a view to selling three hundred to the Chilean army. 'The Centaur would be useful for security work in rough country conditions,' the *Guardian* reported, and could perhaps be used for further domestic repression.[102]

If there were any doubts about the notion that halting British arms sales and breaking off diplomatic relations could put pressure upon Chile to improve its human rights record, the Foreign Office itself appeared to remove them. Foreign Office documents leaked in 1985 stated that an arms embargo on Chile would be a 'striking political gesture on our behalf' against human rights abuses. Equally, breaking off full diplomatic relations with Chile 'would be an effective way of demonstrating our concern to the Chileans'. An arms embargo, however, would also 'hazard the defence and other cooperation we enjoy over the Falklands', and a recall of the British ambassador would 'provoke appetites in parliament for a more substantial scaling down of our relations with Chile'; little agonising was needed, therefore, over the ordering of priorities. The documents also revealed that the Foreign Office viewed the possible sale of the Centaur military vehicles as 'politically contentious' and 'to be watched carefully', indicating apparent British preparedness to sell them even though they might be used for domestic repression.[103]

The Chilean regime's economic priorities elicited Western support despite its resort to murder and repression in helping to effect its strategy. Japan's Foreign Minister was particularly enthusiastic, declaring in 1979 that Latin American governments like Chile were 'fighting against un-democratic groups in order to attain democracy' and that 'the military governments of Latin America deserve support'. (All of which was re-ported uncritically in the *Daily Telegraph*, with reference to Chile's 'relative political stability'.)[104]

Three years after the coup Chile had been loaned $350 million in US bilateral aid, making it the largest recipient of US aid in Latin America. Some sanctions were imposed by the Carter administration as a result of human rights abuses, but the subsequent Reagan administration helped Chile to obtain $1 billion from multilateral institutions and in 1984 voted for over $400 million in loans to Chile from the World Bank and the Inter-American Development Bank.[105] In 1982, as the policy of terror continued, the British Trade Minister termed Chile a 'moderating and stabilising force in Latin America' and stated that Britain was further 'interested in deepening and strengthening political relations'.[106]

The British press – whilst often mentioning the appalling human rights abuses in Chile – generally concurred with the latter line. 'General Pinochet's main achievement has always been the restoration of order after the chaos' of the Allende years, the *Times* suggested, apparently confirming the meaning of 'order'. It even commented that 'too many people demonstrating in the streets can diminish and destroy that asset'.[107] The *Daily Telegraph*, meanwhile, similarly noted that 'the General, and Chile, have had some very good years since the bloody coup against Salvador Allende ... there was an economic miracle. Pinochet brought stability and prosperity to all but the very poor.'[108]

By the mid-1980s, however, it was clear that the Chilean economic experiment had failed in the important dimensions of overall economic growth and in maintaining a favourable climate for investors generally. It was at this point that the Reagan and Thatcher governments suddenly discovered that the Pinochet regime had been seriously abusing human rights. In December 1984 Britain voted at the UN to condemn Chile for human rights abuses, and the United States later followed by sponsoring a draft UN resolution condemning Pinochet for failing to protect human rights.

Commenting on this turnaround, the *Daily Telegraph* noted that the United States was abandoning its 'arms length position towards Chile by which it maintained a business like relationship'. Previously the USA had – apparently – 'as in the case of South Africa, pursued a policy of quiet diplomacy in the field of human rights'.[109] The *Financial Times* stated in 1985 that 'for almost a decade General Pinochet was able to boast of having restored a sense of stability to Chile, albeit at the cost of political liberty', perhaps highlighting the meaning of 'stability'. 'So far,' it continued, 'Chile has been remarkably successful in winning the support of the international banking community, largely because the government has bent over backwards to follow the orthodox prescriptions of the International Monetary Fund.' But now 'Chile's experiment in free market economics has gone sour through a mixture of world recession, falling copper prices, over-borrowing and poor management.' The *Financial Times* stated that 'the US has been a good ally to Chile; but over the past year it has become understandably concerned by General Pinochet's refusal to establish a serious dialogue with even the moderate opposition'.[110] Why the United States had remained unconcerned about human rights when its corporations were earning large profits from the economic climate provided by the regime is left unmentioned. Simply, human rights abuses can be condemned when regimes do not promote Western economic interests and ignored when they do. Yet the relevance of this principle to systematic British and Western policy priorities throughout the postwar era – in fact, an obvious leitmotif of history – cannot be stated in the propaganda system.

National interests and human slaughter I: Uganda

The case of Uganda in the early 1980s highlights further Britain's 'national interests' in the face of human slaughter.

Milton Obote assumed power in 1980 following fraudulent elections in which the Commonwealth Observer Team was inundated with complaints of bribery, intimidation and violence by Obote's party, the Ugandan People's Congress (UPC), against other parties. In a genuinely free and fair election it was widely contended that the main party opposed to Obote would have won. But Obote's UPC undertook measures such as dismissing district commissioners and replacing them with its own supporters to facilitate vote-rigging, and sacked the Chief Justice and two other judges 'to ensure that election malpractices would go unpunished'. 'Voting took place to the resounding echo of gunfire in many areas,' Oliver Furley comments in his analysis of the conflicts in 1980s Uganda. The Commonwealth observers, 'apparently disgusted at the way the elections were proceeding, actually left before the final results', subsequently issuing a public statement saying the elections were as free and fair as could be expected in the circumstances, though voicing private misgivings.[111] Britain immediately recognised the new regime, the first country to do so.

The subsequent story was one of sheer horror as the Obote regime fought a civil war in which it indulged in atrocities on a colossal scale, culminating in near-genocide. Extra-legal executions, torture, abductions and killings of people in detention centres soon became commonplace; bodies were found in dumps by the dozen. According to Amnesty International, the victims included 'innocent and unarmed men, women and children who simply happened to be in an area of armed conflict'. One person testified: 'I saw people being forced to talk by bayoneting, shooting at the ankles and in the knees. Sometimes they would tie your private parts with plastic packs for milk and then they would burn them'.[112] According to Amnesty International, in one army massacre, at Namugongo in May 1984, soldiers:

> entered the theological college, apparently searching for guerillas. Staff and students were interrogated, fired at and beaten. Four individuals, including the Vice-Principal and another priest, were arrested. The four were held in military custody in Kampala and tortured before being transferred to police custody and released uncharged next day. The Reverend Godfrey Bazira was shot in the leg, beaten and taken away. When his body was discovered later, one eye was found to have been gouged out and there were other marks of torture and gunshot wounds. Over the next two days many other people in Namugongo village and the surrounding area were beaten, tortured and killed by soldiers. Many women were raped.[113]

Another report noted that in the military barracks that served as detention centres inmates:

> … live in intensely crowded conditions, often in their own excrement. They are frequently deprived of water and hence have to drink their own urine to survive. Suspects are beaten with such instruments as hammers, wooden clubs, iron bars and barbed wire and other methods of torture include burning the genitals with strips of plastic and the severing of arms and legs.[114]

Ugandan army actions took the form of near-genocide in the Luwero Triangle area of the country; independent reports in 1984 and 1985 asserted that as many as 300,000 people had been killed there, either through slaughters by the army or through starvation as a result of deliberate army and government practices. When an Amnesty International team visited the area in 1986 they 'saw rows of skulls and other bones and human remains laid out at the roadside or stuck on sticks'.[115] Nevertheless, when the US government publicly stated, in an August 1984 report, that 100,000–200,000 people in the Luwero Triangle had been killed by the Ugandan army in the previous three years, the British Foreign Office reportedly replied that there was 'no evidence to substantiate' the figures.[116] It was also alleged that a British special investigation had found 'no evidence' to support the US figures and 'dismissed' them as an 'exaggeration', but Foreign Office sources later said they had been misquoted and that there never was any special investigation.[117] Finally, the British government changed track and accepted that its view of conditions in Uganda did not differ from that of the USA as expressed in its August 1984 report.[118]

The problem was that Britain had supported the Obote regime throughout the period in which it was indulging in gross atrocities. In early 1982 Britain had agreed to send military instructors to head a Commonwealth team to train the Ugandan army. By 1984 other Commonwealth members had withdrawn, leaving the British team with sole responsibility. 'Britain has no intention of leaving in spite of the atrocities that the Ugandan army is committing,' *The Times* reported.[119] It had been reported in June 1982 that a team of former British soldiers was beginning to train Ugandan recruits for a 'special force' to take over 'internal security' from the army, a contract which had the 'discreet approval' of the Foreign Office.[120] The official British army training team remained in Uganda throughout the period of mass slaughter. Indeed, within a fortnight of the 1984 US report detailing atrocities in the Luwero Triangle, Britain and Uganda signed an agreement formalising the military training mission. The following April Britain announced an increase in its military training team personnel and a renewal of the contract.[121] According to Richard Dowden, writing in *The Times* in 1986 after the fall of Obote:

> The High Commission staff in Kampala and the Foreign Office in London maintained throughout the Obote period that atrocities were not taking place or that the reports were greatly exaggerated. Now, in private, they say they could not get access to Luwero, where most of the massacres happened. But the Red Cross knew what was going on, as did British journalists and church leaders; they all passed on information. ... As late as August last year when journalists were travelling freely throughout the Luwero district in local taxis to visit the killing sites, the High Commissioner, Colin McClean, appears not to have gone there.[122]

It was not until June 1985, a month before Obote's fall, that Britain called in the Ugandan High Commissioner in London and threatened to cut off aid.

The US reaction to its own reports of mass slaughter was instructive. A month after the 1984 US government report, the US press reported that Chester Crocker, the Assistant Secretary of State for African Affairs, 'pledged continued US support to the government of President Milton Obote of Uganda, despite American allegations of mass murder and torture by the Ugandan army'. Crocker stated that the Ugandan government was 'working to restore law and order and national unity' in a context of 'armed dissidence'.[123]

British trade links with Obote's Uganda continued despite the massacres; it was reported in August 1984, five days after the US report appeared, that two UK trade missions were to go to Uganda that November with British government backing.[124] In 1983, Foreign Office Minister Malcolm Rifkind had visited the country; upon leaving he referred to British–Ugandan relations as 'very cordial', stating that Britain was releasing another £4 million in financial support. Ed Hooper and Louise Pirouet, writing in a December 1984 Minority Rights Group report, commented

that 'on the recent occasions that British and Ugandan government representatives have met the meetings seem to have been typified by the signing
of trade deals and friendship pacts rather than by real attempts to rectify
the human rights situation'.[125] Britain had substantial commercial interests
in the country and the Obote regime maintained a favourable attitude
towards British investments and an adherence in its economic strategy to
World Bank and IMF guidelines. In May 1982 Uganda was granted a $70
million reconstruction loan from the World Bank whilst Ugandan ministers
outlined the benefits of their new economic programme to foreign investors. These included tax holidays, the free repatriation of profits and
dividends, interest on loans in any approved foreign currency and an
initial complete exemption from corporation tax. The *Financial Times*
reported: 'Western donors have welcomed the plan for its commitment to
a mixed economy and intention to dismantle an inefficient system of
state-controlled companies.'[126] But as Victoria Brittain wrote in the
Guardian, the Ugandan 'recovery programme' 'is based firmly on benefiting
the production section of the economy. It leaves Uganda's massive social
needs in areas such as health and education to some distant future stage',
perhaps to oblivion.[127]

Throughout the period of mass murder, sections of the British press
frequently lent their support to the government's stance. This support
included the assertion that the Ugandan army's resort to gross human
rights violations was due to its 'indiscipline' and that, therefore, the
presence of the British army training team could be justified in terms of
helping to combat this failing. Thus *The Times* stated, on the subject of the
signing of the 1984 agreement formalising the British training mission,
that 'the memorandum of understanding was completed, ironically, amid
criticism of indiscipline within the Ugandan army'. 'The allegations of
indiscipline ... reinforce the argument for sending a British team,' *The
Times* continued, paraphrasing the Foreign Office view.[128] The *Financial
Times* also noted Obote's 'failure to control his badly trained army'.[129] The
Daily Telegraph correctly observed in April 1982 that 'the chances of an
innocent person being knocked off in Uganda today are in fact probably
greater than they were under Idi Amin'. But the reason for the atrocities
under Obote was that the government was 'unable to restrain its very
largely untrained army from killing at random'.[130]

A somewhat different version of reality was provided by Amnesty
International, which later noted:

> The Obote government and its apologists tended to attribute army human rights
> abuses to army indiscipline, but there is no doubt that the army was deliberately
> deployed in situations where it was sure to abuse civilians and that the govern-
> ment made no serious attempt to curb its abuses. In fact, some of the worst
> abuses were committed by the better disciplined elite units, such as the Special
> Brigade and paramilitary Special Police Force.[131]

Support for the government from the *Daily Telegraph* extended to the initial British denial of the extent of the killings. It reported, for example, that 'even some American diplomats in East Africa have admitted privately their bafflement' over the figure of 100,000–200,000 deaths. It continued: 'The British High Commissions in East Africa follow the Foreign Office line that the American claims must be viewed with scepticism.'[132] Editorially, the *Daily Telegraph* commented that the Foreign Office's reaction to the US report on the killings might be 'a little complacent' and identified a 'tendency on the part of the British government to be rather too polite' to Obote – a severe reprimand indeed, given that the regime was murdering hundreds of thousands of people.[133]

One *Financial Times* article in October 1982 appeared with a photo of the Ugandan President with the caption 'President Obote: "we are succeeding"'; it commented that Uganda 'has managed, unlike an increasing number of ailing African states, to comply with the tough conditions attached to [IMF] loans'.[134] In an eight-page survey in the same month, the *Financial Times* declared that 'painfully and slowly, Uganda is pulling itself out of the state of chaos, bloodshed and anarchy' of previous years (at a time when human rights violations were, in fact, increasing). 'There can be little doubt that human rights have been abused over the past two years,' it continued, 'although not on the scale sometimes suggested by critics.' 'Fundamentally,' it went on, 'the greatest challenge facing [Obote's] administration is the restoration of the basic institutions of society and government, of moral values and confidence in the rule of law' – no small challenge, indeed, when the corpses of the dead were continually being discovered, fifty found in May 1982 and eighty in June, for example.[135] The extent of human rights violations was, therefore, downplayed with the *Financial Times* observing the 'arbitrary abuse of power' by government officials, including 'harassment and detention' of opposition figures and widespread 'reports' of human rights abuses. Some of the government's methods were 'disquieting' – not the systematic use of murder to eliminate opponents, but the 'broadcasting of party slogans on state radio, or appointing sympathisers to lucrative jobs'.[136]

After the Obote regime had fallen and Amnesty International observed the former killing sites complete with rows of skulls and other human remains, *The Times* could still comment faithfully that 'as the old mother country which had always been aware of [Uganda's] potential ... Britain has felt a particular responsibility towards its people'.[137]

The irrelevance of human rights

The West's promotion of socio-economic conditions in the Third World favourable to its commercial interests is a root cause of much human rights abuse. Without an understanding of this such horrors may be merely ascribed to evil individuals rather than to deeper, structural causes and to the international context. The fact that Britain did not conduct such abuses itself does not absolve planners from a partial responsibility for them. Indeed, by profiting from the conditions in which they took place and by helping to maintain an international order which in fact requires such conditions to prevail, they are systematic contributors to these horrors. That Britain's national interests regularly lie in clear contradiction to the welfare of peoples of other lands – and who are indeed the victims of both domestic and international oppression – signifies the degree to which the fundamental bases of British foreign policy (and therefore domestic society) require change.

Notes

1. Circulation figures for March 1994 (*Daily Telegraph* 42%, *Financial Times* 12%, *The Times* 16%, *Guardian* 17% and *Independent* 13%). Editors: *A UK media directory*, Vol. 1, March 1994.

2. John Madeley, *Diego Garcia: A contrast to the Falklands*, Report No. 54, Minority Rights Group, London, 1985, p. 3.

3. *Africa Research Bulletin*, Vol. 28., No. 11, 1 November 1991, p. 10361A.

4. Madeley, pp. 3–8.

5. Ibid., pp. 3–8.

6. Martin Walker, 'Britain evicts for base aims', *Guardian*, 10 September 1975.

7. Madeley, p. 3.

8. 'Jingoism is not the way', *Financial Times*, 5 April 1982.

9. 'After Lord Carrington', *Financial Times*, 6 April 1982.

10. 'It may need force', *Daily Telegraph*, 15 April 1982.

11. 'The right thing is right', *Daily Telegraph*, 19 April 1982.

12. 'A national crisis', *Daily Telegraph*, 5 April 1982.

13. 'The fleet under way', *Daily Telegraph*, 7 April 1982.

14. Memorandum submitted by the British Council of Churches, in House of Commons, Foreign Affairs Committee, *UK policy towards South Africa and the other states of the region*, 18 July 1990, London, HMSO, p. 187.

15. See the memoranda submitted by Oxfam, Save the Children Fund, Actionaid and the CIIR, in House of Commons, Foreign Affairs Committee, *UK policy towards South Africa and the other states of the region*, 20 June 1990, London, HMSO, pp. 72–91.

16. Ibid.

17. Geoff Berridge, *Economic power in Anglo-South African diplomacy: Simonstown, Sharpeville and after*, Macmillan, London, 1981, p. 29.

18. Berridge, pp. 34–5.

19. Agrippah Mugomba, *The foreign policy of despair: Africa and the sale of arms to South Africa*, East African Literature Bureau, Kampala, 1977, p. 46.

20. Alex Callinicos, *Southern Africa after Zimbabwe*, Zed, London, 1981, p. 79.

21. William Minter, *King Solomon's mines revisited: Western interests and the burdened history of Southern Africa*, Basic Books, New York, 1986, p. 216.

22. Minter, p. 279.

23. Ibid., p. 24.

24. Memorandum submitted by the United Kingdom–South Africa Trade Association, in House of Commons, Foreign Affairs Committee, *UK policy towards South Africa and the other states of the region*, 20 June 1990, London, HMSO, p. 38.

25. Quoted in House of Commons, Foreign Affairs Committee, *UK policy towards South Africa and the other states of the region*, 4 July 1990, London, HMSO, p. 171.

26. Berridge, p. 35.

27. Minter, pp. 102, 190.

28. Alun Roberts, *The Rossing file: The inside story of Britain's secret contract for Namibian uranium*, CANUC, London, undated, p. 12.

29. Ibid., p. 32.

30. Ibid., p. 4.

31. CIIR and the British Council of Churches, *Namibia in the 1980s*, CIIR, London, 1986, pp. 17, 33; Minter, p. 199.

32. CIIR and the British Council of Churches, p. 23.

33. Anthony Parsons, 'Britain and the security council', in Erik Jensen and Thomas Fisher (eds), *The United Kingdom—the United Nations*, Macmillan, London, 1990, p. 53.

34. E. Baring to Secretary of State for Foreign Affairs, 11 December 1945, PRO, CAB 129/6, CP(46)12.

35. Consul General in Johannesburg to Department of State, 17 February 1950, *FRUS*, 1950, Vol. V, p. 1812.

36. Memorandum of conversation by the Chargé in South Africa, 6 March 1950, *FRUS*, 1950, Vol. V, pp. 1816–17.

37. Minter, pp. 131–2.

38. Policy Statement of the Department of State, 1 November 1948, *FRUS*, 1948, Vol. V, Part 1, pp. 524–32.

39. Mugomba, pp. 30–2.

40. Berridge, pp. 115–16.

41. Ibid., p. 129.

42. Ibid., pp. 117–20.

43. Minter, p. 135.

44. Berridge, p. 153.

45. Minter, p. 225.

46. Mugomba, pp. 61–2.

47. Linda Freeman, 'All but one: Britain, the Commonwealth and sanctions', in Orkin (ed.), p. 145.

48. She continued by saying that 'anyone who thinks that the ANC is going to run the government in South Africa is living in cloud-cuckoo-land', expressing Western fears. Cited in Freeman, p. 144.

49. Minter, p. 310.

50. *Weekly Hansard*, Issue No. 1510, 7 February 1990, Col. 875.

51. Patrick Wintour, Ben Laurance, Alan Travis, 'EC urged to join UK in lifting sanctions', *Guardian*, 12 February 1990.

52. *Weekly Hansard*, No. 1511, 14 February 1990, Col. 284.

53. Memorandum submitted by the Anti-Apartheid Movement, in House of Commons, Foreign Affairs Committee, *UK policy towards South Africa and the other states of the region*, 4 July 1990, London, HMSO, p. 161.

54. Letter to the *Independent*, 3 February 1990.

55. Shridath Ramphal, 'South Africans still need sanctions', *International Herald Tribune*, 30 May 1990.

56. Jim Jones, 'Two die as S. African police fire on marchers', *Financial Times*, 25 January 1990.

57. David Beresford, 'S. Africa "hit squad" revealed by police', *Guardian*, 16 February 1990.

58. Patti Waldmeir, 'South African police kill township protesters', *Financial Times*, 27 March 1990.

59. Patti Waldmeir, 'S. African deaths may halt talks with ANC', *Financial Times*, 20 April 1990.
60. Michael Holman and Patti Waldmeir, 'Three killed as S. African police fire on blacks', *Financial Times*, 21 May 1990.
61. 'Rebels kill 47 in ambush on train', *The Times*, 15 February 1990.
62. 'Mozambican rebels kill 66 in ambush', *Daily Telegraph*, 17 February 1990.
63. 'Eleven die in ambush by rebels', *The Times*, 23 February 1990.
64. Roger Job, 'Mozambique's harvest is tragedy', *Guardian*, 17 March 1990.
65. *Guardian*, 14 May 1990; 'Rebels kill 18', *Daily Telegraph*, 14 May 1990.
66. David Beresford, 'Diplomacy belies Pretoria's role in Mozambique', *Guardian*, 16 June 1990.
67. House of Commons, Foreign Affairs Committee, *UK policy towards South Africa and the other states of the region*, 18 July 1990, London, HMSO, p. 194.
68. Kieran Cooke and David Buchan, 'UK plan to allow new investment in S. Africa angers EC partners', *Financial Times*, 21 February 1990; John Palmer, 'UK defies Europe on sanctions', *Guardian*, 21 February 1990.
69. Jurek Martin, 'US plans economic aid for S. Africa', *Financial Times*, 24 May 1993.
70. *Africa Confidential*, Vol. 34, No. 9, 30 April 1993.
71. Frances Williams, 'Stability vital, Gatt tells South Africa', *Financial Times*, 3 June 1993.
72. Memorandum submitted by UKSATA and the Southern African Association, in House of Commons, Foreign Affairs Committee, *UK policy towards South Africa and the other states of the region*, 20 June 1990, London, HMSO, pp. 40, 52, 55.
73. 'First, South Africa's violence must stop', *Independent*, 5 May 1993.
74. Martin Woollacott, 'Where political rights matter less than economic needs', *Guardian*, 5 May 1993.
75. Ben Laurance, 'Mandela reassures investors', *Guardian*, 5 May 1993.
76. Blum, p. 237.
77. Blum, pp. 238–41; See also *Covert action in Chile, 1963–1973*, A staff report of the Select Committee to Study Governmental Operations with Respect to Intelligence Activities (US Senate), 18 December 1975.
78. CIIR, *Chile*, CIIR, London, 1986, pp. 8–10.
79. Cited in Noam Chomsky, *Turning the tide*, Black Rose, Montreal, 1987, pp. 67–8.
80. CIIR, *Chile*, pp. 25–7.
81. See Latin America Bureau (LAB), *Chile: The Pinochet decade*, LAB, London, 1983.
82. CIIR, *Chile*, p. 16; Alejandro Foxley, 'The neoconservative economic experiment in Chile', in Samuel and Arturo Valenzuela, *Military rule in Chile: Dictatorship and oppositions*, Johns Hopkins University Press, London, 1986, p. 44.
83. Heraldo Munoz, 'Chile's external relations under the military government', in Valenzuela and Valenzuela (eds), p. 307.
84. Jon Barnes, 'Birds of a feather: Britain and Chile', in LAB, *The Thatcher years: Britain and Latin America*, LAB, London, 1988, p. 57.
85. Michael Field, 'New envoys to Argentina and Chile face old problems', *Daily Telegraph*, 21 February 1980.
86. 'Britain ends arms embargo on Chile after sales study', *Daily Telegraph*, 23 July 1980.
87. 'Arms for Chile and double standards', *Sunday Telegraph*, 14 September 1980.
88. David Watts, 'Labour MPs angry at decision of Chile', *The Times*, 18 January 1980.
89. Letter to *The Times*, 23 January 1980.
90. Caroline Moorehead, 'Amnesty and unions deplore lifting of Chile arms embargo', *Times*, 25 July 1980.
91. 'Mr Ridley criticised over torture in Chile', *The Times*, 9 September 1980.
92. '"Tortured doctor" challenge', *Daily Telegraph*, 7 February 1980.

93. 'Frightened woman', *Daily Telegraph*, 8 February 1980.

94. Florencia Varas, 'Miss Wilson describes her days of torture', *The Times*, 11 September 1980.

95. Lindsay Mackie and Patricia Keatley, 'Chile embargo lifted despite torture', *Guardian*, 8 September 1980.

96. Letter to the *Times*, 22 January 1980.

97. Barnes, pp. 60–61.

98. CIIR, *Chile*, pp. 27–8.

99. Martin Walker, 'Chile navy likely to buy Hermes', *Guardian*, 15 June 1983; 'Chilean visit is condemned', *Daily Telegraph*, 19 August 1982.

100. Nicholas Ashford, 'British readiness to sell arms to Chile regime alarms US', *The Times*, 21 November 1983; Martin Walker, 'Nuclear deal with Chile is on', *Guardian*, 10 February 1983.

101. Duncan Campbell, 'Chile defence pact confirmed', *New Statesman*, 7 June 1985.

102. Patrick Keatley, 'Whitehall backs arms sale to Chile', *Guardian*, 2 May 1985.

103. Barnes, p. 61.

104. 'Loss of trade with Chile', *Daily Telegraph*, 10 September 1979.

105. CIIR, *Chile*, p. 29.

106. Letter from Janet Johnstone, Director of Amnesty International's British section, to the *Guardian*, 30 November 1982.

107. 'Poor old Pinochet', *The Times*, 17 June 1983.

108. 'Chile's state of siege', *Daily Telegraph*, 29 November 1984.

109. 'Pinochet's prospects', *Daily Telegraph*, 25 March 1986.

110. 'Challenge to Gen. Pinochet', *Financial Times*, 6 September 1985.

111. Oliver Furley, *Uganda's retreat from turmoil?* Institute for the Study of Conflict, London, 1987, p. 10.

112. 'Ugandans "tortured by barbed wire"', *Guardian*, 2 September 1982.

113. Amnesty International (AI), *Uganda: The human rights record 1986–1989*, AI, London, 1989, p. 8.

114. Ed Hooper and Louise Pirouet, *Uganda*, Report No. 66, Minority Rights Group, London, 1989, p. 16.

115. Amnesty, *Uganda*, p. 10.

116. Michael Getler, 'Britain unable to verify reports of Uganda toll', *International Herald Tribune*, 16 August 1984.

117. Hooper and Pirouet, *Uganda*, p. 18.

118. William Pike, 'Switch in UK view on Uganda', *Guardian*, 26 August 1984.

119. 'Bad news from Uganda', *The Times*, 9 August 1984.

120. Richard Hall, 'London force for Uganda', *Observer*, 6 June 1982.

121. 'UK agrees to increase instructors in Uganda', *The Times*, 15 April 1985.

122. 'How the British failed Uganda', *The Times*, 22 February 1986.

123. 'Crocker promises Obote continued US backing', *International Herald Tribune*, 5 September 1984.

124. A.J. McIlroy, 'British trade missions flying to Uganda', *Daily Telegraph*, 11 August 1984.

125. Hooper and Pirouet, *Uganda*, p. 18.

126. Quentin Peel, 'World Bank lends $70m to Ugandan government', *Financial Times*, 28 May 1982.

127. 'The capitalist lifeline that skirts Uganda's graveside', *Guardian*, 4 June 1982.

128. 'UK–Uganda pact signed', *The Times*, 18 August 1984.

129. 'Hard road for Uganda', *Financial Times*, 30 July 1985.

130. 'Amnesty in Uganda', *Daily Telegraph*, 15 April 1982.

131. Amnesty International, *Uganda*, p. 7.

132. A.J. McIlroy, 'East Africa leaders rally behind Obote', *Daily Telegraph*, 31 August 1984.

133. 'Uganda's plight', *Daily Telegraph*, 17 August 1984.

134. Quentin Peel, 'A critical test case for Africa', *Financial Times*, 19 October 1982.

135. *Financial Times*, 22 October 1982; 'Ugandans "tortured by barbed wire"', *Guardian*, 2 September 1982.

136. *Financial Times* survey: 'Uganda', 22 October 1982.

137. 'A new chance for Uganda', *The Times*, 31 January 1986.

CHAPTER 6

THE SPECIAL RELATIONSHIP:
US AGGRESSION, BRITISH SUPPORT

Mutual Anglo-American support in ordering the affairs of key nations and regions, often with violence, to their design has been a consistent feature of the era that followed the Second World War. The United States firmly supported British actions in Kenya, Malaya, British Guiana, Kuwait, Jordan and elsewhere, and for its part Britain became the 'junior partner in an orbit of power predominantly under American aegis'.[1] This role included generally acting as the world's most significant supporter of US aggression abroad, under both Conservative and Labour governments, though the level of that support varied.

There were some major exceptions to this policy of mutual support, notably in the US refusal to back the British invasion of Egypt in 1956. The United States also manoeuvred to undermine the British position – and to replace it with its own pre-eminence – elsewhere in the Middle East and Asia as the postwar period progressed. Nevertheless, as outlined in Chapter 1, the Washington connection was deemed so vital to Britain's power status and world role that this rivalry was not allowed to upset the fundamental strategic priorities on which both parties were agreed. In short, Britain has lent consistent support to US foreign policy and aggression since 1945 both because of its vital need to preserve its own power status and because the United States, as the most powerful Western nation, led the crusade to uphold and expand perceived Western interests in the Third World.

The special relationship remains a centrepiece of British foreign policy in the 1990s: Britain provided unflinching support – the only major nation to do so – for the belligerent US stance that led up to the war against Iraq. Britain's role in the crisis was crucial, giving the impression of a united 'allied' policy when there was severe scepticism and outright disapproval of the US position among other European states. This is considered in Chapter 7. This chapter examines earlier US interventions and Britain's support for them.

US foreign policy since 1945 has involved a variety of forms of aggression: direct military interventions, primarily in Korea (1950–53), the Dominican Republic (1965), Southeast Asia (1962–75), Grenada (1983), Panama (1989) and Kuwait (1991); large-scale involvement in or organisation of numerous coups and destabilisation campaigns, perhaps the most prominent being in Italy (1948), Iran (1953), Guatemala (1954), Brazil (1964) and Chile (1973), but also, amongst others, Congo (1960), Ecuador (1963), British Guiana (1964), Cambodia (1970), Australia (1975) and Jamaica (1976); and the supply of arms and/or aid to rebel (often effectively terrorist) organisations to overthrow or destabilise governments in Cuba (from 1959), Laos (1950s and 1960s), Iraq (early 1970s), Angola (from 1975), Cambodia (1980s), Afghanistan (1980s) and Nicaragua (1980s).[2]

British governments' consistent postwar support for US foreign policy has helped to legitimise US aggression internationally, often by Britain acting as an apologist for atrocities committed by the United States or at its behest. The extent of British support for US actions does not end at the level of the state, however. The propaganda system also contributes intimately and is as much part of the special relationship as are interstate relations. Consistently conducted under the mantle of containing the supposed Soviet threat, US aggression abroad had other first-order priorities, which were generally concealed by the information system.

The US war against Southeast Asia

The United States' intervention in Southeast Asia was one of the clearest examples in the postwar period of sustained and calculated aggression by a Western state and it is therefore of interest to consider the reactions to it on the part of British governments of the time.

First, it is necessary to recap on the background to the war. After the French defeat by the nationalist–communist Viet Minh movement in 1954, and with the Viet Minh controlling the north of Vietnam, the 1954 Geneva Accords called for national elections to be held in 1956 throughout the whole of Vietnam and for the uniting of the country. The United States refused to sign the Geneva agreement in the knowledge that, as the CIA noted, 'if the scheduled national elections are held in July 1956, and if the Viet Minh does not prejudice its political prospects, the Viet Minh will almost certainly win'.[3] The US instead set about bolstering the regime of Ngo Dinh Diem in the south of the country; the regime in the south became a US client with Washington paying almost all of its military budget and two-thirds of its combined civil–military budget in 1955–58. It also quickly developed into a highly repressive police state which by 1958 held at least 40,000 political prisoners and had killed 12,000 people.[4] Crucially, the regime reversed the land reforms already undertaken by the Viet Minh in the south and from which a considerable portion of the impoverished peasantry, who comprised the overwhelming majority of the population, had benefited. These measures were accompanied by the elimination of opposition in the countryside and a programme of population transfers funded by the United States.[5]

By the late 1950s, it had become clear that the Diem regime and its US backers had no intention of allowing the uniting of the country through free elections and implementation of the Geneva Accords. The armed conflict that began around 1961 in South Vietnam between the North Vietnamese regime and its newly created National Liberation Front in the South on the one hand and the Diem regime on the other was the result of the political repression and economic disenfranchisement of a substantial proportion of the southern population, and of the failure to achieve a political solution, as outlined in the 1954 agreement, to the question of the unification of the country.

Three further points aid an understanding of the war. First, it was not a true civil war. As the historian Gabriel Kolko writes, 'the history of Vietnam after 1954 was only incidentally that of a civil war' and 'the process of conflict after 1954 was essentially a struggle between a radicalised Vietnamese patriotism, embodied in the Communist Party, and the United States and its wholly dependent local allies'.[6] US military involvement in Vietnam throughout the 1960s and 1970s was geared to the support of successive wholly unrepresentative South Vietnamese regimes – regimes that only existed because of US aid – largely against their own population as much as against North Vietnam.

Second, the conflict was very much between alternative systems of economic development. That practised in North Vietnam and in the areas under the control of the Viet Minh in South Vietnam – in brief, a more equitable system in which land ownership was expanded for the benefit of the impoverished – reflected priorities necessarily viewed as heretical by the USA and its Western allies, whose plans for 'development' in the Third World generally excluded any meaningful progress for the majority peasantry. As noted in Chapter 1, the prime importance of Southeast Asia to Western planners was the region's raw materials and market opportunities. In 1952, for example, the United States noted that if Indochina fell out of the Western orbit, other nations would follow and the 'principal world source of natural rubber and tin and a producer of petroleum and other strategically important commodities' would be lost in Malaya and Indonesia. In the 1960s, Kolko comments, 'raw materials, though less publicly cited than earlier, were still prominent in the decision makers' vision. This included the preservation of existing markets.'[7] The main US goal, which provided the underlying reason for intervention in Vietnam, was to prevent South Vietnam (and Southeast Asia) from adopting a course of development outside the framework of US control, in the knowledge that, if meaningful progress were made by the impoverished here, 'the rot [might] spread' elsewhere.[8]

Third, the customary explaination of the Vietnam War as primarily a war against communism and as part of the East–West confrontation does not accord with reality. (The 'war against communism' thesis is applied from the period of the attempted French reconquest through to direct US intervention.) For example, British foreign policy analyst F.S. Northedge writes that 'from the American switch from single-minded anti-colonialism before 1954 to single-minded defence of ex-colonial peoples against communist infiltration stemmed the whole tragedy of the Vietnam war'.[9] (The USA's 'single-minded anti-colonialism before 1954' in fact involved the USA paying the bulk of France's military expenses in its attempt to defeat the Viet Minh – an effort that resulted in the deaths of between a quarter of 1 million and 1 million Indochinese civilians – and US political support, backed by Britain, for the attempted reconquest, discussed in Chapter 1.) Similarly, Lord Beloff, one of the most distinguished historians of British foreign policy, writes that the United States 'found itself embroiled in Southeast Asia in a post-colonial situation through intervention against communist aggression in Vietnam'.[10] (Note how, in Northedge's view, the United States was acting in 'defence' of the South Vietnamese and how, in Beloff's, it was intervening 'against communist aggression'.)

Certainly, the North Vietnam regime was controlled by the Vietnamese Communist Party and adopted Maoist principles in its political and economic plans for national development. Substantial Soviet and Chinese aid was delivered to the Vietnamese, the first arms supplies arriving from China in 1950, four years after France commenced the war of reconquest. Yet attempts to portray the war as simply 'against communism' and as part of an East–West confrontation downplay the fact that the Viet Minh movement was a primarily nationalist movement fighting for the independence and unity of the country free from colonial or neocolonial control. According to US academic Harry Piotrowski, Viet Minh leader Ho Chi Minh 'grafted the national liberation movement onto communism, which gave him a vision of the future, the certainty of an historic process that promised victory and an organisational blueprint'. Communist ideology, according to Piotrowski, 'scarcely played a role in motivating the resistance'.[11]

US military actions in the war included: massive bombing of territories and civilians, often without even a pretence of having any military objective and aimed, deliberately, at striking fear and terror into a virtually defenceless civilian population; the use of weapons such as napalm and chemical defoliants (eventually sprayed over 20 per cent of the forest land in South Vietnam); and numerous massacres of civilians conducted by troops on the ground, often the systematic and deliberate result of 'pacification' efforts ordered at the highest levels. The result was that whole nations were left utterly devastated, with millions killed and the survivors traumatised.[12]

In considering the special relationship it is instructive to consider briefly the British stance towards the war.

First, British troops took covert part in the war. According to Bloch and Fitzgerald, the SAS:

... fought in Vietnam where they were attached to Australian and New Zealand SAS squads despite declared British government policy that no British troops would be involved in the Vietnam war. Some were seconded to Fort Bragg, home of the United States special forces, and then inducted into the US army.[13]

They add:

During the Vietnam war the [British] monitoring station at Little Sai Wan in Hong Kong provided the Americans with intelligence up until 1975. ... The [US] N[ational] S[ecurity] A[gency] co-ordinated all signals intelligence in South-East Asia, and Little Sai Wan was linked to this operation. Its intercepts of North Vietnamese military traffic were used by the American military command to target bombing strikes over North Vietnam.[14]

Britain trained US, Vietnamese and Thai troops at its jungle warfare school in Malaya in the late 1960s, and for several years one of Britain's leading counterinsurgency experts, a veteran of the British war in Malaya, advised the Nixon regime on Vietnam policy.[15]

At the diplomatic level, the Macmillan, Douglas-Home, Wilson and Heath governments of the 1960s and 1970s all effectively supported the US war to varying degrees. Conservative governments were especially enthusiastic but Labour was also consistently sympathetic to the basic US objectives and actions. Despite occasional opposition expressed over specific US military actions, one will search in vain for British government statements questioning the basic right of the United States to conduct the war; it was taken as given that the US was justified in embarking upon the crusade in the first place and was therefore generally given British political backing both for this basic right and for most of the specific acts of military violence that arose from it. Britain thus acted as an effective apologist for US atrocities; the refusal of the 1960s Labour government to break with its ally even as the scale of terror rose to unprecedented heights confirms the extent of the special relationship and the degree of seriousness one might accord to Britain's professed support for the grand principles of peace and human rights.

The aggressor in Vietnam could never – by definition – be the United States. In 1962, as US aircraft were bombing South Vietnam and spraying chemical defoliants over the Vietnamese countryside – a tactic begun the previous year – the British Undersecretary of State for Foreign Affairs could still state that 'the threat to peace in Vietnam does not arise from United States action but from the policies of the North Vietnam government'.[16] In March 1965 Prime Minister Wilson could state: '... we fully support the action of the United States in resisting aggression in Vietnam'.[17] This 'resisting' of 'aggression' in Vietnam by then involved implementation of the late 1964 decisions to escalate the bombing of North Vietnam and of the early 1965 decision to begin the Rolling Thunder bombing campaign, lasting for most of the year, as well as the widespread use of napalm and chemical poisons and various efforts to 'pacify' the population.

The myth that the South Vietnamese were being 'defended', and with the best US intentions, has been long-standing, and was often promoted by British governments. Prime Minister Douglas-Home, for example, informed the House of Commons in March 1964 that in recent talks with President Johnson 'I reaffirmed my support for United States policy which ... is intended to help the Republic of Vietnam to protect its people and to preserve its independence'.[18] The Foreign Secretary could similarly tell MPs in 1964 that the South Vietnamese regime enjoyed 'the obedience of the mass of the population' (perhaps technically correct in the sense that obedience was being engineered at the point of a gun and through general repression, but the clear inference here is surely that the regime was popular).[19]

The strategic hamlet programme that began in the early 1960s, in the course of which Vietnamese peasants were herded, often with violence, into thousands of villages surrounded by concentration-camp-style fortifications – a programme intended to control the population and deprive the liberation movement of support – was also seen as a justifiable, defensive operation. Britain, it will be recalled, had practised similar methods in Malaya in the shape of the 'villageisation' policy, and a British expert served as adviser during the US version of it in Vietnam. 'The "strategic hamlet" programme', Edward Heath, then Lord Privy Seal, noted in 1963, 'is giving improved security to villagers and a chance to build up again the traditional system of Vietnamese village councils and communal activity.'[20]

As the terror mounted following the major US escalations of bombing of 1965, the Labour government became more guarded in public in expressing support for US policy and professed that its position as co-chairman in the peace negotiations precluded it from taking sides. In the numerous discussions of Vietnam in the House of Commons in the second half of the 1960s, Labour governments refused to condemn basic US policy, expressing only an occasional titter of opposition, for example over the saturation bombing of Hanoi and Haiphong in 1968, but proved incapable of declaring that the war was immoral and in unequivocal contradiction to stated British values. Neither did similar possible qualms affect the Heath government that succeeded Labour. When the 'bastion of the free world' (in the words of Lord Stamp) launched another saturation bombing campaign in April 1972, in response to North Vietnam's intervention in the South, the Undersecretary of State for Foreign Affairs declared the 'American reaction is understandable' and Heath said this 'surely is an attitude to be respected'.[21] In response to a question in the House of Commons noting that the US violence was resulting in the wholesale destruction of houses, numerous civilian casualties and 'pellet bombs dropped on individuals', the Foreign Office Minister replied, '...

it is not for us to make protests about individual types of weapons used.'[22] During the Christmas 1972 terror bombing, meanwhile, the *Observer* reported that 'the British government has no intention of joining in the international condemnation'; whilst the Foreign Office was making no comment publicly, 'private comments leave no doubt that British official thinking supports Mr Nixon's action'. Apparently, there were merely 'some slight misgivings' over the use of 'B52 saturation bombing on populated areas, since it is conceded that this can cause indiscriminate damage and loss of life'.[23]

'Our greatest ally': Guatemala, Grenada and Libya

Other cases of US aggression abroad are also instructive in gauging the fundamental foreign policy priorities of the United States and the level of British support for them. One example of the pursuit of these priorities came in Guatemala in 1954, when the United States organised and financed an invasion of the country and the overthrow of President Jacobo Arbenz under the pretext of the international communist threat.

The brief background is that the preceding Arevalo government, which came to power in 1944, enacted several reforms intended to improve social and economic conditions for the poor majority, including legislation to protect employees, expansion of health and education services, and the establishment of a social security system. These measures were further promoted under the Arbenz government democratically elected in 1950 with 60 per cent of the vote – the first time in Guatemalan history that power had passed peacefully and on schedule from one president to another. Richard Immerman notes in his study of the period that Arbenz's 'overriding objective was to build upon the ongoing reforms and to establish Guatemala's independence in relation to the international political and economic structure', to be pursued 'with an emphasis on capitalist modernisation'.[24]

The centrepiece of Arbenz's programme was agrarian reform: prior to the 1952 land reform, 2.2 per cent of the population held over 70 per cent of the land, whilst around three quarters of the population accounted for only 10 per cent of the land. The reforms, which redistributed hundreds of thousands of acres to previously landless Guatemalan peasants, led Arbenz increasingly into conflict with the country's largest landowner, the US-owned United Fruit Company, which devoted its holdings to the production of bananas for export at the expense of growing staple foods for the malnourished population. Arbenz's priorities thus confirmed a 1949 CIA assessment that the preceding Arevalo programme was 'distinctly unfriendly to US business interests', whilst it threatened Guatemala's position as 'a place for capital investment', in the words of the State Department.

Alleging increasing communist subversion in Guatemala, the CIA organised an invasion, provided arms and training to the invading forces, and conducted bombing raids in the country. At the United Nations, meanwhile, Britain (and France) aided the USA by abstaining on a Guatemalan request for the Security Council to consider its complaints about external aggression, and the request was consequently rejected. This prompted President Eisenhower and Secretary of State Dulles to express satisfaction with the British 'willingness to cooperate in regard to the UN aspect' of US policy and that this 'cooperation' had contributed to the 'happier situation in Guatemala'. Immerman comments that, 'having overcome the final obstacle' in the UN, the USA brought the CIA campaign 'to a triumphant conclusion without further interruption'. A new ruling junta took over, repealed the agrarian reforms and the expropriation of United Fruit Company land, and eliminated the threat of independent, nationalist development. With Guatemala's popular democratic experiment overturned, the way was paved for a succession of regimes that assured that wayward socio-economic priorities would not be pursued. The response of these regimes to any popular movement seeking to alleviate the impoverishment of the majority of the population was its physical extermination, amounting to around 100,000 deaths by government forces over the next four decades.[25]

If any moral qualms were expressed by British planners on the overthrow of a democratically elected government, I could not find them in the declassified British files. A Foreign Office memorandum written just after Arbenz's overthrow noted 'the feeling of distaste over the Guatemalan affair' and that the British ambassador at the UN had termed Britain's position there 'barely respectable'. Britain disapproved of the USA denouncing the Arbenz government when its case was still *sub judice* at the UN and the Organisation of American States (OAS), and it disapproved of the US designation of Guatemala as a security threat to the US. However, the British position was that 'we should be happy to see Arbenz disappear but would not exert ourselves to remove him'. Britain's attitude towards the country that *had* helped remove him was expressed thus:

> If the Americans had quietly worked for the overthrow of the Arbenz government, but nevertheless preserved the decencies of international justice, I think a different impression would have been left behind about the whole affair. ... We are glad Arbenz has gone, but, like Henry II with Becket, we do not like the circumstances attending his removal.[26]

This Foreign Office memorandum did not elucidate further how it would have been possible for the USA 'quietly' to have overthrown the government whilst simultaneously preserving international justice. Rather, it suggests that, in the British official mind, the overthrow of a democratically elected government was compatible with international justice – giving, perhaps, an interesting insight into official British values. Significantly, while the US actions were taking place the British understanding was that 'on the whole [the Arbenz government] adhered to the Constitution and the opposition were not unduly fettered up to the beginning of the recent crisis'.[27] Anthony Eden later recalled in his memoirs that:

> Anglo-American solidarity was of overriding importance to us and to the West as a whole. I believed that even if we did not entirely see eye to eye with the United States government in their treatment of the Guatemalan situation, we had an obligation as their principle ally to go as far as we could to help them.[28]

Following the fall of Arbenz, British officials considered whether to recognise the junta that had just seized power by violent means in contempt for the democratic process. A Foreign Office memorandum stated that 'to withhold recognition would be contrary to our established practice and to our proclaimed principles' and that Britain had recognised the current Bolivian regime 'even though it achieved power by violent and unconstitutional methods'.[29] 'We need a friendly Guatemala', another memorandum read, 'because we want the Guatemalans to be as reasonable as possible over British Honduras [a British colony, claimed by Guatemala] and because we have a very favourable balance of trade with them, and they might at any time ... clamp a 100 per cent surcharge on tariff duties on our imports, which would do us great damage.'[30] Britain subsequently recognised the new regime, the possible loss of the enormous Guatemalan market apparently being deemed of greater importance than the overthrow of democracy.

Another facet of the situation was that the elections held by the new junta were more than a little irregular. The British legation in Guatemala reported to Foreign Secretary Anthony Eden that the elections for the Constituent Assembly were held on such short notice that 'electoral campaigning was impossible'. 'The voting was not secret and there was therefore the possibility of intimidation. Finally, the voters in most districts were presented with a single list of candidates' who happened to support the junta. In the so-called plebiscite for the presidency, meanwhile, 'it was only possible to vote "yes" or "no", with no alternative candidate to Colonel Castillo Armas', who had led the overthrow.[31] The following month Eden was informed that Armas had been made president by the Constituent Assembly until 1960. 'Please convey to His Excellency the President the good wishes of Her Majesty's Government and accept the assurance of my highest consideration,' the Foreign Secretary replied, in the customary diplomatic formulation.[32]

Nearly three decades later, the destabilisation and eventual invasion of Grenada in the early 1980s reflected the traditional pattern of US response to any perceived threat to the pursuit of its customary priorities. The New Jewel Movement (NJM) under the leadership of Maurice Bishop had overthrown the previous government in a popular, bloodless coup in 1979. It then instituted measures including a greater role for the trade unions, expanded health care and educational opportunities, whilst emphasising development for the majority in what was an impoverished society. In 1982 the World Bank noted that 'government objectives are centred on the critical development issues and touch on the country's most promising development areas'.[33] The NJM's nominally Marxist programme involved a form of popular democracy in which mass organisations for women, youth and the self-defence forces played prominent roles. In its 1984 report on Grenada the Latin America Bureau notes that 'it is no exaggeration to say that the popular organisations for the first time permitted the mass of Grenadians to participate in the running of their own affairs'. This involved 'a form of continuous direct democracy' which embodied 'considerably greater popular participation than allowed for, and still less realised, in any of the Westminster-style systems working elsewhere in the Caribbean'.[34]

The USA was hostile to the Grenadian revolution; it lobbied international lending organisations to block loans to Grenada and it spread scare stories to discourage tourism to the island. It also concocted a series of 'Soviet threat' propaganda fantasies, alleging the construction of an airport runway for Soviet jets, Soviet delivery of huge quantities of weapons, etcetera.[35] Meanwhile Britain drastically cut its aid programme to Grenada after the NJM came to power, and it excluded the country from a programme of emergency relief following the hurricane damage of 1979–80. In November 1979 Britain rejected applications from Grenada for the delivery of a small quantity of armoured cars, Grenada allegedly not being a suitable destination for such arms sales, unlike the murderous regimes of General Pinochet in Chile and the military junta in Argentina. Foreign Office Minister Nicholas Ridley further demonstrated British values by stating that 'Grenada is in the process of establishing the kind of society of which the British government disapproves, irrespective of whether the people of Grenada want it or not.' Chris Searle comments in his book on Grenada that 'while the entire population of Grenada were engaged in mass consultations to formulate the national budget in [a] unique and unprecedented process of mass democracy and participation', Richard Luce of the Foreign Office, touring the eastern Caribbean, 'peevishly complained that he would not extend his visit to Grenada as there was no democracy there'; this being true, under the correct appreciation of democracy.[36]

The collapse of the Bishop regime and the takeover by a military junta in October 1983 provided an opportunity for a US invasion, which had been rehearsed in previous military exercises in the Caribbean.[37] This invasion involved bombing raids – which destroyed much civilian property and a mental hospital, killing more than thirty patients – and violations of the Geneva Convention in the treatment of detained Grenadians.[38] The

primary pretext for the illegal invasion was to save American lives, a tried
and trusted excuse for Western intervention abroad; the evidence suggested
that the United States had deliberately kept on the island the nationals it
was supposed to be rescuing as an excuse for an invasion.[39] The British
Foreign Secretary played along as required, noting in the House of Commons that the USA's 'decisive action' had been taken 'first and foremost'
to 'protect innocent lives, including up to 1,000 Americans whose safety
was of paramount concern'.[40] British leaders were privately outraged at
the US invasion of a Commonwealth country, and even Margaret Thatcher,
the prime minister, declared that, despite her hatred of communism, 'that
does not mean we can just walk into' other countries.[41] Yet customary
deference to the senior partner precluded Britain from openly condemning
a violation of international law and the charters of the UN and the OAS,
and from refuting the ideological framework of the operation which
required the USA to designate Grenada a 'Soviet–Cuban colony'.[42] Whilst
every European government and virtually the entire world condemned
the invasion in a United Nations vote of censure against the USA, the
junior partner necessarily abstained.

Once in place, US occupation forces could ensure that a more acceptable government was installed in Grenada, reversing the gains of the NJM
years and restoring socio-economic conditions to the regional (and global)
norm. A report by a British labour movement delegation two months
after the invasion noted that 'the Governor General [the British queen's
representative, who continued to preside over, in name at least, the
Grenadian government throughout the NJM years] has assumed dictatorial
powers and is surrounded at all times by US "advisers"'. The report
added that recent measures enacted by the Interim Council included the
'suspension of welfare programmes, purges of the civil and education
services, closure of state industries, [and the] suspension of development
programmes approved by international aid organisations'. The Interim
Council was 'being further pressured by the large landowners, the Chamber
of Commerce and American advisers to take further steps to ensure
dependency on American aid, investment and military presence'. At least
2,000 Grenadians were being detained 'not in any attempt to identify
those responsible for the killings of October 19th [during the takeover by
the military junta], but rather to find out all details of the NJM and
Labour Movement and intimidate its members'. Furthermore, 'surveillance
and harassment of civilians involved in any form of progressive organisation' were widespread, whilst the women and youth organisations had
been 'effectively silenced' and 'there is clearly a purge of all popular
organisations'.[43] British aid to Grenada was subsequently resumed, rising
through 1984 and 1985, and the country was rendered an effective US
client state, dependent on US aid, the experiment in popular democracy
successfully destroyed.

In contrast to the invasion of Grenada, the 1986 US bombing of Libya produced ecstatic levels of support on the part of the British government, which was virtually alone in the face of near-universal international condemnation of the action. US bombers took off on their mission from British bases, and Thatcher told the House of Commons that the US raid was undertaken 'in self-defence', adding that 'terrorism has to be defeated; it cannot be tolerated or side-stepped'. Thatcher failed to note that 'our greatest ally', as she termed the United States, had itself been organising and controlling Contra terrorist operations for the previous five years in Nicaragua (see below). The Foreign Secretary, Geoffrey Howe, also expressed his profound loathing for terrorism, noting that 'state-sponsored' terrorism 'is quite distinct from traditional terrorism' and that 'we are dealing with countries that recruit, train and finance groups of people whom they dispatch to promote terrorism in other countries' and who resort to 'brutality and onslaught, sustained and organised by a sovereign state and managed, financed and dispatched through the agencies of government'. There was 'overwhelming evidence', Howe added, 'that Colonel Gaddafi's government is just such a government'.[44] There was in fact even more overwhelming evidence that the government for which Howe was apologising was conducting just such operations in Nicaragua on a far larger scale than Qadafi could ever have dreamed of.

Destroying development in Nicaragua

The US war against Nicaragua provides further evidence of Britain's support for US aggression but is also a case study of the British press's role in providing ideological support for the United States, reflecting that provided by the government. The war was widely reported and the subject of hundreds of press articles. It might therefore have been expected that, as a result of the sheer amount of resources devoted to providing information about the war, an accurate picture would have been forthcoming. In fact, the extent of ideological conditioning attained in the press coverage of the war provides further evidence of the existence of a propaganda system.

The Nicaraguan revolution of 1979 had overthrown the Somoza family dictatorship which had ruled the country since 1936 with constant US backing. 50,000 people had died during the revolution, which was supported by practically all sections of society except Somoza's immediate entourage, the army and the regime's henchmen of the National Guard. The Somoza legacy was especially grim, even by the generally appalling standards of West-supported regimes in the Third World: two thirds of children under five were malnourished; less than one fifth of under-fives and pregnant women received health care; nine out of ten rural homes had no safe drinking water; over half the population was illiterate. The UN estimated that over 60 per cent of the population lived in critical poverty, two thirds of them without an income sufficient to cover their most basic needs and one third enduring 'extreme poverty'. As a result of the economic policies pursued by the Somoza regime, the richest 5 per cent of the population accounted for almost one third of national income whilst the poorest half received only 15 per cent. Export crops, enriching the large landowners and US agribusiness interests, took up 90 per cent of agricultural credit and 22 times more arable land than that used to grow basic food crops to feed the malnourished population.[45]

The central aim of the new revolutionary government, led by the Sandinistas, was to alleviate the appalling social conditions endured by the majority of the population. In a 1983 report the World Council of Churches gave the following assessent of the state of Nicaragua four years after the revolution:

> What we see is a government faced with tremendous problems, some seemingly insuperable, bent on a great experiment which, though precarious and incomplete at many points, provides hope to the poor sectors of society, improves the conditions of education, literacy and health, and for the first time offers the Nicaraguan people a modicum of justice for all rather than a society offering privilege exclusively to the wealthy ... and the powerful.[46]

An Oxfam report two years later noted:

> The cornerstone of the new development strategy, spelled out by the Sandinista Front some years before taking power, was to give priority to meeting the basic needs of the poor majority. This was to be achieved by involving people in implementing change at a local level, through their neighbourhood groups, peasant associations and other organisations; at a central level, representatives of these organisations were to cooperate closely with the government ministries.[47]

The report concluded that 'in Oxfam's experience of working in seventy-six developing countries, Nicaragua was to prove exceptional in the strength of that government commitment'.[48] A nationwide campaign led to a fall in the illiteracy rate from 53 per cent to 13 per cent, inspiring UNESCO to award Nicaragua the 1980 Literacy Prize. By 1984 there were 127 per cent more primary schools and the resources allocated to education had increased fivefold compared with 1978–79. In 1982 Nicaragua won the World Health Organisation award for the greatest achievement in health by a Third World nation. Within three years of the revolution around 70 per cent of the population had access to health care, compared to just over one quarter before it. Peasant farmers became the main beneficiaries of the land reform programme as thousands of families received titles to land.[49] Former Mexican ambassador and novelist Carlos Fuentes, writing in 1983, noted that the Sandinista government's spending on literacy and health care extended 'to more Nicaraguans in three years than in the past three centuries'.[50]

Sandinista success in devoting resources to the Nicaraguan poor for the first time in their history was indeed striking. Similar developmental priorities had been pursued elsewhere in Latin America, however, most notably in Cuba in the first few years after the 1959 revolution. These initiatives too had resulted in real progress in the conditions of the poor majority, in particular in education and health where, one 1970 independent report noted, 'no country in Latin America has carried out such ambitious and nationally comprehensive programmes'. The report further noted: 'Cuba's centrally planned economy has done more to integrate the rural and urban sectors (through a national income distribution policy) than the market economies of the other Latin American countries.'[51] The US response to the Cuban revolution had been one of immediate hostility: organising an invasion of the country and a programme of terrorism directed against the Castro regime, including bombings by exile groups from bases in the USA and numerous sabotage raids.[52] These actions reflected the USA's traditional aim of preventing independent development that did not conform to its requirements: principally, a favourable economic climate for its business interests. The cut-off in US aid to Cuba, the imposition of an economic blockade and the further threat of US intervention, meanwhile, forced Castro into an increasing reliance on the Soviet bloc, eventually obliging Cuba to become a dependent Soviet ally, and thus further justifying US attacks against the country – and its international isolation – as part of the Cold War.

Nicaragua was a repeat performance. In the final years of the Carter presidency the United States provided a safe haven for the exiled henchmen of the Somozan National Guard, permitted military training camps to be established on US soil and authorised covert funding to anti-Sandinista political, press and labour organisations. On coming to office in January 1981 President Reagan ignored constant Nicaraguan calls for a normalisation of relations, immediately froze US aid to Nicaragua and cancelled a proposed sale of wheat. The economic isolation of Nicaragua was stepped up through the 1980s, and involved the blocking of international loans, pressure on allied governments to withhold aid and the imposition of an economic embargo. In March 1981 an expanded programme of CIA activity inside Nicaragua was authorised, which included assistance to political opponents of the Sandinistas. In November 1981 the CIA was allocated $20 million to build a 500–man force to conduct political and paramilitary operations against Nicaragua. This force would complement the 1,000 former Somoza supporters already being trained by the military emissaries of the neo-Nazi Argentinian junta, the cost for the training being met by the USA.[53] The Contras, whose leadership consisted almost entirely of former high-ranking National Guardsmen, thus were created and sustained by the United States and its allies in the region: Argentina and, as the main base for operations against Nicaragua, Honduras.

The Contras lacked virtually any domestic legitimacy. Recruits to the Contra cause consisted almost entirely of Miskito Indians, some of whom went willingly, disaffected by the Sandinista policy of moving Miskitos away from the areas near the Honduran border in the early stages of the war, a policy that caused thousands to flee over the border. Many of the recruits, however, were kidnapped and forced to serve. The extent of support for the Contras within Nicaragua was described as follows by the Defense Department in a leaked National Security Council paper of July 1983: 'support for democratic resistance [i.e. the Contras] within Nicaragua does not exist'.[54]

Reflecting the background of its leaders, the US proxy army was effectively a terrorist organisation rather than a guerrilla force; it conducted numerous atrocities against civilians, which were well documented by human rights organisations. The chairpersons of Americas Watch and Helsinki Watch, for example, concluded: 'there can be no doubt ... that a planned strategy of terrorism is being carried out by the Contras along the Honduran border' and that 'the US cannot avoid responsibility for these atrocities'.[55] Former CIA director Stansfield Turner stated in 1985: 'I believe it is irrefutable that a number of the Contras' actions have to be characterised as terrorism, as state-supported terrorism.' Former Contra spokesman Edgar Chamorro stated in an affidavit to the World Court that the Contras were advised by the CIA to 'kill, kidnap, rob and torture'.[56] Americas Watch noted in 1984 that the Contras were 'engaged repeatedly in kidnappings, torture and murder of unarmed civilians, mostly in villages and farm cooperatives'.[57] Practices such as the slaughter of civilians, including children, the severing of limbs and mutilation were regular occurrences that served to sow fear amongst the peasant supporters of the Sandinistas. In 1982–84 alone, over 7,000 civilians were killed by the Contras; the 'prime targets' , according to Oxfam, were 'individual leaders and community organisers who have worked hardest to improve the lives of the poor'. The Contra atrocities included the 'systematic killing' of project workers, community leaders, health promoters and teachers.[58]

A secret July 1982 Defence Intelligence Agency report (leaked the following year) further noted that Contra activities included the 'assassination of minor government officials' and the 'burning of a customs warehouse, buildings belonging to the Ministry of Construction, and crops'. One of the Contra factions claimed credit for the bombing of a Nicaraguan civil airliner, the hijacking of a Costa Rican airliner and the explosion of a bomb unloaded from a Honduran aircraft at Managua airport.[59] CIA manuals explicitly advised the Contras how to 'neutralise carefully selected and planned targets' such as judges, magistrates and police and state security officials.[60] Terrorism conducted by the Contras was complemented by sabotage operations by its patron – the CIA – in particular against economic targets such as oil installations. The US mining of Nicaraguan ports was declared illegal by the World Court, a judgment dismissed by the United States government.

In fact, the whole US war was illegal. In June 1986 the World Court rejected US claims that it was exercising 'collective self-defence' in its policy towards Nicaragua and asserted that the United States 'by training, arming, equipping, financing and supplying the Contra forces' had acted 'in breach of its obligation under customary international law not to intervene in the affairs of another state'.[61] The war caused many thousands of deaths, drove over 150,000 people from their homes and caused billions of dollars' worth of destruction to the Nicaraguan economy.

Washington's state-sponsored terrorism in Nicaragua was part of its wider policy in Central America, which also entailed support for the regimes in Guatemala and El Salvador. In relation to Guatemala, Reagan referred to President Rios Montt in December 1982 as a 'man of great personal integrity', 'totally dedicated to democracy in Guatemala', who 'wants to improve the quality of life for all Guatemalans and to promote social justice'; the Guatemalan President, Reagan said, was getting a 'bum rap' and a 'bad deal' on criticism of his regime's human rights record. This was at a time when human rights organisations were estimating that between 3,000 and 8,000 people had been killed and 200,000 driven from their homes by the regime. Montt had already stated on Guatemalan television that he had 'declared a state of siege so that we could kill legally'.[62] Between 1981 and 1984 it is estimated that 50,000–75,000 people were killed or 'disappeared' and 1 million were displaced from their homes in the Guatemalan government's counterinsurgency campaign.[63]

In El Salvador, around 40,000 people were killed by government forces in the civil war of the early 1980s as US military aid inundated the regime; the US government provided consistent excuses for the terror, prompting human rights groups to term the Reagan administration 'an apologist for some of the worst horrors of our time'.[64] Between 1980 and 1983, Amnesty International 'received regular, often daily reports identifying El Salvador's regular security and military units as responsible for the torture, "disappearance" and killing of noncombatant civilians from all sectors of society'. Furthermore, 'the vast majority of the victims' were 'characterised by their association or alleged association with peasant, labour or religious organisations, with human rights monitoring groups, with the trade union movement, with refugee or relief organisations or with political parties'.[65]

Thus, in contrast to Nicaragua, elsewhere in Central America the forces attempting to secure real developmental change to benefit the majority were being systematically repressed or simply eliminated by their governments, under the patronage of the great power to the north. In Nicaragua under the Sandinistas, however, as Americas Watch reported in 1982, even torture had been 'effectively eliminated': and there was 'widespread agreement, even among the government's strongest critics, that physical torture is not practised in Nicaragua today'.[66] And, according to Oxfam America, referring to its work in Nicaragua, Honduras, El Salvador and Guatemala, 'only in Nicaragua has a substantial effort been made to address inequalities in land ownership and to extend health, educational and agricultural services to poor peasant families'.[67]

Britain's role was one of giving basic support for US policy in the region, consistent with the particularly vital special relationship between Thatcher and Reagan. Foreign Secretary Geoffrey Howe 'absolutely endorsed' the supposed US objectives of democracy and development in Central America: the US, 'in trying to maintain and strengthen the forces of democracy in an area threatened with a communist takeover' (in the reporter's words), was pursuing these objectives 'with the skill we would expect of them', Howe noted.[68] 'We support the United States' aim to promote peaceful change, democracy and economic development' in Central America, Prime Minister Thatcher stated in January 1984, by which time the US aim of destroying the prospects for peaceful change and real economic development was clear for all to see.[69] The Under-Secretary of State at the Foreign Office could similarly note the following year – three years after Contra operations in Nicaragua had begun – that 'the American government have stated time and again that they are seeking a solution by peaceful means to the problems of Central America'. Indeed, 'no country would benefit more from a solution by peaceful means in Central America than the United States', he continued.[70]

Basic political support by Britain for US objectives was coupled with specific actions in line with US priorities. Britain was the only European country that agreed to send observers to the 1982 elections in El Salvador, which were conducted in the midst of massacres and the repression of civil liberties and in which only the parties of the right and centre-right participated. In November 1983 Britain and West Germany were the only European Community (EC) states that abstained on a UN resolution expressing 'deep concern' at the violation of human rights in El Salvador. In 1984, the British government instructed its World Bank delegation to stop 'opposing or abstaining on all proposals' and to support all 'developmentally-sound projects' in El Salvador, before reintroducing a small aid programme to the country and offering military training to a few Salvadoran military officers.[71]

By contrast, Britain was the only European government not to send observers to the 1984 elections in Nicaragua, won by the Sandinistas. Though the elections were regarded by independent observers as free and fair, Britain's view, expressed by the Foreign Secretary, was that 'free and fair elections could not be regarded as having taken place'. 'In El Salvador', Howe assured the House of Commons, 'a real transfer of power took place; but that was not the position in Nicaragua.' In other words, the wrong side won.[72]

Britain and the United States are the only major aid donors that gave more aid to Nicaragua in the last seven years of the Somoza dictatorship than in the first seven years of Sandinista rule. This was the case even though Nicaragua under the Sandinistas, according to a British government minister, had 'a good record in the spending of development aid'. According to the British charge d'affaires in Managua, Nicaragua had a 'very impressive record on social development', one which was 'amazing' in comparison with El Salvador and Honduras, the latter receiving 100 times more British aid than Nicaragua.[73]

During this period Britain lobbied in favour of US positions in international forums. Foreign Office documents leaked in 1985 stated that, with regard to Britain's policy of helping to block loans to Nicaragua, 'We shall need to stick to our present line of claiming that our opposition is based on technical [that is, rather than political] grounds.' 'If we can find them!' another Foreign Office official appended to the note.[74] Britain could not bring itself to support the principle of the inviolability of international law, and abstained on a United Nations vote condemning the USA for mining Nicaraguan ports. Throughout the US war, Britain preferred to maintain what Thatcher called 'the fundamental alliance between Great Britain and the United States'.[75]

In an effort to frame an understanding of the US war against Nicaragua (and by extension against Central America), three key points deserve mention and can form a basis for considering the extent of ideological servility demonstrated by the propaganda system.

The first is that whilst the Nicaraguan government did not create a paradise on earth in Nicaragua, it was engaged in a development programme that independent organisations consistently praised for offering real socio-economic advance for the poor majority and that alleviated the appalling levels of poverty that had been the legacy of the previous decades. The success of this programme stood in marked contrast to the situation in other states of the region and, indeed, to virtually the entire Third World. Since it might be argued that the alleviation of poverty remains the overwhelming priority for the majority of Third World societies, one might therefore regard success in this sphere as the dominating fact of Sandinista rule.

The second key point is that the Nicaraguan revolution was a nationalist one, directed against the super-exploitation of the country's resources by a regime controlled by a tiny elite allied to sectors of US business; this had little or nothing to do with the East–West conflict. That many Sandinista leaders were Marxists and expressed the intention of creating a socialist state was a reality but one that did not diminish the essentially nationalist orientation of development priorities. The revolution's leaders, like those in Cuba before, consistently called for good relations with the United States and had no desire or intention of trading one dependency (on the USA) for another (on the Soviet Union). The Sandinistas' domestic policies allowed for around 60 per cent of the economy to be controlled by the private sector throughout the 1980s. Democratic elections, judged by independent observers to be free and fair, were held in 1984 and again in 1990.

The central goal of the US propaganda machine, however – for which there were several historical precedents – was to portray its war against the Sandinistas as part of the East–West conflict and essentially a war against the Soviet Union itself. The publicly stated basis for US policy towards Nicaragua was to prevent the establishment of a Soviet client. In reality, the evidence suggests the establishment of such a relationship was the USA's very intention, since it would serve as a pretext for continued aggression. Basic US thinking was outlined by two National Security Council officials, who recommended – though the plan was not carried through – the sinking of a Mexican oil tanker in a Nicaraguan port. They noted in a 1984 memo:

> It is entirely likely that once a ship has been sunk no insurers will cover ships calling in Nicaraguan ports. This will effectively limit their seaborne trade to that which can be carried on Cuban, Soviet bloc or their own [ships].[76]

The United States froze aid, helped to prevent international loans to Nicaragua, and put pressure on allied governments to halt aid and arms sales, forcing Nicaragua to turn elsewhere. In 1983 Secretary of State George Schultz was mandated by the National Security Council to 'press Western European governments at the highest level to cease financial support for the Sandinistas'.[77]

After France announced, in January 1982, that it was delivering a small arms package to Nicaragua, the USA applied pressure and stalled the delivery; it became clear that arms sales from West European governments, previously sought by the Sandinistas, would not be forthcoming in future. Reliance on the Soviet bloc for arms was therefore the only alternative in the face of increasingly frequent Contra raids into Nicaraguan territory, and the constant threat of US invasion signalled by US–Honduran military exercises off the Nicaraguan coast and the example of the invasion of Grenada in 1983. Nicaragua's subsequent defence build-up in turn presented frequent public relations opportunities for the USA to depict the Sandinistas as a Soviet ally embarking upon an offensive military course living up to, therefore, the rationale used for the original US aggression. The Reagan administration simultaneously concocted a series of disinformation campaigns, alleging Nicaraguan plans to invade neighbouring states as a Soviet proxy, Soviet plans to construct a launching pad in Nicaragua for military intervention elsewhere, and so on.

The real threat of the Nicaraguan revolution is the third key point. This has been referred to as the 'threat of a good example' (the title of the Oxfam report cited above), that is, the danger that the type of development pursued by the Sandinistas would be successful in Nicaragua and might spread to other states in the region, threatening US business operations and their traditional control over other states' resources. Rather than the fantasy of preventing the creation of a 'Soviet bridgehead' on the Central American mainland or preventing the USSR from dominating the world by subsuming the massive resources of Nicaragua to its will, the principal US goal in the war against Nicaragua was clearly the destruction of this threat of a good example; the war was, therefore, a continuation of traditional US foreign policy priorities.

The US ambassador to Nicaragua, Lawrence Pezzullo, noted that 'our problem with the revolution is not that it wants to bring change to a society that sorely needs change. ... But if that policy parallels Cuban policy, this is going to be very difficult for us to accept.'[78] Economist Xabier Gorostiaga, head of the National Institute of Socio-Economic Research in Nicaragua, noted that under the Sandinistas the country had become a 'term of reference' for other Third World states and that 'we are under attack because we may become a model'.[79] The US press report that broke the story of the November 1981 authorisation of CIA operations against Nicaragua noted that the CIA plan included efforts to 'destroy vital Nicaraguan targets, such as power plants and bridges' which would 'disrupt the economy and divert the attention and resources of the government' away from badly needed social programmes.[80] These economic targets – rather than military targets – became the primary focus of Contra operations, which forced the Sandinista government to spend more and more on defence, thus helping to discredit it and reverse the gains made by the population.

The propaganda system in action I

It is instructive to review the reporting of the war by the British press and in particular to gauge the extent to which state ideology was followed. In attempting this I looked at just over 500 articles (reports, editorials and features) on Nicaragua in the *Financial Times*, *Times* and *Daily Telegraph* for the three years 1981–83, accounting for virtually every article on the subject appearing in these three newspapers. Since this period coincided with the first three years of the Contra war and the first three years of the Reagan administration, it was judged to be an ideal time frame for a systematic analysis of reporting on the basic issues involved. In addition, some articles written in the later years of the 1980s are analysed below. The results of the survey are striking, providing further evidence of the existence of a British propaganda system and the special relationship that it has with the US propaganda system.

The alleviation of poverty: a minor issue

On the subject of Sandinista successes in devoting resources to the Nicaraguan poor for the first time in history, out of just over 500 articles I found *one* full article. This appeared in *The Times* and noted the 'remarkable success' of the literacy campaign and that in its first eighteen months half a million people had been taught to read. Even this remarkable exception ended by stating; 'when you talk about reality in Nicaragua, the literacy campaign stands out as one of the few positive signs'; thus the article ignored the other great strides in socio-economic welfare achieved by a government with meagre means.[81] One other exception deserves attention, a feature by James Curran, the editor of *New Socialist*, who was permitted to write in *The Times* that:

> An all-party British parliamentary delegation concluded that 'there is much to praise in Nicaragua. The new government has made a determined attack on poverty by raising the living standards of the poorest and has made impressive achievements in the fields of literacy, health and education.'[82]

Apart from these two articles, press coverage of this issue was limited to a handful of throwaway sentences (for example, Sandinista 'moves towards a redistribution of income have favoured the poorer strata of society', in one *Financial Times* article, 'imaginative policies on literacy and social welfare', in another[83]) Only a few of these throwaway sentences could be discovered: fewer ten mentions in all the articles reviewed.

The fact that the impoverished were markedly better off under the new regime eluded the newspapers under analysis. The *Times* stated merely that 'most Nicaraguans continue to prefer the Sandinistas to the heirs of the Somoza dictatorship', and this lone remark was made in reference to the choice between the current regime and the US-organised terrorist force engaged in the systematic slaughter of civilians in the border areas, and this hardly testified to the real popularity of the Sandinistas amongst the peasantry and the latter's drastically improved social conditions.[84] The *Daily Telegraph* also managed only to state that 'Nicaraguan peasants cannot be said to be well off under the Sandinistas, but they are no worse off than under Somoza'.[85] The couple of mentions (the odd sentence) in the *Daily Telegraph* of Sandinista successes in alleviating poverty were 'balanced' by reporting on a regime 'as oppressive as the previous dictatorship' (under the headline 'Everywhere a stench of Havana')[86] – or indeed a regime that was 'even more unspeakable' than the 'wholly unspeakable Somoza dictatorship'.[87]

It would take considerable intellectual acrobatics to designate Sandinista successes in alleviating poverty – remarkable by many standards – as unworthy of much comment by any objective indicators. This might particularly be the case when compared to the appalling conditions elsewhere in the region – surely well known to every reporter who had ever visited the area. The daily lot of Salvadorans or Guatemalans, for example, frequently consisted, as it had for Nicaraguans under Somoza, of attempting simply to elude starvation, if they could stay alive long enough in the face of state terrorism often directed to eliminating them. The absence of significant press comment on the Sandinista achievements was even more remarkable in view of the sheer number of articles that appeared on the subject of Nicaragua in these years. One might reasonably conclude – and this is supported by the evidence below – that reporting was conditioned by a different set of priorities, one that conformed to an ideological framework in which the facts about real development successes were ignored in favour of the stream of disinformation emanating from Washington and London. Whatever the specific reason – which is ultimately unimportant – readers of these newspapers were not enabled to view the conflict in terms of alternative forms of development, but instead their newspapers framed their accounts of the US war against Nicaragua primarily using a more respectable lens: that of the conflict with the Soviet Union.

Following the required doctrine

In the three newspapers considered, the standard account of the basic issues of the war hardly ever went beyond the notion that it should be seen as part of the East–West confrontation. This was a crucial formulation: once an issue is framed in this way by an omniscient first principle (or basic assumption), the details fit conveniently into place: US policy is more easily justified since the ultimate enemy is the Soviet Union. The reader is effectively forced to take 'sides'. As the *Daily Telegraph* informed its readers, 'anyone who sees a role for the Western Alliance cannot be neutral, even when the battlefield is far away'.[88]

In August 1981, the *Daily Telegraph* began an article by noting that 'in a move to head off Soviet influence in the western hemisphere' a Reagan official was meeting officials of the 'Left-wing' Sandinista government; in the next sentence it had become 'the pro-Marxist Sandinista junta'. The reader was informed that the meeting was 'aimed at keeping the Nicaraguans from falling under the spell of the Kremlin'.[89] That the basis of US policy was to *prevent* Nicaragua falling into the arms of the Soviet Union was taken as given: it passed unnoticed that by sponsoring a war in the country and attempting to exclude Nicaragua from Western sources of arms and aid, the USA was deliberately forcing Nicaragua into the Soviet bloc. The *Daily Telegraph*'s correspondent in Nicaragua could note, in 1983, that the Sandinistas' slide towards communism 'is not happening as swiftly as it did in Cuba, undoubtedly because the Reagan administration, with the hindsight of the Cuban experience, is doing its utmost to prevent it'.[90]

The Times offered a variation on this theme, occasionally noting that US policy might have the unfortunate effect of pushing Nicaragua into the Soviet bloc, a result that would be unintended and unfortunate. *The Times* stated, for example, that 'in mounting their propaganda campaign against Nicaragua, the Americans run the risk of driving Nicaragua closer to the Soviet Union'.[91] The *Financial Times* concurred that 'the real problem' with US policy towards Nicaragua was that 'it may push the Nicaraguan government further into the Soviet camp'.[92] Elsewhere the newspaper noted that there were 'glaring inconsistencies' in Reagan's apparent policy to 'halt communism' in the hemisphere.[93] Such attitudes meant that a US official could be quoted as stating that 'the purpose of US policy in [Central America] is to create conditions in which the area can be removed from East–West conflict', eliciting no comment from the reporter.[94] In all the articles I found one reference (in the *Financial Times*[95]) to the basic US strategy of wearing down the Sandinistas in order deliberately to push them increasingly into the Soviet bloc.

The *Financial Times* noted in November 1981 that the Reagan administration had recently been trying to improve relations with Nicaragua 'since it fears that the Sandinistas could become a pro-Soviet Trojan horse in the US back yard'.[96] *The Times* similarly stated that it was because of the shock of the Nicaraguan revolution in 1979 'and the fear that Nicaragua, and then the other countries of Central America, would one by one join Cuba in the Soviet camp, that the Americans have decided to make such an issue of El Salvador'.[97] Also, 'the Reagan administration ... sees Central America purely as a stage for the apparently perennial confrontation between East and West'.[98]

For the *Daily Telegraph* the issue was one of the 'pro-Russian regimes now threatening in America's backyard' and that, by April 1983, 'Nicaragua is now a fully-fledged Soviet-Cuban satellite'.[99] 'No deal can be done with the Sandinistas,' *Daily Telegraph* editors stated, since 'they are not agrarian reformers, they are totalitarian Marxists' who were 'thoroughly *incubanated*'.[100] The principal question, the newspaper's correspondent in Managua declared, was how Reagan would prevent the 'red stain' from 'spreading throughout Central America'. This was no easy task, to be sure, since Nicaragua, 'in Washington's book', had been 'targeted by the Communists in Moscow and Havana' as 'the toehold long sought on the Central America mainland', whilst in the Sandinistas 'the Kremlin has willing apprentices'.[101] The issue was momentous, and the State Department could have put it no better:

> The establishment of a Soviet client state on the American mainland, hard by America's main shipping lanes, constitutes a major threat to the United States' and the West's security, moving the front-line of Soviet–Western confrontation from the old world to the new. ... Communist invasion by proxy is just being

contained in the four other Central American states thanks to United States support.

Worse still, *Daily Telegraph* editors noted, 'Cuba is now planning to open a new front in Belize ... to take Guatemala from the flank, Honduras from the rear, and eventually provide an incursion route into Mexico itself.'[102]

In all the articles there were few exceptions to such a portrayal of Washington's war against Nicaragua. The only (near-) dissent from the official line occurred in the occasional comment that the roots of the Central American upheavals were the appalling social conditions in the region, not any Sandinista desire to become stooges of the Kremlin. Even these comments were accompanied by qualifications.

Thus *The Times* could note:

> ... the turmoil in Central America is not primarily caused by outside subversion. It results from the fact that most of the countries in the region have suffered from years of misgovernment, usually at the hands of military regimes backed by the United States.

'Misgovernment' was, in fact, the repression, often elimination, of the population while economic climates were fostered that enriched ruling elites and the transnational business interests allied to them, 'backed by the United States'. *The Times* continued by declaring that, since 'the solution does not lie ... in simply trying to stamp out insurgent groups by military means', the 'danger is that by concentrating on that Washington is repeating past mistakes'. The *Times* framework of analysis here did not permit it to state that there was no alternative but for Washington to destroy militarily the threat of independent development represented by the guerrillas in El Salvador and the government in Nicaragua. Instead Washington was merely making a 'mistake', presumably unaware of what it was doing. *The Times* continued by stating that 'in the case of Nicaragua' the US 'should acknowledge that that country is far from being a fully-fledged member of the Soviet block but that Washington's present policies could drive it in that direction, just as they drove Cuba in the 1960s', thus repeating the formula noted above.[103]

Whilst these domestic sources of upheaval could occasionally be recognised, there were next to no suggestions that the 'Soviet threat' scenarios promoted by Washington were mere propaganda. *The Times* could therefore correctly note that 'there is a difference between totalitarian communist/Marxist movements encouraged or even directed from outside and indigenous pluralist movements which have a left-wing colouring but are basically coalitions of revolt against the corrupt exercise of power'. Yet, in describing the US attitude, it could only manage to state that 'the rhetoric from Washington is close to suggesting that all leftist movements are implanted in Latin America by the schemers of the Kremlin or Havana'.

This, the newspaper concluded, 'is a dangerous over-simplification'.[104] The view conveyed by *The Times* was that the US administration was so overwhelmingly ignorant that it did not recognise the real source of upheavals in the region, instead genuinely believing that they were all (or primarily) caused by the machinations of the Kremlin. According to *The Times* the US attitude was one that 'refuses to see that the crying need throughout much of Latin America is for sound social and economic reforms'. The administration, in bewildering ignorance, apparently saw 'all leftist movements' as 'part of an international conspiracy'.[105]

Similarly, the *Financial Times* could note that 'most Americans find it hard to believe that a few thousand guerillas in El Salvador or a left-wing government in Nicaragua can contribute grounds for a national emergency'. However, 'the fact of the matter', the *Financial Times* declared, 'remains that the hard core of right wingers largely responsible for administration policy-making believe the rhetoric, and Mr Reagan does too'.[106] The *Financial Times* also noted:

> ... that one of the poorest countries in Central and Latin America with a population of less than 3m should pose such a threat to US interests might seem an irrational fear to many in Europe but for the White House this fear exists and has to be considered. ... Nor is it new, since it has lain behind the policy of American intervention in the area whether in the Dominican Republic, the Bay of Pigs or more recently Grenada.

The US administration's reasoning is indeed irrational if we actually believe its rhetoric, here parroted by the *Financial Times* as Nicaragua 'strategically straddl[ing] Central America' and acting 'as a springboard to further the aims of international communism'. It ceases to be irrational when we glance into the real world, with the real threat recognised to be the example for the region's impoverished set by the Nicaraguan revolution.[107]

The *Financial Times* on a few occasions correctly noted that 'the fundamental causes of this instability [in Central America] do not come from outside interference so much as from long-standing domestic problems of poverty, endemic violence and political instability'. However, it also took as given that the Reagan administration saw the conflicts in the region 'too readily as part of the global East–West confrontation'. In the same article *Financial Times* editors pondered the recently stated US goals for the region of 'democracy, reform, freedom, economic development' – goals not easy to square with US actions regarding El Salvador and Nicaragua. The newspaper noted that 'it is not easy to be confident that, in practice, American policy in the region is best adapted to achieving these goals. ... On the contrary, it is legitimate to fear that some elements of this policy could prove counter-productive.' That these goals could be taken seriously at all is surely evidence of the profound sympathy in educated circles for Britain's ally's foreign policy motivations.[108]

Overall, the story was one of basic subservience to the ideological framework promoted by the Reagan White House to justify its attacks on Nicaragua. The goal of destroying independent development in Nicaragua that might alleviate grinding poverty in that country and might set an example to others elsewhere receives no mention in the three years of reporting (and none that I could find throughout the rest of the war). The closest these three newspapers were capable of getting was to allude to the domino theory. The theory was not that Nicaragua could inspire independent development elsewhere but that, as the *Financial Times* put it, 'its home-grown experiment in Marxism is being used by Cuba and the Soviet Union as a springboard to further the aims of international communism, destabilising America's own backyard'.[109] The domino theory, therefore, also remains firmly a part of the 'East–West conflict' propaganda line.

The morality of immorality and the legality of illegality

The level of ideological treatment of the issues and support for basic US objectives is particularly striking in considerations of the legal and moral questions of the US war. Thus one *Times* editorial referred to the World Court's decision to accept as admissible Nicaragua's suit against the USA for conducting military activity in the country, mining harbours and supporting the Contras. 'To the international lawyer,' *The Times* stated, 'sovereign states must be equal, but to statesmen they cannot be' since spheres of influence 'are still a powerful fact of international life'.

> Just as sovereignty in practical international affairs is a relative principle, so self-determination is a phrase that should be much more closely examined, and Washington's current rhetoric in favour of Latin American democracy deserves more credence than it gets. The present Nicaraguan government has no clear mandate for establishing and then exporting the ideology of a Marxist Nicaragua allied with Cuba and the Soviet Union. President Reagan [has] recently given certain limits of United States tolerance clear definition. The legal arguments of the Hague cannot obscure these extra-legal facts of the matter.[110]

The US then, according to *The Times*, should not concern itself too much with the verdict of the World Court. The first sentence of the above extract is particularly interesting: it amounts to saying that Nicaragua is not entitled to full self-determination. The editorial appeared on 30 November 1984, just after the Nicaraguan elections. Yet, according to *The Times*, Nicaragua had 'no clear mandate' even for 'establishing' a Marxist ideology – even though Nicaraguans had just democratically voted for the Sandinistas. One need not wonder whether *The Times* would accept that by the same reasoning a democratically elected government could have a mandate to establish a 'capitalist' ideology.

Elsewhere, *Times* editors stated that the old 'military dictatorship' had been 'succeeded by a new-style repression which the November election has merely helped to extend'. Nicaragua was a society 'unable to live in peace with its neighbours or with the United States', the editors further observed, identifying the victim as the aggressor. Thus the United States was seen as the party on the defensive, expressing its 'readiness to meet Sandinista or Cuban force with selective counter-force'.[111]

The Times also had a few words to say about the morality of the war. One editorial on this subject appeared in August 1987, after six years of Contra activities had resulted in thousands of civilian casualties in a reign of terror well-documented by human rights groups. Americas Watch, for example, found in 1985 that the Contras 'have attacked civilians indiscriminately; they have tortured and mutilated prisoners; they have murdered those placed *hors de combat* by their wounds; they have taken hostages; and they have committed outrages against personal dignity'. The United States, meanwhile, 'has directly solicited the Contras to engage in violations of the laws of war'.[112] According to *The Times*, however, 'United States aid to the Nicaraguan insurgents is correct on grounds of both realpolitik and morality'. 'All great powers have local spheres of influence', which may be 'regrettable, but it is inevitable'. Nicaragua 'is within the United States' sphere', Nicaragua 'is subverting El Salvador' and Nicaragua is 'a potential foothold on the American mainland for the Soviet Union'. *The Times* then noted: '... at this point America's critics and Nicaragua's friends triumphantly announce: in that case, it must be acceptable for the Soviet Union, within *its* sphere of influence, to crush Solidarity' in Poland. This, however, was 'the point at which United States realpolitik joins with morality' since 'there can be no moral equivalence between a society with plural institutions and one without them. Solidarity, unlike the Nicaraguan government, was not encouraging armed insurrection in the Soviet Union and among its neighbours.' The United States is thus pardoned from supporting terrorism on the grounds that it has plural institutions. The logical intellectual extension of this is that the USA can do whatever it likes, perhaps obliterate an entire nation, and still remain on the moral high ground.[113]

In a 1987 editorial entitled 'the Contra question', *Times* editors posed the question 'When is a terrorist a freedom fighter?' Replying to their own question, they stated, 'the Contras do not deny that some of their number have committed atrocities'. But, they continued, 'there seems little doubt that they would not, for example, plant bombs in department stores, or use methods associated with people who are unambiguously terrorists'. 'They want the world to believe – and may well be telling the truth when they say it – that their military activity is directed against the regular forces of the Nicaraguan army,' the editors suggested, belying the reality that the prime targets of Contra terrorism were the 'individual leaders and community organisers who had worked hardest to improve the lives of the poor' (Oxfam, noted above). *The Times* could therefore declare that the Contras were in 'a different category from the Provisional IRA'; in fact this is certainly true, since the number of horrendous murders that have been committed by the IRA is far fewer than the number committed by the Contras. Yet this '[did] not mean that the United States, let alone Britain, should embrace their cause unreservedly', the editors continued. But anyway 'US support for the Contras is not unreserved'. Rather it is 'prudent aid to a friendly force, such as great powers have given down the ages and always will'. 'Moral questions', the editors added philosophically, 'have a habit of being resolved by considerations of power'. Indeed they do, and in this task these powers receive considerable ideological support from apologists for these horrors.[114]

Contra activities, *Times* editors continued elsewhere, were 'the essential pressure' without which it was 'certain' that 'no genuine easement will occur in the tightening grip of the "revolution"'.[115] 'The rebellion has had an effect,' the newspaper noted in 1986, the praiseworthy effects being to help 'reduce the Nicaraguan economy to its present straits' and forcing the Sandinista government 'to spend half its budget on defence'.[116] (*Financial Times* editors agreed that these were worthy successes, noting that 'Reagan can claim' that 'he has brought the Nicaraguan economy to its knees'.[117]) The Contras were a 'necessary element' who 'deserve no less support than the democratic forces within Nicaragua itself', *The Times* concluded.[118]

The inability to distinguish between the slaughter perpetrated by the USA's allies in the region (the governments of El Salvador and Guatemala, and the Contras) and the incomparably more benign Sandinista government in Nicaragua was a persistent theme of reporting by these newspapers. *The Times* noted that out of the 'acceptable faces' in the Sandinistas, the US administration and the Contras, 'it is not always easy to discern the villains of the piece', an assertion that is surely true if the real villains of the piece are supported by the onlooker in question.[119] In April 1983, after years of sheer terror conducted by government forces in El Salvador, the *Financial Times* could comment that 'it is less clear' that El Salvador 'has the kind of regime with which the US ought to be associated', though 'one should not doubt Washington's sincere desire to promote reform'.[120]

The *Daily Telegraph*, in a 1984 editorial, admitted no such problems, instead seeing a clear difference between the governments of El Salvador and Nicaragua. 'The Sandinista regime in Nicaragua', it commented, 'far from being a popular democracy, is an example of creeping totalitarianism.' Meanwhile, 'in El Salvador, however, largely as a result of United States pressure, there is patchy and uncertain progress towards a more democratic state of things. Land reform has been half-completed and the first round of the election for the Presidency held.' *Telegraph* editors were therefore able to distinguish between the mass murder which had taken the lives of around 40,000 people in early 1980s El Salvador under despotic regimes with only a pretence of 'democracy' and the generally popular rule of the Sandinistas who were contributing to significant social progress, in fact confirmed a few months later with Sandinista success in the November 1984 elections; by distinguishing in favour of the former.[121]

Thus the story of the British Press's coverage of Nicaragua is one of intellectual apologia for the US-sponsored manipulation and suppression of the real issues, and a clear demonstration of the special relationship that exists between US interests and the British press. In Orwellian style, *Daily Telegraph* editors noted in 1983: '... the Reagan administration has failed to fight its propaganda battle abroad, hence British and European public opinion has been subjected to wholly one-sided propaganda'.[122]

Notes

1. Balfour to Bevin, 9 August 1945, *Documents on British Foreign Policy*, Ser. 1, Vol. III, p. 17.

2. See especially Noam Chomsky, *Turning the tide*; Chomsky and Edward Herman, *The Washington connection and Third World fascism*; Kolko, *Confronting the Third World*; Blum; John Prados, *Presidents' secret wars: CIA and Pentagon covert operations since world war II*, William Morrow, New York, 1986.

3. Kolko, *Vietnam*, p. 84.

4. Ibid., pp. 89–90.

5. Ibid., pp. 94–5; Neil Sheehan, *A bright shining lie: John Paul Vann and America in Vietnam*, Picador, London, 1990, p. 183.

6. Kolko, *Vietnam*, p. 107.

7. Ibid., pp. 76, 113.

8. Chomsky and Herman, p. 305, citing US officials.

9. Northedge, pp. 218–19.

10. Lord Beloff, 'The end of the British Empire and the assumption of world-wide commitments by the United States', in Louis and Bull (eds), p. 255.

11. Harry Piotrowski, 'The structure of the international system', in Schraeder (ed.), p. 177.

12. See, for example, Chomsky and Herman, pp. 312–28.

13. Jonathan Bloch and Patrick Fitzgerald, *British intelligence and covert action: Africa, Middle East and Europe since 1945*, Junction, London, 1987, p. 44.

14. Ibid., p. 64.

15. Fred Halliday, *Arabia without Sultans*, Penguin, Harmondsworth, 1974, p. 359; Bloch and Fitzgerald, p. 74.

16. House of Commons debates, 5th Series, 1961–62, Vol. 655, 14 March 1962, Col. 1318.

17. House of Commons debates, 5th series, 1964–65, Vol. 709, 25 March 1965, Col. 735.

18. House of Commons debates, 5th series, 1963–64, Vol. 690, 3 March 1964, Col. 1128.

19. Ibid.

20. House of Commons debates, 5th series, 1962–63, Vol. 676, 29 April 1963, Col. 702.

21. Letter to the *Daily Telegraph*, 15 May 1972; House of Commons debates, 5th series, 1971–72, Vol. 835, 17 April 1972, Col. 17; ibid., 25 April 1972, Col. 1274.

22. House of Commons debates, 5th series, 1971–72, Vol. 837, 15 May 1972, Col. 20.

23. Robert Stephens, 'Britain silent on bombing', *Observer*, 24 December 1972.

24. Richard Immerman, *The CIA in Guatemala: The foreign policy of intervention*, University of Texas Press, Austin, 1982, pp. 62–3.

25. Ibid., pp. 28, 64–6, 82–3, 171–3.

26. Memorandum by K. Pridham, 8 September 1954, PRO, FO 371/108945/AG 10345/6.

27. Guatemala to Foreign Office, 9 July 1954, PRO, FO 371/108930/AG1015/129.

28. Anthony Eden, *Full circle*, Cassell, London, 1960, p. 135.

29. Memorandum by R. Barclay, 22 July 1954, PRO, FO 371/108947/AG1051/6.

30. Memorandum by M. Man, 16 July 1954, PRO, FO 371/108947/AG1051/8.

31. R. Allen to A. Eden, 14 October 1954, PRO, FO 371/108935/AG1015/245.

32. Foreign Office to Guatemalan Minister for Foreign Affairs, 8 November 1954, PRO, FO 371/108935/AG1015/255.

33. Blum, p. 310.

34. Latin America Bureau (LAB), *Grenada: Whose freedom?*, LAB, London, 1984, pp. 37, 39.

35. See Blum, pp. 312–13.

36. Chris Searle, *Grenada: The struggle against destabilisation*, Readers and Writers, London, 1983, pp. 55–6.

37. The Latin America Bureau, for example, writes that logistical preparation for a US invasion had been under way since 1981 and that 'the principal issue facing the Reagan administration was less military organisation than the political means by which an invasion might be arranged and justified' (LAB, *Grenada*, p. 80).

38. Ibid., pp. 92–3.

39. William Gilmore, who conducted a study of the legal basis for the invasion, notes that 'there is evidence to suggest that the internal situation on the island did not pose "an imminent threat of injury to US citizens"' and that 'it does not appear from the record that the United States government made any direct attempt to put the undertaking given to it by the RMC [the military junta] to the test by seeking permission for such flights to land for the purpose of facilitating an evacuation of its nationals' (*The Grenada intervention: Analysis and documentation*, Mansell, London, 1984, pp. 61, 63. See also LAB, *Grenada*, p. 84).

40. House of Commons debates, 6th series, Vol. 47, 1983–84, 25 October 1983, Col. 146.

41. Quoted in John Dickie, *'Special' no more: Anglo-American relations: Rhetoric and reality*, Weidenfeld and Nicolson, London, 1993, p. 188.

42. Cited in Tony Thorndike, 'Grenada', in Peter Schraeder (ed.), *Intervention in the 1980s: US foreign policy in the Third World*, Lynne Rienner, London, 1989, p. 249.

43. *Grenada: Report of a British Labour Movement Delegation*, LMDG, London, December 1983, pp. 2, 41.

44. House of Commons debates, 6th series, Vol. 95, 1985–86, 16 April 1986, Cols. 875, 880, 953.

45. Dianna Melrose, *The threat of a good example?*, Oxfam, Oxford, 1985, p. 11; Holly Sklar, *Washington's war on Nicaragua*, Between the Lines, Toronto, 1988, p. 36.

46. Cited in Melrose, p. 12.

47. Ibid., p. 13.

48. Ibid., p. 14.

49. See Melrose, pp. 14–36.

50. Carlos Fuentes, 'Nicaragua and sundry hobgoblins', *International Herald Tribune*, 22 January 1983.

51. Jerome Levinson and Juan de Onis, *The alliance that lost its way: A critical report on the Alliance for Progress*, Twentieth Century Fund, Chicago, 1970, p. 309.

52. Blum, pp. 208–10.

53. Sklar, p. 100.

54. Cited in Sklar, p. 145.

55. Cited in Noam Chomsky, *Turning the tide*, pp. 12–13.

56. Cited in Sklar, p. 177.

57. Ibid., p. 140.

58. Melrose, pp. 27–9.

59. Sklar, p. 116.

60. Peter Kornbluh, 'Nicaragua', in Schraeder (ed.), p. 243.

61. Sklar, p. 314.

62. Harold Jackson, 'Reagan steps up Central American offensive', *Guardian*, 6 December 1982; Chomsky, *Turning the tide*, p. 31.

63. CIIR, *Central America*, CIIR, London, 1988, pp. 21–2.

64. Americas Watch, Helsinki Watch and the Lawyers Committee for International Human Rights, cited in Chomsky, *Turning the tide*, p. 33.

65. Cited in Philip Geyelin, 'Terror in Central America: Playing with the facts', *IHT*, 16 June 1984.

66. Cited in 'Nicaragua has ended torture, US body says', *The Times*, 15 May 1982.

67. Cited in Chomsky, *Turning the tide*, p. 129.

68. Philip Webster, 'Howe fully endorses Reagan policies', *The Times*, 3 August 1983.

69. House of Commons debates, 6th series, Vol. 52, 1983–84, 16 January 1984, Col. 6, written answers.

70. House of Commons debates, 6th series, Vol. 77, 1984–85, 24 April 1985, Col. 872.

71. James Ferguson, James Painter and Jenny Pearce, 'Under attack: Central America and the Caribbean', in LAB, *The Thatcher Years*, pp. 30–34.

72. House of Commons debates, 6th series, Vol. 67, 1984–85, 9 November 1984, Col. 326.

73. Melrose, pp. 45–8.

74. Hugh O'Shaughnessy, 'Secret FO block on Nicaragua aid', *Observer*, 12 May 1985.

75. House of Commons debates, 6th series, Vol. 74, 1984–85, 26 February 1985, Col. 178.

76. Cited in Kornbluh, p. 243.

77. Kornbluh, p. 244.

78. Cited in Alan Riding, 'US envoy earned trust of Nicaraguans', *IHT*, 26 August 1981; see also Jenny Pearce, 'Star-spangled clanger', *Guardian*, 15 January 1982.

79. 'Nicaraguan flea worried by American elephant', *Guardian*, 2 July 1983.

80. Patrick Tyler and Bob Woodward, 'US is said to approve anti-Nicaragua actions', *IHT*, 11 March 1982.

81. Michael Leapman, 'Reading a new chapter in Nicaraguan politics', *The Times*, 16 March 1981.

82. James Curran, 'Give Nicaragua a chance', *The Times*, 3 August 1983.

83. Hugh O'Shaughnessy, 'Nicaraguan people rally to the Sandinistas', *Financial Times*, 6 May 1983; 'Central American role for the UN', *Financial Times*, 6 April 1983.

84. 'CIA arming enemies of Sandinistas', *The Times*, 4 April 1983.

85. Frank Taylor, 'Nicaragua rebels set for victory, says CIA chief', *Daily Telegraph*, 24 May 1983.

86. Peter Kemp, 'Everywhere a stench of Havana', *Daily Telegraph*, 17 August 1982.

87. 'Inter-American dilemmas', *Daily Telegraph*, 11 April 1983.

88. Ibid.

89. Frank Taylor, 'Nicaragua overture by Reagan', *Daily Telegraph*, 11 August 1981.

90. Frank Taylor, 'High noon in Nicaragua', *Daily Telegraph*, 19 May 1983.

91. 'Wrong approach to Central America', *The Times*, 11 March 1982.

92. 'US policy in El Salvador', *Financial Times*, 29 April 1983.

93. Reginald Dale, 'The shadow of Vietnam', *Financial Times*, 11 August 1983.

94. Geoffrey Matthews, 'Four-nation peace drive in Central America launched by Colombia', *The Times*, 14 April 1983.

95. Hugh O'Shaughnessy, 'Nicaraguan people rally to the Sandinistas', *Financial Times*, 6 May 1983.

96. William Chislett, 'Prison sentences sharpen Nicaraguan discontent', *Financial Times*, 6 November 1981.

97. 'A debatable Cuban domino', *The Times*, 6 November 1981.

98. John Carlin, 'Four-nation attempt to defuse war threat', *The Times*, 11 May 1983.

99. 'Reagan's big heave', *Daily Telegraph*, 26 April 1983.

100. The struggle', *Daily Telegraph*, 29 April 1983. Emphasis in original.

101. Frank Taylor, 'Reagan seeking mandate for Central American policy', *Daily Telegraph*, 25 April 1983.

102. 'A British presence', *Daily Telegraph*, 3 October 1983.

103. 'Jaw-jaw si, war-war no', *The Times*, 3 December 1981.

104. 'When the killing has to stop', *The Times*, 4 March 1982; see also James Curran, 'Give Nicaragua a chance', *The Times*, 3 August 1983.

105. 'President Reagan's awkward guest', *The Times*, 18 March 1981.

106. Reginald Dale, 'The shadow of Vietnam', *Financial Times*, 11 August 1983.

107. 'Diplomacy in Central America', *Financial Times*, 18 November 1983.

108. 'US policy in El Salvador', *Financial Times*, 29 April 1983.

109. 'Diplomacy in Central America', *Financial Times*, 18 November 1983.

110. 'Limits of the law', *The Times*, 30 November 1984.

111. 'The fourth frontier', *The Times*, 10 December 1984.

112. Cited in Sklar, p. 187.

113. 'Voice of Managua', *The Times*, 27 August 1987.

114. 'The Contra question', *The Times*, 31 October 1987.

115. 'A revolution gone sour', *The Times*, 8 February 1985.

116. 'Aid for the contras', *The Times*, 17 March 1986.

117. 'Elusive peace in Central America', *Financial Times*, 3 July 1987.

118. 'Second wind', *The Times*, 14 June 1985.

119. 'A revolution gone sour', *The Times*, 8 February 1985.

120. 'US policy in El Salvador', *Financial Times*, 29 April 1983.

121. 'Myths and Nicaragua', *Daily Telegraph*, 3 May 1984.

122. 'Castro's two card trick', *Daily Telegraph*, 1 August 1983.

PART FOUR

THE CURRENT ERA

CHAPTER 7

THE PRACTICE OF
INTERNATIONAL ORDER

The era in which Britain engaged unilaterally in military interventions, colonial wars and coups to pursue its first-order objectives largely passed in the 1960s. Since then the priorities outlined in Chapter 1 have been pursued chiefly by lending diplomatic, and sometimes material, support to the foreign policy, and aggression abroad, of the United States. The decline of Britain's global power was evidenced above all in the Middle East: in the failed invasion of Egypt in 1956 and, as a consequence of budgetary pressures at home, in the military withdrawal from the Gulf in 1971. Though Britain retained a foothold in the region through close relationships with one important oil producer, Kuwait, and traditionally close allies Oman and Jordan, the Western ability to control events in the Middle East now lay primarily with the United States.

The situation was similar elsewhere. When, in the 1970s, revolutionary movements succeeded in overthrowing pro-Western regimes in a number of Third World states – including Angola, Nicaragua, Ethiopia, Mozambique and Grenada – Britain could generally only sit on the sidelines; it was the United States that, through a variety of means, sought to subvert many of these new regimes. This was in marked contrast to the 1940s and 1950s – the first wave of Third World upheaval following the Second World War – when Britain had played a decisive unilateral role in preventing the appearance of unacceptable regimes. For Britain, the 1970s was marked rather by the turn towards Europe and the joining of the European Community (EC) in 1973.

The wave of Third World revolutions, the US defeat by Vietnam and the increased economic power the Organisation of Petroleum Exporting Countries (OPEC) in the 1970s considerably undermined the goals of Anglo-American postwar planning outlined in the documents of the early postwar years. Britain lost the ability to shape even fundamental world events to its requirements, and the apparent loss of US hegemony signified by these developments resulted in the particularly aggressive foreign policy of both nations under Thatcher and Reagan in the 1980s. These administrations sought to recover their own declining or lost power, the United States in particular attempting to reassert the control over the international system it had exercised in the 1940s and 1950s. It was no surprise that for Britain under Thatcher this entailed a unilateral military intervention in a colonial situation – the Falklands in 1982 – reminiscent of the previous period. At the same time, foreign policy took the same road under Thatcher as it had under Attlee in the late 1940s: in attempting to secure the twin goals of maximising national influence on the world stage and contributing to a reassertion of Western hegemony in the international system, Britain opted for a revitalised partnership with the United States. The crucial difference between the two periods was that Britain was in a position to offer mainly diplomatic, rather than military, support for the new agenda.

The collapse of the Soviet Union has offered new opportunities to fulfil largely the same Western agenda regarding the Third World as outlined after the Second World War. In the current era, British foreign policy remains consistently opposed to the grand principles – such as promotion of human rights and economic development in the Third World – widely assumed to be consistent with it. Yet the relative decline of British power has restricted Britain's ability to impose its requirements abroad unilaterally. Britain remains an important individual actor on the world stage but one whose foreign policy is evermore enmeshed with those of the other leading industrialised states – those in the G7 and European Union, for example – and the international institutions – the World Bank, the IMF and, to a large extent, the UN – that they control.

Due to this relative decline in unilateral power, the reality of British foreign policy as regards the upholding of these grand principles can now best be understood in a wider international context: by continuing to consider its support for US aggression abroad, but also by recognising Britain's influential role in the international institutions that effectively manage the global economy and shape the international order. Although – as will be discussed in Chapter 8 – Britain's unilateral actions can still be important, it is now increasingly in this set of relationships that British foreign policy – and its contribution to the abuse of human rights, and human suffering – can be understood.

Britain was the only major state to support the US invasion of Panama and to unstintingly support the US defeat of Iraq, itself playing the secondary role in the coalition, whilst impressing upon the United States that it was Washington's only reliable European ally. Britain also plays a prominent role in continuing the Northern states' plunder of the Third World, chiefly through its support for IMF and World Bank programmes and the international debt and trade regimes (these are considered in Chapter 8). Timorese, Cambodians, Bosnians and other unpeople, meanwhile, continue to impede Britain's pursuit of its national interests in the so-called 'post-Cold War' era.

Continuing conflicts

Respectable commentators are unanimous in asserting that, with the demise of the Soviet Union, the framework of international affairs has changed fundamentally.[1] Previously, two interrelated required truths were: the Cold War was the dominating fact of the postwar world; and, second, the need to contain the Soviet Union provided the overriding basis for Western foreign policies. Now that not even the best and brightest can continue to parrot these formerly required propaganda notions, the structure of international affairs must logically be fundamentally different.

Whilst the 'Soviet threat' has disappeared, however, new demons are deemed to be on the horizon: Third World nations with nuclear weapons, international terrorists, Islamic fundamentalists, drug traffickers, population growth, migration, etcetera. These are the 'challenges', 'threats' or 'risks' to Western 'security interests' in the current era, widely identified through-out the propaganda system, essentially to replace the 'Soviet threat'.[2] Instead of being able to relax secure in the knowledge that it won the Cold War, the West should not lower its guard: there are further evils for which it needs to prepare through continued high defence spending, planning for military intervention, arms sales abroad to promote 'security' in key regions, and so on.

Glancing into the real world, on the other hand, we find that inter-national affairs have undergone some structural changes with the dis-appearance of the Soviet Union but that the fundaments of the system remain the same. The current ('post-Cold War') era entails the promotion by the Western states of the same priorities as outlined in Chapter 1; this is logical, since the structure of domestic society (which to a large extent determines national interests and foreign policy) has not changed, and also since containment of the Soviet Union was often merely the pretext for foreign policy actions. These priorities are now being pursued under different pretexts and with instruments modified to suit new circumstances.

The different pretexts include the new so-called threats noted above; in fact practically anything, however tenuous, will do. The US invasion of Panama in 1989, for example, was pursued partly under the pretext of deposing and arresting a drug trafficker – General Noriega – and partly under the time-honoured pretext of 'protecting American lives'. This was the case even though Noriega had engaged in drug trafficking with US knowledge, while remaining on the CIA payroll, for a couple of decades before the invasion.[3] The war against Iraq in 1991 was justified on the basis of the principle of standing up to aggression. That this was somewhat inconsistent – given numerous past acts of aggression by, or supported by, the Western states – did not appear overly to concern commentators within the propaganda system (see below).

Opportunities for military intervention are even greater than before. In the most important region – the Middle East – there is now no danger of a nuclear war with the Soviet Union, so the Western field of manoeuvre is virtually unhindered. The use of massive force against a country by the United States and its allies can take place without any fear of substantial retaliation, as in the case of Iraq. Yet if military intervention in the major areas is easier (war against peripheral countries like Panama can continue as before, virtually at will), it is also less of a requirement in the new era. On this point, the demise of the Soviet Union has affected matters somewhat. In the past, states threatened with intervention or a Western-imposed economic blockade could at least appeal to the Soviet Union as an alternative source of aid or arms, as in the cases of Cuba, Nicaragua, Vietnam, Angola and others. Since this is no longer an option, Third World states now have little alternative but to adopt the economic prescriptions of the IMF, World Bank and their Western backers. The G7 states thus wield enormous power: economic disciplining keeps the Third World (which now, basically, includes the former Soviet empire) in line and ensures that so-called development proceeds along the appropriate guidelines.

A further Western instrument for organising the world appropriately is the United Nations. 'The Security Council', the journalist Richard Gott has written, is 'a tightly-run ship organised chiefly by the British on behalf of the Americans. ... While the Americans provide the economic arm-twisting, the British supply the diplomatic expertise.'[4] Of the Security Council's other three permanent members, France is firmly in tow, having lost its previous foreign policy rationale of Gaullist 'independence' from the superpowers, Russia is largely dependent on the G7 states for aid and investment, and China, whilst clearly the most undisciplined member which often pursues a genuinely independent line, can effectively be bought off through threats of economic sanctions over human rights abuses. The former deputy director of the State Department's Policy Planning Staff, Francis Fukuyama, has stated that the UN 'is perfectly serviceable as an instrument of American unilateralism and indeed may be the primary mechanism through which that unilateralism will be exercised in the future'.[5] Thus the UN can continue to be obstructed or ignored when it infringes upon US interests (Israel, former Yugoslavia, Cuba), and mobilised when it serves them (Iraq, Somalia). In the latter cases, use of the UN has the significant advantage that the US will not be called upon to do all the dirty work: other nations will help pay the financial costs and risk the loss of lives. The ability to use the United Nations to serve Western interests is what is meant by the idea now current that the end of the Cold War enables the UN's reactivation. (Today's orthodoxy has it that the Cold War – and Soviet obstructionism – paralysed the United Nations, yet in the last quarter of a century of the Cold War (1965–90) the three Western members of the Security Council – the USA, Britain and France – cast 85 per cent of the vetoes cast in the council.)[6]

The first of the two major postwar conflicts – the West–South conflict – thus remains firmly in place, though the pretexts and instruments used to conduct it have been modified. The current era is, in short, one of the virtually complete supremacy of the Northern triad: the USA, the European Union (EU) and Japan – at least, that is, until Third World states opposed to the current international order acquire fully functioning weapons of mass destruction, especially nuclear weapons. This would be a logical step to deter outside intervention in their particular region; indeed, there should be little surprise that it is in the Middle East – the West's major preoccupation – that weapons proliferation is most widespread. These developments increasingly pose threats to continued Western control over key regions in the Third World; thus they are deemed 'security threats'.

The second major conflict of the postwar world – that between the United States and the West – is also continuing, with the prospect that, without the alleged Soviet threat and the United States's reliance on its security guarantee to discipline its allies, the EU and Japan will increasingly assert their independence from US foreign and economic policy. Resorting to war against Iraq was particularly useful to the United States in this regard, serving to demonstrate clearly US military dominance at a time when Western Europe was questioning the future viability of NATO and the desirability of the US military presence in Europe. The case of those Europeans arguing for greater military (and political) independence from the US was dealt a heavy blow by the Gulf War, which helped the United States to prevent the emergence of a European defence (and consequently political) identity that would undermine continued US pre-eminence through NATO.

This latter goal was recognised as basic in a Pentagon draft document leaked in March 1992, which stated that the United States should prevent 'the emergence of European-only security arrangements which would undermine NATO'. The document noted that the US mission would be to '[convince] potential competitors that they need not aspire to a greater role or pursue a more aggressive posture to protect their legitimate interests', whilst the 'less visible' victory at the end of the Cold War was defined as 'the integration of Germany and Japan into a US-led system of collective security and the creation of a democratic "zone of peace"'. Thus the essence of US strategy is to 'establish and protect a new order' that accounts 'sufficiently for the interests of the advanced industrial nations to discourage them from challenging our leadership', whilst maintaining a military dominance capable of 'deterring potential competitors from even aspiring to a larger regional or global role'. A 'dominant consideration underlying the new regional defence strategy' is said to be the requirement that 'we endeavour to prevent any hostile power from dominating a region whose resources would, under consolidated control, be sufficient to generate global power'. These regions include Western Europe, East Asia, the former Soviet Union and the Middle East. The US press noted that the document 'articulates the clearest rejection to date of collective inter-nationalism' and is 'conspicuously devoid of references to collective action through the United Nations'. The draft document was criticised by the White House and State Department and revised, but it is hardly open to doubt that its themes reflect the basic current concerns of US planners.[7]

The ability of the US to assert its hegemony within the industrialised world is now severely constrained, however, by the sheer economic power of Japan, the increasing integration of the EU and the widening of the area of Third World-style exploitation of cheap labour and natural resources to include Eastern Europe and the former Soviet Union. In the latter, the business corporations and economic interests of Germany and Japan are better-placed than those of the USA to be the primary beneficiaries. With the USA's junior partner Britain helping to prevent further EU integration and vetoing a greater degree of Western European independence from the US in the military sphere – in line with its traditional practice – Japan presents a greater problem than the EU for continued US pre-eminence.

A 'stable international order'

In October 1991 the US Deputy Secretary of State, Lawrence Eagleburger, outlined the US goal of a 'stable international order' in which the United States would continue its 'burden of world leadership' and in which 'the maintenance of the world's free trading order ought to be our highest priority in foreign policy'. A danger was that 'the multipolar world to which we are returning is one in which nations will be tempted to go their own way with little regard for the common good or for the inter-national order'. Saddam Hussein 'has given us a glimpse of what that world could look like', Eagleburger noted.[8] But presumably far less evil eminences could be tempted to 'go their own way' with 'little regard for the common good'. Thus US goals, logically, remain the same as in the Cold War era: 'international order' (that is, world capitalism under US domination) will be maintained, whilst the primary threats to it are in-dependent deviations that challenge that domination.

The benefits of such an order are apparent. If Latin America becomes a 'stable' hemisphere with 'open economies', the Assistant Secretary for Inter-American Affairs Bernard Aronson notes, it 'offers increased op-portunity for American workers and businesses'.[9] Another US official explains that 'there's no part of the world where the US export sector has greater market opportunities than in this hemisphere'. The economic recovery of Central America is 'one of the most hopeful signs for the future of the US economy'.[10] Aronson adds elsewhere:

... the 1990s will see the most profound and fierce competition for capital that the world has seen in the postwar era. Only those countries that can inspire confidence and open up their systems to new investment will be able to survive in this environment.[11]

The rest can presumably wither and die; unable to contribute to international order.

The results are striking in those countries that have pursued these priorities for some time. In Brazil, for example, according to the US State Department, 2 per cent of national income goes to the poorest 20 per cent of the population, whilst 65 per cent goes to the richest 20 per cent.[12] 65 per cent of all houses in urban centres and 93 per cent of those in the countryside lack sewerage.[13] Millions of children live on the streets. By the early 1990s, one third of all children under the age of five suffered from malnutrition; 350,000 of them die each year and at least 50 million people (out of a population of 150 million) do not get enough food to eat, though the country has abundant supplies of food and is a major food exporter. Powerful land owners dominate the Brazilian Congress and impede reform that would benefit the majority, whilst economic policy generally is directed towards the rich, with the support of the international financial institutions and the leading Western states.[14]

'We use American economic strength to promote the development of other market economies,' the US Under-Secretary for Political Affairs has correctly noted.[15] Other options are on offer, however, to prevent deviations that might upset 'international order'. As General Colin Powell, former chairman of the US Joint Chiefs of Staff, explained: '... we must insure that our world is sufficiently secure to allow us to work on our economies and to keep the international trading system growing and prosperous.' In not every crisis, however, Powell continued, can one expect from the United States 'a quick sniff of gunpowder to resolve conflicts'.[16] But retaining the option is always useful.

US military forces are now unambiguously structured for intervention in the Third World, commensurate with the US military strategy of focusing 'on major regional threats that could harm US interests', according to the Secretary of Defence.[17] Thus in June 1991, the press reported, the United States was building 8,650 cruise missiles, ideal weapons for destroying targets at distance without risk of reprisals and used against Iraq both in the war of 1991 and the raids of 1993.[18] US scientists are developing a new generation of miniaturised nuclear weapons 'designed for use primarily in the Third World'.[19] A 1991 US military report (the Reed Report) recommended that US nuclear weapons be targeted at 'every reasonable adversary' around the world and that a nuclear expeditionary force be established to counter 'nuclear weapon states [that] are likely to emerge' and 'despotic' states that 'seek to deter the United States and other powers from interfering with their regional aggressions'. Moreover, the report states, 'we are not comfortable that we can count on deterrence to deal with many lethal Third World threats'; it recommends 'first use' of nuclear weapons if US forces were faced with superior conventional forces or the threat of 'impending annihilation'. The report also recommends the use of nuclear weapons as a response to conventional or chemical attack and urges the USA to 'retain an option to leave ambiguous whether it would employ nuclear weapons in retaliation to gross acts on the part of an aggressor'.[20]

Michael Quinlan, recently retired as Permanent Under-Secretary of State at the UK Ministry of Defence, provides an interesting insight into the current utility of nuclear weapons. The United States, Quinlan argues, is the only 'credible candidate, in terms of global reach, influence and acceptance' to be 'the prime possessor of nuclear weapons'. Britain, as one of the 'partner countries of the United States in seeking stable international order' should 'accept a duty of backing the United States in bearing the nuclear task'. This would involve 'clear political support' and 'other forms of help, for example in deployment, where such help is appropriate in order to sustain the role effectively'. It is important to note that this notion envisages a role for nuclear weapons 'beyond the classic central task of providing a secure counterbalance to Eastern military power', a role reflecting 'a nonspecific concept of helping to underpin world order in whatever context it might be threatened'. In this view, the nuclear armoury therefore needs to be 'unmistakeably evident to whomever it may concern' so that 'even in adverse circumstances nuclear force could be brought to bear rapidly, accurately, under close control and in measured amounts wherever it is needed'. In short, a nuclear weapon capability acts 'in support of world order'.[21]

Just after the US bombing of Iraq in June 1993, Martin Walker wrote in the *Guardian* that 'Iraq [had] just become the first test-bed' of 'a new American defence and foreign policy for the post-cold war world' (in fact rather like in the Cold War world, but concealed). Its 'crucial symbol' was the aircraft carrier *Theodore Roosevelt* where, Walker noted, an experiment was under way to replace half its strike force of fighter-bombers with a battalion of marines 'able to intervene on land at will with their helicopters and gun-ships, and air cover from the rest of the F-14s'. There was to be improved sea-lift capacity, the arrival of a new cargo plane capable of carrying three times the load of the current Hercules C130, and an expansion of the marines with improved armour, Harrier jump jets and a 'fleet of fast-moving armoured reconnaissance vehicles'. 'Rather like the British Army of the 19th century,' Walker continues, 'the US armed forces are being reshaped to fight small wars rather than big ones', and are taking on the role of an 'imperial police force'.[22]

US general Colin Powell, noting that the US military's 'forward presence' remains 'the key element' in its military strategy, has stated that, in the

Middle East, the US forward presence will be 'somewhat larger than in the past'. This will entail 'a carrier battle group almost full-time and an amphibious ready group', as part of an overall military structure and strategy to 'project power', 'to fight in low-intensity conflicts' as well as in 'mid- or high-intensity conflict' and 'to deploy rapidly to any region in the world'. These forces are said to be required 'to deal with our enduring needs in a changing world'.[23]

British military strategy reflects the same priorities. 'The old distinction between "in" and "out of area" is no longer relevant for defence planning,' the 1993 Defence Estimates stated. To promote Britain's 'wider security interests through the maintenance of international peace and stability', the military require a:

> Graduated range of military options, from the employment of small teams of Special Forces to the mounting of an operation requiring the deployment of a division with maritime and air support, as circumstances demand. We have therefore identified for planning purposes an intervention capability.

British plans to ensure a worldwide intervention capability include the replacement or refurbishment of its air transport fleet and the building of a new helicopter carrier.[24]

The Ministry of Defence is also considering the acquisition of conventionally armed cruise missiles, and the Royal Navy is reportedly keen on the submarine-launched variety.[25] Having abandoned plans for a nuclear tactical air-to-surface missile (TASM) for the RAF, the government is proposing to adapt some of the Trident strategic missiles to provide a 'sub-strategic' nuclear force, to be carried on Trident submarines.[26] Britain, the Defence Secretary has stated, is 'one of the world's most formidable military powers' and 'it is the government's intention that that should remain the case ... for many years to come'.[27]

This overall strategy of preparing for war against the Third World represents a clear continuation of the pursuit of basic postwar goals. A senior British officer later to be Chief of the Defence Staff told NATO in 1977: '... in the future [NATO] might have to wage peripheral wars to keep its share of the world's resources.'[28] This observation reflected the view of the US ambassador to India, Chester Bowles (expressed in 1956): 'The very suggestion that the day may come when the Atlantic nations may no longer take what they need from the natural resources of Asia and Africa will be dismissed by many as preposterous.'[29] In order to continue to take their needs, resort to war – preferably short and sharp – may be required. A leaked national security document of the early days of the Bush administration reveals that 'in cases where the US confronts much weaker enemies, our challenge will not be simply to defeat them, but to defeat them decisively and rapidly'. Any other outcome would be 'embarrassing' and might 'undercut political support'.[30]

The defeat of Iraq

The war against Iraq in 1991 was the largest commitment of British forces to a military operation since the Falklands War of 1982 and exemplified the traditional British commitment to the maintenance of 'international order'. Whilst the United States clearly led the 'coalition' forces in defeating Iraq, Britain's military played a decisive role as 'junior partner' (*Daily Telegraph*).[31] Furthermore, Britain's diplomatic stance during the crisis that led up to the war – considered below – was virtually indistinguishable from that of the United States, serving to give the impression of a united coalition when the position of many other European states was decidedly less supportive.

The number of people killed in the conflict remains uncertain, with reasonable estimates varying from around 35,000 (with 240 'allied' deaths) to 100,000–120,000 Iraqi troop deaths and 5,000–15,000 Iraqi civilian deaths.[32] Yet the conflict was, according to John Major, 'perhaps the most successful military operation we have ever known'.[33] A consideration of the reality of the war reveals something of the reality of official British values and of the values of the 'mellower and more advanced nations of the world' as they maintained 'international order'.

A central feature of the war was the use of an array of the most devastating weaponry – including the testing of new weapons in combat, such as the Tomahawk cruise missile – and the 'much more general process of precise targeting of people throughout the war', in the words of Paul Rogers of the Bradford School of Peace Studies. The US navy alone dropped 4,400 cluster bombs and the US and British air forces dropped thousands more, some of which produced a hail of about half a million anti-personnel shrapnel fragments, similar to the Multiple Rocket Launch System bombs that release 8,000 anti-personnel fragmentation grenades as they detonate.[34] 'Cluster bombs are perfect child-killers,' Eric Hoskins – a Canadian doctor and coordinator of a Harvard study team on Iraq – notes.

> In appearance they are toy-like; an elongated coke-can attached to a tiny parachute. ... When a child comes across one of these unexploded 'toys' and pulls on the parachute, he or she loses an arm or an eye, or more commonly a life. What evil and malignant mind designs these killing devices, I do not know. Most hospitals in Iraq contain at least one child victim of such obscene creativeness.

Of the 100,000 tons of bombs dropped on Iraq and Kuwait, only 7 per cent were 'smart' or precision-guided; an estimated 75 per cent of all bombs dropped missed their target. The 'allied' bombardment 'effectively terminated everything vital to human survival in Iraq – electricity, water, sewage systems, agriculture, industry and health care', Hoskins notes. 'Food warehouses, hospitals and markets were bombed. Power stations were repeatedly attacked until electricity supplies were at only 4 per cent of prewar levels.'[35] In fact, this was deliberate policy: a draft congressional report of February 1992 acknowledged that 'senior commanders made deliberate exceptions to the policy of limiting damage to certain power installations', the US press reported.[36] This targeting of Iraq's life-support installations had hardly even a pretence of military significance.

The war made the children of Iraq 'the most traumatised children of war ever described', according to a Harvard study team of child psychologists. The team noted:

> The children strive to understand what they saw: planes bombing, houses collapsing, soldiers fighting, blood, mutilated and crushed bodies. The children fight to forget what they heard: people screaming, desperate voices, planes, explosions, crying people. They are haunted by the smell of gunfire, fires and burned flesh.

The team asked themselves 'if these children are not the most suffering child population on earth'.[37] Another Harvard medical team concluded three months after the end of the slaughter that in the coming year typhoid, cholera, malnutrition and other health problems 'caused by the Gulf war' will kill 'at least 170,000 more children than would have died under normal conditions', the press reported. This figure was 'conservative', according to the leader of the team. Most of the expected deaths would be 'the delayed result of the US bombing campaign that destroyed power plants needed to run hospitals, water purification stations and food factories'.[38]

Eight months after the end of the onslaught, as the result of the war itself and the sanctions, deaths among children under five had nearly quintupled. Almost 1 million children were malnourished and more than 100,000 were starving and at risk of dying in the near future. Typhoid, hepatitis, meningitis and gastroenteritis had reached epidemic levels, whilst raw waste filled city streets and was flowing untreated into the rivers that Iraqis had turned to for drinking water.[39]

The systematic destruction of Iraq was accompanied by colonial-style slaughter: what RAF Marshall David Craig termed 'more and more like butchery' in reference to the massacres at Mutla Ridge.[40] On the roads out of Kuwait, retreating Iraqi forces were disposed of in a way that would have impressed nineteenth-century British imperialists. According to a US military officer, the US air force was given 'the word to work over the entire area, to find anything that was moving and take it out'.[41] A US navy pilot was reported to have stated that the retreating Iraqis had fixed white flags to their tanks and were riding with turrets open but were bombed because allied rules of engagement required the pilots to bomb the tanks unless the soldiers had abandoned them.[42]

Bob Drogin of the *Los Angeles Times* reported:

> Here, on a forgotten road hit by allied air strikes Iraqi military units sit in gruesome repose, as scorched skeletons of vehicles and men alike, black and

awful under the sun. For 60 miles ... hundreds of Iraqi tanks and armoured cars, howitzers and anti-aircraft guns, ammunition trucks and ambulances are strafed, smashed and burned beyond belief.

'Most were retreating', Drogin notes, from the 'fast approaching allied blitzkrieg'. 'At one spot, snarling wild dogs have reduced two corpses to bare ribs'; 'giant carrion birds claw and pick at another' whilst men's 'hair and clothes are burned off, skin incinerated by the heat'. 'The grim reality of war', Drogin states, 'is a horror to behold'.[43]

Michael Kelly also witnessed the scene, noting that for 50 to 60 miles 'the road was littered with exploded and roasted vehicles, charred and blown-up bodies' whilst at Mutla Ridge the US marines had 'cut to shreds' vehicles and soldiers 'trapped in a two-mile nightmare traffic jam'. 'Nine men in a flat-sided supply truck were killed and flash-burned so swiftly that they remained naked – skinned and black wrecks in the vulnerable positions of the moment of first impact'. 'Another man had been butterflied' by a bomb; 'the cavity of his body was cut wide open and his intestines and such were still coiled in their proper places, but cooked to ebony'.[44]

The *Guardian* reported that: 'The allied bombing of Iraqi troops retreating from Kuwait at the end of the Gulf war was a military decision which the [British] government fully agreed with.' 'It was very important indeed that they should not succeed in escaping', Defence Secretary Tom King stated.[45]

Another method of killing was the use of earthmovers and ploughs mounted on tanks, which resulted in the burial alive of thousands of Iraqi soldiers along 70 miles of trenches. 'Not a single American was killed during the attack,' a US *Newsday* reporter noted, and 'every American in the assault was inside armoured vehicles, impervious to Iraqi small-arms fire'.[46] *Independent* journalist Robert Fisk noted that 'US and British units participated in thousands of hasty burials in the desert'. Six months after the end of the war 'allied' forces had failed to provide 'even the vaguest statistics of the Iraqi death toll', in violation of the Geneva Convention, all of whose basic rules on the matter 'the Gulf war allies appear to have ignored'.[47]

The most exhaustive study of the effects of the conflict on civilians is perhaps that by the US human rights organisation Middle East Watch (MEW); it is therefore worth citing in some detail.[48] In its summary, MEW states that 'allied aircraft bombed wherever and whenever they wanted' in what 'quickly became a rout'. It notes that despite the 'exceptional opportunity to conduct the allied bombing campaign in strict compliance with the legal duty to take all feasible precautions to avoid civilian harm, we find that the actual conduct of the war fell short of this obligation in several significant respects'. This divergence emerged 'both in the choice of the means and methods to prosecute the air war and in the selection of targets for attack'. 'In some instances', therefore, the 'coalition forces appear to have violated the laws of war'. For example, despite having the technological ability to conduct aerial attacks at night – to reduce civilian casualties – 'in several attacks in urban areas, allied planes dropped their bombs during the day, needlessly killing hundreds'. MEW notes that an RAF Tornado squadron leader 'who bombed a suspension bridge ... admitted that the bridge was in the centre of a populated area and that his aircraft dropped its laser bombs in the morning. "Yes, there will be civilian traffic", the pilot said, purporting to justify the daytime attack by speculating, "but they could well be civilian contractors working on an airfield".'

Regarding 'incidents in which civilian vehicles were attacked on Iraqi highways', MEW states that 'even if it is assumed that these civilian vehicles were not deliberately targeted, these allied attacks appear to have been indiscriminate, in that they failed to distinguish between military and civilian objects'. MEW continues by noting that 'numerous witnesses described incidents in which civilian structures, most typically houses in residential areas they lived in or knew well, were destroyed or damaged in areas where they believed there were no conceivable military installations or facilities nearby, including anti-aircraft artillery'. 'These accounts', MEW states, 'suggest that some civilian casualties during the war were not the product of inaccurate bombing – mere misses – but of attacks that, pending convincing justification from the allies, appear to have been indiscriminate.' Interestingly, the report declares that 'Basra, which was largely off-limits to foreign reporters during the air war, appears to have suffered considerably more damage to civilian structures than Baghdad, where a small international press force was present.'

MEW also considers the bombing of Iraqi food warehouses, other agriculture-related facilities and the electricity system – which was almost completely destroyed – and on which Iraq was reliant for essential services such as water purification, sewage removal and treatment, the operation of hospitals and agricultural production. The 'consequences of denying almost the entire civilian population of an energy-dependent country an essential service such as electricity are grave indeed', the report states. Sewage treatment stations were brought to a virtual standstill and water treatment plants were rendered inoperable, a situation made even worse 'by the destruction of the factories that had produced the chemicals used to purify water'. MEW dismisses the allies' self-exoneration:

> The apparent justification for attacking almost the entire electrical system in Iraq was that the system functioned as an integrated grid, meaning that power could be shifted countrywide, including to military functions such as command-and-control centres and weapons-manufacturing facilities. But these key military targets were attacked in the opening days of the war. The direct attacks by the allies on these military targets should have obviated the need simultaneously to destroy the fixed power sources thought to have formerly supplied them. If

these and other purely military targets could be attacked at will, then arguably the principle of humanity would make the wholesale destruction of Iraq's electrical-generating capability superfluous to the accomplishment of legitimate military objectives.

The message is clear: if you mess with the powerful, you will be destroyed, along with your children and any other defenceless unpeople who happen to get in the way of the maintenance of 'international order'. A vile regime led by a gangster and murderer in the shape of Saddam Hussein (an ally of the West prior to August 1990) is an easy touch, having chosen a target for aggression – oil – that, by definition, the West and its allies have the right to control.

The Western quest for continuing control over Middle Eastern oil has little to do with security. If economic security were the real issue, clear policy alternatives are available. Michael Shuman of Washington's Institute for Policy Studies notes that 'greater energy efficiency could enable the United States to reduce its dependence on foreign oil supplies and the associated military risks of the Persian Gulf'. He states further that 'before the United States sent its troops to Saudi Arabia, it was calculated that investing *a single year's* budget for the Rapid Deployment Force in efficiency improvements could eliminate the United States' need for Middle East oil, as well as the risks posed by the force itself'. Shuman continues by stating:

> Looked at another way, had the United States invested as much as a quarter of the price it is paying for the war against Iraq on energy savings, the country could have permanently unplugged itself from Persian Gulf oil. Just increasing the efficiency of American cars by three miles per gallon could replace all US oil imports from Iraq and Kuwait.[49]

One would be hard pushed to find discussion of such a way of eliminating dependence on imported oil in the massive number of academic and other studies concerning the 'defence' of Western 'security interests' in the Middle East. Serious scholars must concern themselves with the logistics of military intervention to secure the oilfields, the need to maintain in power the friendly ruling families in the Gulf and the dangers to Western access to oil posed by Islamic fundamentalists. This latter mode of thinking appears to have certain advantages. Control over the world's oil supplies is a significant lever for control of the international economy. By adopting greater self-sufficiency, the rationale to assure that control – intervention to protect vital Western interests – is lost. Military planning is therefore the preferred option, sacrificing the possibility of energy security – in the real sense of the term – at home.

The ease with which brute violence was effected depended on two factors. The first was the necessary avoidance of a diplomatic, peaceful solution to the crisis, which would have precluded the US display of military might and threatened its ability to impose its own order on the crucial region. The second – in relation to Britain – was the ability of the British propaganda system to confine discussion of the crisis and the results of the war to that required by state ideology, thus implicitly helping to garner the acquiescence or support of the population for British policy. This crucial element will therefore be considered in some detail below.

On the first point, from the beginning the United States and Britain ruled out the possibility of negotiations and a diplomatic settlement of the Kuwait crisis. This was made plain at several stages in the crisis before the war began, the world being required to accept that the commitment to reverse this aggression was complete, non-negotiable and deserving of no 'linkage' with other issues or 'rewarding' of Saddam Hussein. This position was virtually unique. After Israel had invaded Lebanon in 1982, killing around 20,000 people in the process, the Western response was one of acquiescence and continuing contact and dialogue with the aggressor state (and, in the case of the United States, the continuing provision of arms to Israel and subsidy of the Israeli economy). After the South African invasion and occupation of Angola, and the virtual destruction of that country as well as Mozambique through sponsorship of terrorism in the 1970s and 1980s, the West pursued a policy of 'constructive engagement' (linkage) with Pretoria, ostensibly to encourage it to mend its ways.

In the case of Iraq, however, the press reported that 'Britain will not support negotiations with President Saddam Hussein until he has withdrawn from Kuwait': Thatcher stated, three weeks after the invasion of Kuwait in August 1990, that it was 'most unlikely' that a negotiated solution to the Gulf crisis could be found.[50] At the end of August, diplomatic efforts by the UN Secretary-General and Jordan's King Hussein were 'premature' in the UK view, with Washington also believing 'the time is not ripe for such initiatives'.[51] A month after the invasion, the press reported that Foreign Secretary Douglas Hurd had made clear that 'any further political initiatives to solve the Iraqi crisis would not be welcomed'; Hurd himself said that there was 'no room in the immediate future for some speculative political initiative'.[52] In December 1990, John Major stated that there could be 'no question of negotiations, concessions, partial solutions or linkage to other issues'.[53] This position continued until the outbreak of war in January, with Major noting a week before that 'there would be no negotiations and nothing to be gained by Saddam Hussein if he attempted to negotiate'.[54]

The press followed suit. According to *The Times*, any talks 'must not … develop into negotiating postures of give-and-take' and Saddam must capitulate completely 'on terms sufficiently humiliating to put paid to his claims to pan-Arab leadership and cripple his military might'.[55] Shortly before the outbreak of war, *The Times* declared that 'unless he leaves with George Bush's blessing, even the best European diplomat is likely to do more harm than good' in negotiations.[56] The *Daily Telegraph* expressed the dilemma succinctly: 'The most difficult decisions could come for President Bush if Saddam ... announced a willingness to withdraw from Kuwait,' the editors wrote with no detectable embarrassment. 'If the restoration of the emirate were achieved, most world opinion would undoubtedly become strongly hostile to armed action against Iraq in pursuit of further objectives.' The United States would then be confronted with 'an immensely taxing dilemma' as to whether US forces could step down from a war footing with Iraq's nuclear and chemical weapons remaining 'intact and capable of future enhancement'.[57] On this reasoning, the idea that the war was fought for the grand principle of reversing aggression and upholding a state's sovereignty can already be safely dispensed with.

At the same time as reporting that the leaders of the 'coalition' were bent on avoiding negotiations, and themselves concurring with this stance, editors could simultaneously comment that the same leaders were seeking a peaceful outcome to the crisis. Thus, for example, the *Daily Telegraph* noted that 'President Bush and his allies must be right to explore every peaceful possibility of forcing Saddam's withdrawal, before resorting to direct action'.[58] Similarly, as the 15 January 'deadline' approached, *Financial Times* editors observed that 'the Americans ... are right to go on trying to reach a peaceful settlement before the UN deadline runs out', at a time when US leaders barely concealed their contempt for others' efforts – by the EC and the Soviet Union, for example – to reach a peaceful settlement through negotiation.[59]

In fact, there may have been a few slim opportunities to reach a negotiated settlement to the crisis, but these were barely (if at all) reported by the British press and dismissed by the US government. In an offer delivered to the United States on 23 August 1990, for example – and reported in the US newspaper *Newsday* – Iraq stated its willingness to withdraw from Kuwait and allow foreigners to leave the country in return for a lifting of economic sanctions, Iraq's gaining 'guaranteed access' to the Gulf through the Kuwaiti islands of Bubiyan and Warbah, and its gaining of full control of the Rumailah oilfield extending slightly into Kuwaiti territory. One Bush administration official specialising in the Middle East stated that 'the terms of the proposal are serious' and described the package as 'negotiable'. According to *Newsday* reporter Knut Royce, this proposal came 'as some [US] government officials now say that they see some hope of a negotiated settlement'.[60]

A further Iraqi proposal was relayed to US officials on 2 January 1991 and reported in *Newsday* the following day. Iraq offered to withdraw from Kuwait if the USA pledged not to attack soldiers as they pulled out, if foreign troops left the region and if there were agreement on the Palestine problem and on the banning of all weapons of mass destruction in the region. A State Department Middle East expert described the proposal as a 'serious prenegotiation position' and other US officials called it 'interesting' since, in the reporter's words, 'it drops previous claims to two Kuwaiti islands and a portion of the oil field, and because it signals Iraqi interest in a negotiated settlement'.[61]

The British press ran a different story. The *Daily Telegraph* noted in October 1990 that 'Saddam shows not the slightest sign of acceding to the essential terms – Iraq's withdrawal from the whole of Kuwait, reinstatement of the previous regime and the release of all hostages'.[62] *The Times* concurred the following month, stating that 'Saddam has said absolutely nothing to indicate that he is prepared to yield one millimetre of Kuwaiti territory, never mind withdraw unconditionally'.[63] The *Independent* reached a similar conclusion, noting that 'at no stage of the crisis has President Saddam indicated a readiness to pull out of Kuwait, except on terms that would, by linking such a move to Israel's withdrawal from the occupied territories, make him a hero to most Arabs'.[64] This stance continued into the new year and the approach of the coalition 'deadline'. Two weeks after the disclosure of the second Iraqi offer noted above, the *Daily Telegraph* observed that 'the opportunities of diplomacy have been fully explored' and *The Times* claimed that Saddam 'has not indicated to any emissary that he has any intention of giving up Kuwait'.[65]

Academic studies have tended to reinforce this version of history. In a study for the International Institute for Strategic Studies (IISS), for example, Roland Dannreuther notes that 'at no time did Iraq give any indication that it might reverse its annexation of Kuwait'.[66] The IISS annual review of world affairs for 1990–91 states correctly that Iraq sought to create conditions to allow it to withdraw from Kuwait under a face-saving formula, but alleges that 'this meant continual emphasis on the "linkage" between the issues of Kuwait and Palestine'.[67]

The propaganda system in action II

The major achievements of the propaganda system during the crisis were, however, to elevate US–UK actions to grand principle, to suppress the gruesome reality of the slaughter, and to frame the relevant issues according to precepts acceptable to the state. Consider first the outrage expressed over Iraq's invasion of Kuwait, an event surely worthy of unreserved condemnation from any civilised quarter. *The Times* (surely correctly) noted that 'the world's disgust should be expressed in the strongest terms' and called for 'a worldwide expression of anger at a small nation's sovereignty rudely shattered by brute force'. 'Iraq should be treated as a pariah, deprived of all diplomatic and economic contact and assistance,' the newspaper continued.[68] Elsewhere, *The Times* declared that Iraq's vile act of taking hostages 'is a crime under international law' and that this 'is not a nicety to be pored over by diplomats, but a fact on which the deterrence of inhuman and unlawful conduct depends'.[69] All the newspapers reasoned similarly, the *Daily Telegraph* arguing that the invasion was an 'intolerable challenge to international order'.[70] Later, the *Financial Times* commented that 'Iraq committed a blatant act of aggression' and added that 'it was the first such major act in the post cold war age'.[71]

But only the first of these two statements was true, since in December 1989, just eight months before Iraq's invasion of Kuwait, the United States had invaded Panama with 26,000 troops; it was the biggest US military operation since the Vietnam War, and resulted in at least 2,000 Panamanian deaths. The invasion was in clear violation of international law and the charters of the United Nations, the Rio Treaty and the Organisation of American States (OAS), to all of which the United States was a signatory. The invasion was subsequently condemned at the United Nations by 75 votes to 20 with 40 abstentions, and by the OAS by 20 votes to 1, the lone dissenter being the USA. British Foreign Secretary Hurd stated that Britain 'fully support[ed] the American action'.[72]

The newspapers under analysis reacted to this particular violation of international law and invasion of one state by another in a slightly different way than they were to respond to the Iraqi invasion eight months later. According to *The Times*, President Bush took a 'difficult, but correct decision' in ordering US troops into Panama, which it described as a 'necessary action'; Washington's only fault lay in 'having failed to act earlier'. The editorial on the day after the invasion provided justifications for the US pretexts for the invasion, somewhat in contrast to the paper's later contention in the case of Iraq that violating international law was a crime and 'not a nicety to be pored over by diplomats'.[73] The *Daily Telegraph* noted that 'there can be no real argument over the central question of the morality or desirability of taking action' and described as 'humbug' the claims of international lawyers that there was no legal pretext for the US invasion.[74] The *Independent* adopted a different approach, arguing – falsely – that the US action was legal since Noriega had declared war on the United States, but suggesting that 'not every action ... that is legal, understandable and effective in the short term proves ultimately to be wise'.[75] The *Financial Times* (which later seemed to have developed amnesia in respect of the invasion) correctly noted, by contrast to the *Independent*, that it constituted a violation of international law and condemned it as opposing 'the standards of behaviour which should govern relations between states'.[76]

Thus two of the quality newspapers under analysis supported the US violation of international law regarding Panama, one could not recognise its illegality but thought it unwise (yet 'understandable') and only one both recognised its illegality and condemned it.

The evident outrage over Iraq's invasion of Kuwait was consistently explained by portraying Iraqi aggression as a violation of sacred principles. More honest appreciations of the threat posed by the invasion were occasionally forthcoming, however. *The Times* explained that 'the horror of Kuwait' lay not so much in the 'totality of the conquest' as in 'the implication of that conquest for a dozen states in an economically crucial region of the world'. Therefore, 'there must be an overriding international concern that such aggression should not triumph'.[77] The *Financial Times* explained that 'from the British point of view, Kuwait has been one of the most important customers of the City of London'.[78] Similarly, the Director-General of the Middle East Association noted that the Gulf states had been 'good friends to the West', adding that their 'political, economic and commercial policies have been helpful to us', to the extent that we have an 'obligation produced by mutual benefit in the past'.[79] Kuwait's previous benefaction towards Britain has been briefly discussed in Chapter 4.

The Western democracies, and particularly the United States and Britain, who played the leading roles in the crisis, were faced with a fundamental dilemma: killing large numbers of people and destroying another state cannot properly be justified in terms of access to oil, 'strategic interests' or the balance of power. Garnering public acquiescence in, or support for, modern-day slaughter requires a grand principle as pretext. This dilemma was addressed by British academic Michael Howard, Professor of Modern History at Yale, who stated that the 'preservation of a stable political balance, the protection of friendly powers, the pre-emption of a hostile hegemony and the assurance of continued access on reasonable terms' to oil were all 'perfectly valid reasons for going to war'. However, these reasons would be 'hardly enough to command the unanimous support of the global community' and 'they would not be universally accepted as adequate reasons for war even within our own societies'. Rather, 'significant elements of the American and British peoples today demand a higher moral justification for killing people'. And 'sometimes the most peace-loving of statesmen feel compelled to go to war', something which, Howard predicted, 'the President may have to do' 'before the end of the year'.[80] The peace-loving US President came to the rescue and officially announced the moral justification for killing people: the 'new world order'.

Thus the world was poised on the fringe of a new era in which the rule of law would replace the law of the jungle and where the United States would lead the world into a new era of international cooperation, with the international community's response to the Iraqi aggression being 'the first political test of how the post-Cold War world will work'.[81]

The grand principle of standing up to aggression for the sake of a 'new world order' thus became the official truth and required reasoning. Prime Minister Thatcher explained in September 1990 that 'the real reason' Britain had sent troops to the Gulf 'was to make it quite clear that in the end of this 20th century you cannot sit back when someone invades another country and takes it by force. If you do that there's no international law, no country is safe. That was the fundamental point of principle.' Thatcher continued by saying that 'there is of course a secondary one, that the majority of the world's reserves of oil are in the Middle East'. But Britain had reacted 'not to the oil factor but to the point of principle'. So principled was the British position that, Thatcher stated, 'you do not negotiate about resolutions of the United Nations'.[82] 'If Iraq's aggression were allowed to succeed', Thatcher continued in the House of Commons, 'no small state could ever feel safe again'[83]; her Foreign Office Minister, William Waldegrave, asserted that 'we cannot allow the forces of international law to be faced down'.[84]

When Major succeeded Thatcher as Prime Minister, Britain's commitment to grand principle remained unchanged. On the eve of the war Major noted that 'the principles at stake are crucial and we must uphold them'. If Saddam was to 'get away with his aggression and gain from it, other small countries in the vicinity, and those elsewhere in the world with large and potentially aggressive neighbours, will all too likely face similar problems and similar dangers'. Yet the 'overriding point' was that progress had recently been made towards establishing 'a more peaceful world in which there is greater respect for the United Nations and its resolutions'; but 'all our hopes for that would fall away if we were to allow Saddam Hussein to get away with swallowing up Kuwait'. Therefore, 'if we are to have that safe world, we must demonstrate conclusively that aggression cannot succeed'.[85]

Press commentators reacted with the appropriate solemnity. The editors of the *Independent* commented that 'it is not just the future of a small state, Kuwait, that is at stake, or the power of the one of the world's most ruthless dictators, but the basis of the future world order'.[86] Peter Jenkins, writing in the *Independent*, noted that oil and the 'commitment to Israel' give the US 'strong interests in the Middle East' but 'over and above' these 'we may be seeing a revival of American idealism, another consequence of the ending of that dirty zero-sum game called the Cold War'. Referring to the 'political freedom' recently achieved in Eastern Europe, Jenkins commented that 'the idea that once inspired American foreign policy, so corrupted by the Cold War, becomes relevant once more to the best hopes of mankind' and 'today we have the makings of a new era of cooperation'.[87] *Financial Times* writer Michael Prowse, even after highlighting Western hypocrisy over the major principle, summed up the required position, by noting that:

> The single most important justification for the US hard line has been to deter future acts of aggression. With the Cold War over, President Bush rightly wants to create a 'new world order' in which weak nations need not fear their stronger neighbours. He is prepared to risk sacrifices today in order to protect future generations.[88]

That the official position was merely laughable was not recognised by the overwhelming majority of media and academic commentators. In the huge majority of cases, commentators failed to point out that previous US and British stances towards acts of aggression were not altogether supportive of the now-proclaimed inviolable principle. It thus took real devotion not to note Western acquiescence in or support for the Turkish invasion of Cyprus, the Indonesian invasion of East Timor, Morocco's takeover of the Western Sahara, South Africa's invasion of Angola, Somalia's invasion of Ethiopia, Israel's invasion of Lebanon etcetera, not to mention Western states' own acts of aggression. Or to ridicule the notion of the United States – a systematic violator of international law, as the historical record shows – leading the crusade to uphold the principle of international law. Rather, commentators added their weight to the state's pretext for war and thereby, one might reasonably suggest, shared in the responsibility for the violence undertaken in the name of that principle. 'World order would suffer if aggression went unchallenged,' Independent editors noted.[89] 'Failure' to act against Iraq, a Daily Telegraph editorial observed, would 'encourage tyrants the world over to prey on weaker neighbours'; surely not a major theme of the postwar world.[90] A Times editorial stated that 'the cause in Kuwait is simple on a world scale, the defence of the weak against aggression by the strong'.[91] The Professor of War Studies at King's College, London, Lawrence Freedman, also noted that 'this is not a one-off trial of will but a test case for those who believe international law is central to world order'.[92]

The fact that there was a history of 'strong' nations intervening in or obliterating 'weak' nations posed few intellectual dilemmas. The Daily Telegraph commented that 'developing countries have recognised the threat which the invasion of Kuwait poses to the creation of a new world order where militarily weak countries will be prey to stronger tyrants'; it was, surely, a notion already understood by countries such as Grenada, Nicaragua, Cuba, Iran, Guiana and others.[93] The newspaper's editorial writers continued elsewhere by stating that 'small, vulnerable nations understand more clearly than ourselves the consequences for their own safety if Saddam's act of aggression is allowed to stand'.[94] An Independent editorial similarly noted the sudden conversion of Britain and the United States to the new role of protecting the interests of small states, stating that 'around the world small nations have realised what it would mean for their own existence if President Saddam were allowed to get away with his act of aggression' – presumably having been oblivious to such concerns before.[95]

The Financial Times explained just after the beginning of the war that it 'came about not because of US hubris and imperialism, or because of oil, or because a handful of feudal Arabian princes demanded it'. Rather, 'it happened because the annexation of Kuwait was an act intolerable to a world which cannot live in peace if the integrity of nations is treated so casually'.[96] And now the West has to 'convince the Arab peoples' that 'the war is being fought – as it is – above all for *their* security'; no small task indeed.[97] *The Times* commented that 'Britain's willingness to wage war in the Gulf is based not only on calculations of national interest' but on the understanding that it is 'necessary to protect civilised values'.[98] Indeed, *Financial Times* editors declared, Britain's role in the war 'reflected its sense of 20th-century history' since 'the British know in their bones that aggressors must not be appeased'.[99]

In a genuinely independent press, one might have expected an open and honest discussion of past Western acts of aggression and intervention and an exposition of the inherent hypocrisy of Western state leaders suddenly saying they would abide by the principle of standing up to aggression. In the huge majority of discussions of the crisis, however, the somewhat wayward past position of the Western states on this matter was simply ignored. But the fact was so obvious as necessarily to merit some attention and therefore needed to be finessed. On the few occasions when past Western acts of aggression were considered, therefore, they received considerable ideological treatment.

Thus the *Daily Telegraph*'s Robert Harvey addressed the issue of Britain's invasion of Egypt in 1956. 'It remains the conventional wisdom that the Americans [who in opposing the invasion and effectively forcing Britain to withdraw] were moral and right,' Harvey notes, 'yet history may deliver a different judgement'. History 'may distinguish between "bad" colonialism – the over exploitation, usually by commercial interests, of resources and labour in the colonies; and "good" colonialism – the attempt to regulate the commerce and social organisation of the peoples affected, and defend them'. Thus the invasion of Egypt is presumably of the former variety: incomparable with the present invasion, as a matter of principle.[100]

Freedman explained that some challenges to the rule prohibiting 'unprovoked aggression against a small neighbour' are 'often ambiguous or geographically self-contained, and do not touch the material interests of other states'. Perhaps he had Panama in mind. However, 'international dramas occur when unambiguous challenges are made in strategically important areas of the world' such as in the case of Iraq's invasion of Kuwait.[101] Elsewhere, he expanded on the differences between the Kuwait crisis and the Vietnam War. 'There are no obvious similarities between the Vietnam war and the Gulf crisis – not in political cause, geographic conditions or historical context', he noted. 'Two differences', Freedman continues, 'are fundamental.' 'First, in Vietnam the United States was intervening in a civil war and its side lacked a popular base'; thus repeating the crucial myth that this was not a war against Vietnam as a whole but a 'civil war'. Freedman goes on to state that the United States could not 'convincingly' demonstrate that the war 'was the result of aggression by one state against another – the North versus the South', but in the Gulf 'there is no doubt that it is confronting a blatant case of aggression'. The second difference was that with Vietnam the 'international community was generally sceptical, to say the least, of the way the war was both justified and prosecuted, whereas in the Gulf the United States is part of a remarkable United Nations consensus'. In fact, during the Vietnam War the majority in the 'international community' (with some important exceptions like Britain) were decidedly appalled at the conduct of the war and utterly condemned it, rather than being 'sceptical, to say the least'. But even this is by the by. There is indeed an 'obvious similarity' between the Vietnam War and the Gulf crisis: both Vietnam and Kuwait were the objects of aggression. In the former, the USA was the aggressor state, eventually pummelling Vietnam (and Cambodia) almost out of existence. In the latter, Iraq was the aggressor state, invading and terrorising Kuwait. The 'similarity' is quite obvious but could not be noted by one of Britain's leading academics.[102]

The *Independent* in its editorials also attempted to explain why the government's position of standing up to this particular act of aggression was perfectly consistent with not standing up to other acts of aggression. 'If a principle is involved,' the editors asked, 'why did the West or the UN not try to reverse Israel's occupation of the West Bank and adjacent territories, India's annexation of Goa, or China's brutal conquest of Tibet?' The truthful answer is that the United States consistently vetoed UN attempts to reverse Israel's occupation of neighbouring lands, whilst it and other Western states cared little about the other two acts of aggression because their 'interests' were not threatened. Yet the *Independent* editors offer three different reasons.

First, 'the Cold War made any such confrontation a threat to world peace'. This allegedly was the reason why the United States did not try to reverse Israel's occupation of Arab lands, even though the Soviet Union had consistently advocated Israeli withdrawal. The second reason was that 'the seizure and destruction of Kuwait was a particularly clear-cut crime against the international order'. This is correct if 'international order' is understood to mean that as defined by Western interests; actions against Goa, Tibet and the occupied territories do not figure since they failed to upset the international order, like the invasion of Panama and the aggression against Nicaragua, even though they were also clear-cut crimes in international law. Third, 'in the case of Israel, persistent threats of destruction from neighbouring Arab states partially justified the occupation, if not Israel's subsequent treatment of the resident populations'. Thus the fact that Israel's action is in violation of international law and repeated UN calls for withdrawal, calls supported by virtually the entire world with the exception of the United States, is not sufficient to obviate justification for the occupation. By the same reasoning, any state could plead 'security interests' as a pretext for aggression (and indeed it is a frequent pretext, in fact, for Western aggression, as in the bombing of Libya and the attack on Nicaragua, to name but two cases).[103]

Later academic studies provided further ideological support for the 'principled' stand against aggression. For example, two leading academics from King's College, London write in their major study of the Gulf conflict that 'there seems little doubt that Bush was influenced most of all by the need to uphold the principle of non-aggression'. President Bush was a 'crusader' for 'the cause of international norms of decency' and the issue arose of 'the West's face – of being seen to acquiesce in something condemned as contrary to the most elementary principles of international law'. The authors do note at one point that Western 'opposition to aggression tended to be extremely selective' and cite the examples of Turkey in Cyprus, Indonesia in East Timor and Israel in the occupied territories. However, they explain the principled stance against Iraq by noting that 'past appeasement provided no grounds against taking on a dictator when the nature of his regime became impossible to ignore'. The West's 'past over-indulgence of Saddam Hussein ... was no reason to continue the practice'. The authors fail to mention the US violation of international law in invading Panama and suggest that President Bush's 'world view' had been forged by the failure of appeasement in stopping Hitler and 'the consequent need to uphold international law in the face of aggression'. This principled stance was matched by Britain since 'as a former imperial power' there was a 'natural tendency towards globalism in British foreign policy'. 'This', the authors note, 'made it responsive to challenges to international order. A readiness to take on aggression was an important part of the national self-image.' This tendency was 'further reinforced by a reasonable record in military interventions'. Prime Minister Thatcher thus 'saw this crisis – as so many others – first and foremost as a matter of principle'.[104]

With such servility on the part of 'independent' commentators, state leaders had little need to fear that reporting of the actual fighting would stray into the realms of the unacceptable. The government-imposed 'media blackout' was not itself responsible for ensuring that reporting took place along guidelines acceptable to those conducting the carnage; the media effectively followed state directives from the beginning, whether there was official censorship or not. The BBC reportedly told its broadcasters to be 'circumspect' about pictures of death and injury,[105] whilst scenes of human casualties amounted to 3 per cent of all news coverage on television. The issue of oil featured in 4 per cent of BBC1's reports, 3 per cent of BBC2's and 5 per cent of Channel 4's.[106] The fiction that this was a 'clean war' with 'surgical strikes' and 'precision bombing', little 'collateral damage' with mass bombardment intended to 'soften up' the enemy and 'knock out' military installations, and that the majority of explosives were 'smart bombs' was duly parroted from the beginning with few attempts to seek out the reality of the violence.[107] *The Times* could, for example, note the 'devastating vindication of the capacity of modern technology applied to air power to offer the military precision traditionally associated only with ground troops'.[108] The *Daily Telegraph* similarly noted the official assertion that the aerial bombing attained 'extraordinary levels of accuracy', adding that the 'destructiveness of the projectiles remains sometimes uncertain'.[109] It noted at one stage that a Pentagon war briefing 'was one of the most impressive expositions of its kind in recent military memory' as US Defence Secretary Richard Cheney and Chairman of the Joint Chiefs of Staff Colin Powell continued the highly effective propaganda campaign to obscure the horrors of the destruction. 'The two men were as confident, balanced, lucid and frank as military secrecy could allow them to be,' the editors added.[110]

That the claims of 'pinpoint accuracy' and other such crude propaganda assertions could have been exposed as fiction is highlighted by a report that appeared in *The Times* on 3 July 1990, six months before the war was launched against Iraq. The article was headlined 'US report highlights failures in Panama' and opened thus: 'Six months after the American invasion of Panama, Washington is looking foolish over the claims it made about the role of Stealth aircraft,' The article then noted:

> A senior air force general knew one bomb missed its target by up to 160 yards but kept silent while Richard Cheney, the US Defence Secretary, boasted to the media about the aircraft's 'pinpoint accuracy'. ... The report further tarnishes the perfect image of the invasion initially painted by the Bush Administration.

Six months later, the media preferred to ignore such a precedent in the latest round of 'pinpoint accuracy' bombing.[111]

When the story of the massacre of retreating Iraqi forces (noted above) broke, it also received considerable ideological treatment. Consider the *Times* version, for example. The massacre at Mutla Ridge, its defence correspondent noted, was one of the 'controversial incidents' of the war and a 'horrific reminder of the consequences of war'. 'Mutla Ridge', the article continues, 'was one of the reasons for President Bush's decision to stop the war when he did', under pressure from the US military to continue it. 'But a visit to Mutla Ridge explains everything' about the Bush decision. The article thus begins by commending the US President. It then proceeds – asking, was the carnage 'justified'? – to lend credence to the official view that the retreating Iraqi soldiers represented a military threat to US forces. Thus 'the convoy moving out of Kuwait City appeared to represent a potential threat'.

> The fleeing Iraqis, armed with guns, as well as stolen merchandise, could have inflicted casualties as they came up against allied units which had swept across Kuwait and southern Iraq. That was the justification for attacking them, even

though they appeared to be following thousands of their colleagues in trying to escape the battlefield.

The report ends by noting that the Iraqis were in fact 'trapped and capable of nothing but surrender' and that 'it was the final "turkey shoot" of the war, and, in retrospect, unwarranted. Further carnage would have been politically unsupportable and terrible publicity. President Bush knew it.' Thus, even though the final position is that it was 'unwarranted', the massacre is the subject of considerable ideological treatment, with its horror mitigated by Bush's magnanimity and the possibility that it was militarily necessary; in sum, it invited few if any moral qualms.[112]

Similarly, consider the following article by Michael Dewar, deputy director of the International Institute for Strategic Studies, one of Britain's leading 'independent' research institutes. On the subject of the 'turkey shoot', the judgement that it was an 'unwarranted and immoral act of carnage on a demoralised and routed force that posed no serious threat to the coalition', Dewar notes, 'is easy to make in hindsight and takes little account of the conditions and realities of war'. Dewar provides a frightening apologia for slaughter. The 'most important' reason why it is 'naive to criticise either Schwarzkopf or Bush for the slaughter' is that 'emotions are heightened in battle. Adrenalin is flowing fast. American pilots flying over Mutla Ridge were in a state of high excitement. They were winning.' Dewar then quotes Napoleon and observes that 'it is in the nature of a retreat that casualties will always be high'. He further states, interestingly, that 'there was essentially no difference' between the slaughter at Mutla Ridge and 'that which took place further north and west in the Iraqi desert' during the US and British pursuit of the Republican Guard, 'except, perhaps, that it was less visible to the media'. He concludes: '... much of the pious comment about Mutla Ridge shows a complete lack of understanding of the realities of battle. The lesson must be: leave the prosecution of war to the generals and the fashioning of the peace to the politicians.'[113]

Iraq was defeated 'decisively and rapidly', as US national security strategy, noted above, demanded. The British Minister of Defence Procurement observed after the war that 'absolutely overwhelming force produces results very fast'.[114] The level of destruction used appeared to pose no moral dilemmas; in fact it was often precisely called for. The *Daily Telegraph*'s Robert Harvey observed that Iraqi aggression and terror against Kuwait 'provides black-and-white justification for employing the devastating military superiority of the West to throw the invader out'. However, there are 'longer term considerations which render the equation more complex', like the fact that 'a dismembered Iraq is not in the West's interests'. The country could be justly pummelled back into the previous century, that is, but it might not be in our strategic interests.[115] The *Independent* noted that 'presumably, military victory would be quicker and cheaper if nuclear weapons were used', but 'politically, the result' would be 'disastrous'.[116] The *Daily Telegraph*'s editor, Max Hastings, quoted from Lord Fisher, a former First Sea Lord, as stating that 'moderation in war is imbecility'. 'Most of us will answer', Hastings continued, 'that, *failing some absolute catastrophe on the battlefield*, the moral and political cost of employing nuclear weapons seems intolerable'; presumably, then, if Britain were really losing, it could justifiably launch a nuclear strike. Against Iraqi forces in the open desert, however, 'no tactical scruples are necessary' and 'the allied armed forces can set about fulfilling Fisher's dictum without qualification'. What is now demanded from our military commanders is 'a commitment without sensitivity or reservation' and a 'killer instinct on the battlefield', something which 'many German commanders' in the Second World War possessed.[117]

The Gulf War became a 'famous military victory' (*The Times*), 'an extraordinary military achievement' (*Financial Times*) and 'an extraordinary triumph' (*Daily Telegraph*).[118] The Queen knighted US military commander Norman Schwarzkopf, whilst Britain's own military commander, General Peter de la Billiere, soon left the army and joined a City bank where, its chief executive noted, 'his knowledge and experience of the Arabian peninsula at the highest levels will greatly enhance our profile in the region'.[119] Once the conflict was over, and the media (and later, academia) had played their legitimising role, all pretence to the grand principle that justified the slaughter could be dispensed with, just as it had been before. Soon, with evident parallels to the Gulf crisis, Serbia sought to carve up and destroy Bosnia, which was recognised as an independent state; but Serbia's actions elicited no British government rhetoric in favour of mobilising all necessary means to combat this particular act of aggression.

Notes

1. See, for example, the various articles in International Institute for Strategic Studies, (IIIS) *New dimensions in international security: Part 1*, Adelphi Paper 265, IISS, London, 1992.

2. See, for example, Edward Mortimer, *European security after the Cold War*, Adelphi Paper 271, IISS, London, 1992.

3. John Weeks and Phil Gunson, *Panama: Made in the USA*, LAB, London, 1991, pp. 13–14.

4. Richard Gott, 'Nations divided by a lost vision', *Guardian*, 28 August 1993.

5. Francis Fukuyama, 'Bush's global backyard', *Guardian*, 9 September 1992.

6. Great Britain, Foreign and Commonwealth Office, *Table of vetoed draft resolutions in the United Nations Security Council, 1946–87*, Foreign Policy Document No. 183, January 1988.

7. Patrick Tyler, 'Pentagon's new world order: US to reign supreme', *International Herald Tribune*, 9 March 1992; Barton Gellman, 'How to stay top nation', *Washington Post*, reprinted in *Guardian Weekly*, 22 March 1992; Martin Fletcher, 'US relaxes "globo-cop" stance', *The Times*, 25 May 1992.

8. United States Information Service, European Wireless File, News Alert, 'Eagleburger sees free trading order as top US goal', 3 October 1991.

9. Bernard Aronson, 'US policy and funding priorities in Latin America and the Caribbean for FY 1992', *US Department of State Dispatch*, Vol. 2, No. 11, 18 March 1991, p. 187.

10. United States Information Service, European Wireless File, News Alert, 'Bush, Calderon to discuss Central American development', 10 October 1991.

11. Bernard Aronson, 'Our vision for the hemisphere', *US Department of State Dispatch*, Vol. 1, No. 7, 15 October 1990, p. 184.

12. Brazil fact sheet, *US Department of State Dispatch*, Vol. 1, No. 15, 10 December 1990, p. 316.

13. 'Pope hits at public and private morals', *Latin American Weekly Report*, 31 October 1991.

14. Jan Rocha, 'Brazil's children starve in the land of plenty', *Guardian*, 25 October 1990.

15. Robert Kimmitt, 'Economics and national security', *US Department of State Dispatch*, Vol. 2, No. 22, 3 June 1991, p. 399.

16. Colin Powell, Speech to UK EC Presidency Conference: 'Europe and the world after 1992', London, 7 September 1992.

17. See Richard Cheney, *Report of the Secretary of Defence to the President and Congress*, USGPO, Washington, January 1991.

18. Simon Tisdall, 'US to build stealth cruise missiles', *Guardian*, 8 June 1991.

19. Martin Walker, 'US develops "micro-nuke" weapons', *Guardian*, 10 September 1992.

20. William Arkin and Robert Norris, 'Tinynukes for mini minds', *Bulletin of the atomic scientists*, Vol. 48, No. 3, April 1992, pp. 24–5.

21. Michael Quinlan, 'The future of nuclear weapons: Policy for Western possessors', in *International Affairs*, Vol. 69, No. 3, July 1993, pp. 489–90, 496.

22. Martin Walker, 'The US saves its fists and uses a sling', *Guardian*, 28 June 1993.

23. United States Information Service, European Wireless File, News Alert, '"Forward presence" is focus of US force structure', 9 October 1991.

24. *Defending our future: Statement on the defence estimates*, HMSO, London, July 1993, pp. 45, 11, 63.

25. Donal Macintyre, 'Britain to consider need for hi-tech anti-missile defence', *Independent*, 16 February 1994.

26. Stephen Bates and David Fairhall, 'Rifkind in battle over defence', *Guardian*, 19 October 1993.

27. Christopher Bellamy and Colin Brown, 'Cuts "will not affect front-line strength"', *Independent*, 27 April 1994.

28. 'Russia and Africa', *Economist*, 9 July 1977.

29. Cited in Minter, p. 115.

30. Cited in Noam Chomsky, 'The weak shall inherit nothing', *Guardian*, 25 March 1991.

31. Mark Tran, 'Saudis propose arms and air support for Iraqi rebels', *Guardian*, 20 January 1991; 'Presenting Britain's case', *Daily Telegraph*, 26 January 1991.

32. Lawrence Freedman and Efraim Karsh, *The Gulf conflict 1990–1991: Diplomacy and war in the new world order*, Faber and Faber, London, 1993, pp. 408–9; 'Greenpeace puts combined Gulf war dead at over 150,000', *Guardian*, 30 May 1991.

33. Mark Tran, 'Saudis propose arms and air support for Iraqi rebels', *Guardian*, 20 January 1991; 'Presenting Britain's case', *Daily Telegraph*, 26 January 1991.

34. Paul Rogers, 'Myth of a clean war buried in the sand', *Guardian*, 19 September 1991.

35. Eric Hoskins, 'Killing is killing – not kindness', *New Statesman and Society*, 17 January 1992.

36. Michael Gordon, 'US says Gulf raids hit civilian sites harder than planned', *International Herald Tribune*, 24 February 1992.

37. Victoria Brittain, 'Gulf war "will haunt Iraqi children for ever"', *Guardian*, 23 October 1991.

38. Susan Okie, 'Child death rate doubles in aftermath of Gulf conflict', *Guardian*, 23 May 1991.

39. Victoria Brittain, '"100,000 Iraqi children starve,"' *Guardian*, 23 October 1991; Patrick Tyler, 'Trade ban starves Iraqis', *Guardian*, 25 June 1991.

40. 'Highway to hell', *New Statesman and Society*, 21 June 1991.

41. Cited in Dilip Hiro, *Desert Shield to Desert Storm: The second Gulf war*, Paladin, London, 1992, p. 387.

42. See Hiro, p. 389.

43. Bob Drogin, 'Desert claims death convoy', *Guardian*, 11 March 1991.

44. Michael Kelly, 'Carnage on a forgotten road', *Guardian*, 11 April 1991.

45. Richard Norton-Taylor, 'King explains bombing of Iraqi retreat', *Guardian*, 7 March 1991.

46. Patrick Sloyan, 'Iraqi troops buried alive say American officers', *Guardian*, 13 September 1991.

47. Robert Fisk, '"Known unto God and the US army high command', *Independent*, 5 August 1991; and 'US withholds death toll from Red Cross', *Independent*, 5 August 1991.

48. Middle East Watch, *Needless deaths in the Gulf war: Civilian casualties during the air campaign and violations of the laws of war*, Human Rights Watch, New York, 1991, pp. 1, 3, 4, 6, 11, 12, 97, 177, 180–81, 187, 233 for the following citations.

49. Michael Shuman, 'Participatory peace policies', in Chester Hartman and Pedro Vilanova, *Paradigms lost: The post Cold War era*, Pluto, London, 1992, p. 133; emphasis in original.

50. Ralph Atkins, 'London to keep the pressure on', *Guardian*, 28 August 1990.

51. Andrew McEwen, 'Britain dismisses diplomatic peace efforts as premature', *Times*, 31 August 1990.

52. Ralph Atkins, 'Hurd dismisses political option', *Guardian*, 3 September 1990.

53. Cited in Louise Fawcett and Robert O'Neill, 'Britain, the Gulf crisis and European security', in Nicole Gnesotto and John Roper (eds), *Western Europe and the Gulf*, Institute for Security Studies of the WEU, Paris, 1992, p. 146.

54. David Sharrock, 'Major tells Emir that only full Iraqi withdrawal will do', *Guardian*, 8 January 1991.

55. 'This dangerous phase', *The Times*, 28 August 1990.

56. 'Shades of Suez', *The Times*, 1 January 1991.

57. 'The testing time', *Daily Telegraph*, 1 September 1990.

58. 'Time for reflection and diplomacy', *Daily Telegraph*, 4 September 1990.

59. 'A last chance for peace', *Financial Times*, 4 January 1991.

60. Knut Royce, 'Middle East crisis secret offer: Iraq sent pullout deal to US', *Newsday*, 29 August 1990.

61. 'Iraq offers deal to quit Kuwait', *Newsday*, 3 January 1991; 'Rumours of a deal emerge', *International Herald Tribune*, 4 January 1991.

62. 'Essential resolution', *Daily Telegraph*, 25 October 1990.

63. 'Diplomacy's last chance', *The Times*, 1 November 1990.

64. 'War's inexorable approach', *Independent*, 10 November 1990.

65. 'Simply right', *Daily Telegraph*, 16 January 1991; 'Containing war', *The Times*, 17 January 1991.

66. Roland Dannreuther, *The Gulf conflict: A strategic analysis*, Adelphi Papers 264, IISS, London, p. 34.

67. IISS, *Strategic Survey 1990–1991*, IISS, London, 1991, p. 58.

68. 'Iraq's naked villainy', *The Times*, 3 August 1990.

69. 'Back to the agenda', *The Times*, 3 September 1990.

70. 'Containing a megalomaniac', *Daily Telegraph*, 3 August 1990; 'Stiffening resolve', *Daily Telegraph*, 4 August 1990.

71. 'Resolution on Iraq', *Financial Times*, 28 November 1990.

72. Hurd, *Weekly Hansard*, No. 1505, Vol. 164, No. 20, 20 December 1989, Col. 357. On the illegality of the invasion see Charles Maechling, 'Washington's illegal invasion', *Foreign Policy*, No. 79, Summer 1990; John Quigley, *The invasion of Panama and international law*, International Progress Organisation, Vienna, 1990; see also Noam Chomsky, *Deterring Democracy*, pp. 149–77 and Weeks and Gunson, *Panama: Made in the USA*.

73. 'Bold throw in Panama', *The Times*, 21 December 1989.

74. 'Justified action', *Daily Telegraph*, 21 December 1989.

75. 'A legal act may not be a wise one', *Independent*, 21 December 1989; On the point that Panama's 'declaration of war' did not in fact constitute a legal justification for the invasion, see Quigley, pp. 15–16.

76. 'Getting rid of Noriega', *Financial Times*, 21 December 1989.

77. 'Uniting for peace', *The Times*, 7 August 1990.

78. 'The limits of an assets freeze', *Financial Times*, 6 August 1990.

79. James Craig, 'Recent developments in Saudi Arabia', speech at the Royal Institute of International Affairs, 24 October 1990.

80. Michael Howard, 'On balance, Bush must go to war', *The Times*, 5 November 1990; *Financial Times* editors also noted this dilemma; 'Mr Bush knows that his policy involves risking a war in which thousands if not hundreds of thousands of people would die. ... Such a risk cannot be justified by arguments over the price of oil, or the balance of power in a strategically important region. ... It can only conceivably be worthwhile if it does have the effect of securing small states everywhere against the designs of their neighbours, and convincing would-be aggressors that war is not a means to an end' – something of which US leaders have been traditionally deeply aware. ('Steps to a new world order', *Financial Times*, 17 September 1990.)

81. US Secretary of State James Baker, speech before the House Foreign Affairs Committee, United States Information Service, *Official Text*, p. 1.

82. London Press Service, Verbatim Service, Thatcher interview on TV-AM, 2 September 1990.

83. *Weekly Hansard*, Issue No. 1533, Vol. 177, No. 152, 6 September 1990, Col. 735.

84. Ibid., Cols. 832–3.

85. *Weekly Hansard*, Issue No. 1543, Vol. 183, No. 33, 15 January 1991, Cols. 742–3.

86. 'Failure to stop dictators bears a higher price than war', *Independent*, 16 January 1991.

87. Peter Jenkins, 'New role for a superpower', *Independent*, 4 September 1990.

88. Michael Prowse, 'Shades of grey over the Gulf', *Financial Times*, 7 January 1991.

89. 'A burden to be shared', *Independent*, 1 September 1990.

90. 'No linkage', *Daily Telegraph*, 10 December 1990.

91. 'No mock heroics', *The Times*, 18 January 1991.

92. Lawrence Freedman, 'Any way you paint it, it's not Cuba', *Independent*, 1 November 1990.

93. 'Saddam contra mundum', *Daily Telegraph*, 22 December 1990.

94. 'Cause for which the West is ready to fight', *Daily Telegraph*, 15 January 1991.

95. 'Failure to stop dictators bears a higher price than war', *Independent*, 16 January 1991.

96. 'A cause for war', *Financial Times*, 17 January 1991.

97. 'The world at war', *Financial Times*, 16 January 1991; emphasis in original.

98. 'Dalyell's disservice', *The Times*, 31 December 1990.

99. 'The British contribution', *Financial Times*, 16 January 1991.

100. Robert Harvey, 'Pointers from the past, lessons for the future', *Daily Telegraph*, 4 September 1990.

101. Lawrence Freedman, 'If we fail in Kuwait, we fail ourselves', *Independent*, 7 August 1990.

102. Lawrence Freedman, 'Haunted by the ghosts of defeat', *Independent*, 20 September 1990.

103. 'Failure to stop dictators bears a higher price than war', *Independent*, 16 January 1991.

104. Freedman and Karsh, pp. 212, 435, 166, 213–14, 75, 110–11.

105. '"Circumspect" BBC', *Guardian*, 15 January 1991.

106. Georgina Henry, 'A credibility war that TV news won', *Guardian*, 20 January 1992.

107. For the similar role of the US press in the war see Marie Gottschalk, 'Operation Desert Cloud: The media and the Gulf war', *World Policy Journal*, Vol. IX, No. 3, Summer 1992.

108. 'No respite', *The Times*, 18 January 1991.

109. 'Rewards of patience', *Daily Telegraph*, 23 January 1991.

110. 'Justified confidence', *Daily Telegraph*, 24 January 1991; see also 'The war of words', *Daily Telegraph*, 28 January 1991; the *Daily Telegraph*'s penchant for Stalin-style disinformation was clearly revealed throughout the war, as editors commented that 'bad presentation could weaken morale at home' and that, with the necessity of winning the war as quickly as possible with minimum casualties, 'it esteems military secrecy far beyond media demands for information'. 'If hard evidence of military incompetence emerges ... then there may well be a media duty to report this. But failing such a development, the genuine public "right to know" what was done well or ill will come when the war is over.' But the issue was not one of 'military incompetence' or what was done 'well' or 'ill'; it was a basic question of the utter horror of the devastation being inflicted by us, whilst the reality of this was being systematically suppressed. The *Daily Telegraph* revealed that it was more concerned to act as an arm of the state than as an independent source of information. See the two editorials 'Voice of authority' (17 January 1991) and 'Waiting for news' (8 February 1991).

111. Susan Ellicott, 'US report highlights failures in Panama', *Times*, 3 July 1990; After the war was over, stories crept out ridiculing the claims of military success made by US leaders during the war. A congressional report, for example, stated that the US claimed that 388 of the 846 tanks in the three Republican Guard divisions were destroyed from the air, when in fact only 166 were. It also noted that the number of Iraqi naval vessels reported sunk by the US was three times greater than the total size of the Iraqi navy. Similarly, the number of Scud missile launchers claimed to have been destroyed was four times greater than the total number of launchers deployed. (Martin Walker, 'Gulf war's lessons for Clinton, *Guardian*, 17 August 1993.) When the next major war comes, it is reasonable to assert that such facts will also be buried for the sake of pandering to state propaganda.

112. Michael Evans, 'The final turkey shoot', *The Times*, 27 March 1991.

113. Michael Dewar, 'A defence of Mutla Ridge', *Guardian*, 11 April 1991.

114. Christopher Bellamy, 'RAF chief tells how war strategy changed', *Independent*, 26 March 1991.

115. Robert Harvey, 'Why the key issues remain to be resolved', *Daily Telegraph*, 7 December 1990.

116. ' ... Will shape the ensuing peace', *Independent*, 18 January 1991.

117. Max Hastings, 'Targeting the force to defeat Saddam Hussein', *Daily Telegraph*, 8 January 1991; my emphasis.

118. 'When to stop', *The Times*, 28 February 1991; 'Light shines into the gloom', *Financial Times*, 2 March 1991; 'Saddam should be treated as a pariah', *Daily Telegraph*, 1 March 1991.

119. John Willcock, 'Billiere, Gulf war commander, joins city merchant bank', *Guardian*, 15 July 1992.

CHAPTER 8

THE ONGOING WAR

In order to gauge further the extent, in the 1990s, of British governments' respect for grand principles it is instructive to review other aspects of British policy. This final chapter begins by briefly considering British military involvement in a number of situations of human rights abuse before analysing in greater detail policy towards Indonesia and East Timor. It concludes by asserting that the control by the world's powerful states over the Third World that has been a a primary goal of postwar planning is currently being exercised primarily through international economic instruments, with Britain playing a significant role in the process.

A 1992 report by Amnesty International – *Repression Trade (UK) Limited*, subtitled *How the United Kingdom makes torture and death its business*[1] – reveals the role of the British government, as well as that of private British companies, in recent human rights violations. In April 1990, for example, the government announced that British army counterinsurgency specialists were helping to train the Presidential Guard in the Philippines. 'The 3,000–strong elite Guard', Amnesty states in its report, 'has in the past been accused of the torture and summary execution of opposition activists.' These executions included the killing of two members of a national youth association in 1988 who, according to a third youth who survived, 'had first been brutally tortured at the hands of the Guard before their execution'. Amnesty also notes that the British construction company, Laing, had built three twelve-feet high gallows to be used by Sheikh Zayed of Abu Dhabi, one of which was exported. 'The gallows were intended to remain outside in desert conditions, ready for immediate use when required'. Another British company – Electronic Intelligence – had installed an electronic torture chamber inside the headquarters of Dubai's Special Branch. The combined effect of its strobe light system and deafening noise generator would be 'to reduce anyone inside the chamber to a screaming, helpless supplicant within moments'. A former director of the company was quoted as saying that the purpose of the equipment was 'to make people talk without physically damaging them'. In another, less recent example, Amnesty noted that during the regime of Idi Amin in Uganda, Pye Telecommunications exported telecommunications equipment to the notorious State Research Centre, 'which improved the operational capacity of Amin's secret police'. 'The Centre is estimated to have killed between 100,000 and 500,000 people in the eight years of Amin's rule.'

The Amnesty report states:

> The United Kingdom Government actively promotes sales of ['security and arms'] equipment from British companies to many countries which have records of grave and persistent human rights violations. This promotion is facilitated through exhibitions such as the British Army Equipment Exhibition (BAEE), which is closed to the public, and to which countries are secretly invited to send representatives. In 1989, the list of guests to BAEE included representatives of 30 countries in which Amnesty International had reports of torture being practised at the time, including Turkey and Chile.

The Amnesty report highlights a standard theme of British foreign policy, namely, the close working relations that British governments have developed with many repressive regimes. Another recent example concerns Cambodia. British army training has extended to the allies of one of the postwar world's worst genocidal organisations: the Khmer Rouge, who killed at least 1 million Cambodians when it was in power in the late 1970s. After repeated denials, the British government finally admitted in 1991 that Britain had 'provided training to the armed forces of the Cambodian non-communist resistance from 1983 to 1989'.[2] President Bush admitted that there was 'tactical military cooperation' between the Khmer Rouge and the other guerrilla factions being trained by Britain. From a secret jungle base near the Cambodian border in Thailand, the SAS trained guerrillas 'in the use of mines and explosives against civilian as well as military targets', according to the US human rights organisation Asia Watch. The British training may therefore have contributed to the statistic that there were about 300 amputees a month, as well as an unknown number of deaths, in the country.[3]

Moreover, according to evidence accumulated in extensive research by the journalist John Pilger, soldiers in the Khmer Rouge itself have been trained by the SAS. Pilger quotes a former SAS trainer in Thailand thus:

> ... we trained the Khmer Rouge in a lot of technical stuff – a lot about mines ... we trained them in Mark 5 rocket launchers and all sorts of weapons. We even gave them psychological training. At first they wanted to go into the villages and chop people up. We told them how to go easy.[4]

There is also evidence that even after 1989 Britain continued to help the Khmer Rouge lay mines; one British intelligence official is quoted by Pilger as saying that the SAS operation is 'the principal direct Western military involvement in Indochina'.[5] 'The training is still continuing,' a former MI6 officer said in July 1991.[6]

A further example concerns Liberia. In 1989, negotiations began between the Liberian regime of Samuel Doe and a British arms manufacturer,

United Scientific Instruments (USI). This involved a barter deal in which the Doe regime would be provided with arms in return for USI's 'exclusive right' to manage timber concessions in certain areas of the country. According to Africa Watch, Doe had presided over a 'reign of terror' with extra-judicial killings and torture and a 'regime ... incapable of respect for the rule of law'.[7] Thousands had been killed after Doe assumed power in a 1980 coup, after which US military and economic aid had poured into the country in the early 1980s. Regarding the deal with USI, *West Africa* magazine gave this report:

> Doe's military shopping list included: 10 Scorpion armoured fighting vehicles, complete with machine guns, night vision laser sights, ammunition and spares, a new radio communication system, training for Liberian soldiers in weaponry and communications systems at the Alvis school in Britain, and an Alvis service engineer seconded to Liberia for two years and freight transport.

The report went on to state that 'in return USI was given a concession which would last the duration of the time it would take Liberia to complete the purchase of the weapons, which was estimated to be five years'. USI pulled out of the deal at the last minute after an uprising and increasing civil war activity, but this was only after three British government departments had scrutinised and approved the deal and an export licence worth £20 million had been granted to the company in February 1990.[8]

Consider also British policy towards the former Yugoslavia. It is not the intention here – in a study essentially of Britain's role in the Third World – to analyse in great detail Britain's role in the Balkans, but a short consideration may not be out of place. One reason for this is that policy towards the war in Bosnia is consistent with the disregard for human rights that has accompanied British policy as an elementary principle throughout the postwar era. The scale of atrocities – over 200,000 deaths in Bosnia, with 2.3 million people forced from their homes – has, logically, been insufficient to force Britain to adopt anything but a conciliatory approach to the aggressors in a conflict in which, as a UN spokesman noted, 'defenceless civilians are being attacked by a modern army'. 'The aggression of the Serbs', he continued, 'is quite transparent.'[9]

It needs to be noted, however, that – again consistent with postwar foreign policy – there is no institutional interest in adhering to the principle of standing up to aggression in motivating policy. The Pakistani ambassador to the UN recalled, in June 1993, the principle which had played some role in a conflict – against Iraq – a few years earlier; now buried. 'If aggression is allowed to stand' in Bosnia, he noted, 'the forces of moderation will lose and the forces of extremism will be strengthened'.[10] At a time when Britain was refusing to contemplate easing the sanctions against Iraq, Foreign Secretary Hurd noted that 'it might be possible to suspend part of the sanctions against Serbia and Montenegro if they make territorial concessions over and above what they have so far offered'.[11] Hurd also contemplated a 'significant' Serb withdrawal from occupied territories, somewhat in contrast to demands on Iraq, where only complete withdrawal from Kuwait was sufficient to satisfy the Western commitment not to capitulate to aggression.[12] Yet Britain has not shown 'double standards' towards reversing Serbian aggression, as has often been claimed; the British policy of effectively rewarding aggression has been consistent with its postwar standards, as long as we adopt the benchmark of policy in the real world rather than the benchmark elucidated by the propaganda system: namely, one based on principle.

'The policy adopted by the Western powers in April 1992, at the outbreak of the war in Bosnia-Herzegovina, was tantamount to accepting the disappearance of a state they had just recognised,' the French aid agency Médecins Sans Frontières wrote in a report on contemporary UN peacekeeping operations.[13] Of all the external actors that contributed to the Bosnian tragedy, the evidence suggests that Britain probably bears principal blame. The *Guardian's* Ian Traynor wrote, for example:

> Britain has dominated the international mediation effort in Bosnia since its inception: Carrington and then Owen led the diplomatic drive; the principal aide to both was Peter Hall, our former Ambassador in Belgrade; the mediators' special envoy in Sarajevo was a young British military officer, Jeremy Brade; and the chief of staff for the UN forces in Bosnia is Britain's Brigadier Vere Hayes.

Traynor also points out that it was Lord Carrington who 'first established ethnic territories as the fundamental organising principle for the future of Bosnia'.[14] The 'peace efforts' in Bosnia have all been geared to the establishment of such ethnic territories, the main obstacle being the government of the independent state to be partitioned. It has been the objects of aggression who have been pressured to agree a deal: Lord Owen warned that the UN forces might withdraw from Bosnia, and British Foreign Secretary Hurd warned that British forces might withdraw, if the Bosnian government does not sign up to a 'peace' agreement.[15]

Britain also played the lead organising role in preventing the lifting of the arms embargo against the Bosnian government. Bosnian Vice-President Ejup Ganic noted that 'the only sticking point is the bloody British. Everyone supports lifting the embargo – except the Foreign Office and John Major.'[16] Thus Bosnia – recognised as an independent state by Britain – is not accorded the same privilege as Indonesia. The British government has consistently justified arms sales to Jakarta by reference to Article 51 of the UN Charter, which accords to each nation the right to self-defence. This principle, then, applies to a government engaged in mass violence in Indonesia itself and in East Timor for three decades (see below), but not to the Bosnian government. Again, however, this is not evidence of 'double standards': in each case, Britain effectively sides with the aggressor.

Another major British contribution has been to help designate the conflict merely a 'civil war' – a concept also promoted by the press who generally refer to the war as one between 'the Muslims', the 'Bosnian Serbs' and the 'Bosnian Croats'. This ideological first principle has greatly aided British policy since, if the conflict were recognised as essentially an inter-state war – with Bosnian sovereignty at stake – the need to reverse such aggression in Europe would be seen to be even more compelling. Yet Serbian and Croatian government involvement in the war is so overwhelming that it can hardly be understood as a civil war. The US government stated in February 1994 that there could be up to 10,000 Croatian regulars in Bosnia, whilst the UN estimated there were up to 5,000. The *Guardian's* Ed Vulliamy wrote in September 1993 that, with columns of Croatian tanks in Bosnia, 'there is no longer any pretence' and that 'this is annexation by Zagreb'.[17] Equally, Serbia has consistently supplied weapons to its allies in Bosnia and there have been persistent reports of Serbian army units operating there. The *Independent's* defence correspondent wrote in February 1994 that 'the Muslim enclaves in eastern Bosnia have been under shell-fire from Serbia proper for months. Serbs from Serbia were involved in attacks on the three enclaves of Srebrenica, Zepa and Gorazde.'[18]

Another important feature of the contemporary era – standing in sharp contrast to policy in Bosnia – concerns the Northern powers' intent to pursue military policies in the Third World. The practice of picking off Third World troublemakers can now be effected with impunity, now that the Soviet deterrent has disappeared. The United States has taken the leading role in this, whilst Britain has lent mainly diplomatic support.

Virtually the last act of the Bush administration, for example, was to launch forty to fifty cruise missiles against Baghdad in January 1993, in order, the administration argued, to destroy a 'nuclear fabricating plant'. The defect in the pretext was that, according to a spokesperson for the International Atomic Energy Agency, the plant was 'absolutely out of action' and was 'no longer involved in production of electronic components for enriching uranium'. The US press noted that 'the US attack was largely designed to send a political message to the Iraqi regime that virtually any building in the country can be struck with force and precision'.[19] The US raid was given 'full support' by the junior partner, as were the Clinton administration's cruise missile attacks in June 1993.[20]

The US administration stated that the latter attacks were in response to an alleged Iraqi plan to assassinate George Bush, evidence which the United States refused to make public. Whatever the truth of the plot, the *Middle East Economic Digest* reported that White House officials indicated 'the raid was directed as much at other perceived threats in the region as it was at Iraq itself'. President Clinton stated that the raid was a warning not only to Saddam but to 'other governments that foster terrorism'. Other US officials admitted that the bombing of the World Trade Center in New York was 'very much on our minds and an explicit part of the discussions' when the raid on Baghdad was being planned.[21] Baghdad was simply the convenient target at the time for demonstrating the instruments of violence at the disposal of the chief guardian of international order.

Prime Minister John Major stated the attack was a 'justified and proportionate exercise of the right of self-defence', although the UN charter does not justify such an act as self-defence.[22] Also significant was the reaction from the Russian and German governments, both of which stated that the US raid was 'justified'; the Russian statement noting that it stemmed 'from the right of any state to individual and collective self-defence' in accordance with the UN Charter.[23]

Somalia also became an object of United States aggression once the US had managed to pick out one General Farah Aideed as the primary rogue in that country's civil war. Rakiya Omaar, formerly of Africa Watch, wrote that 'UN peace keepers in Somalia enjoy the most liberal rules of engagement ever given to UN forces' and that 'nearly 300 Somalis had been killed and many others injured by late March' 1993. 'Few of these incidents have led to investigations, let alone prosecutions,' she continued. 'An American found to have killed a young boy was merely demoted one grade and fined one month's pay.'[24]

During the US deployment in Somalia several massacres took place, with at least 54 people killed in one US attack and around 100 in another, both in July 1993. In the first, *Africa Confidential* reported, women and children were killed and 'at least 30 of those who died were religious and intellectual leaders from various clans', not armed supporters of Aideed. 'These are precisely the elders whom it is UN policy to support in its bid to defeat the warlords,' it noted. Among those killed was a religious leader who had met the UN special representative in Somalia for discussions three days before. 'The house bombarded by US Cobra gunships and Blackhawk helicopters was described by the UN as a "command and control centre" but was well-known as a conference centre,' the report continued.[25]

US leaders declared, with the support of the media, that the intervention in Somalia was undertaken for 'humanitarian reasons', an incredible proposition given the postwar history US interventions in the Third World. The first landings were televised live at prime viewing time in the United States, just as the 1986 bombing of Libya had been. It is more reasonable to suggest that the intervention was undertaken because of the US establishment's need to demonstrate the ongoing importance of the military and of continued high defence spending now that their previous rationale, the Cold War, had been removed. According to *Africa Confidential*, President Bush ordered the intervention to show that 'the USA can intervene anywhere' and 'to show the financial costs of US leadership of the new order and so help protect the US defence budget against President-elect

Bill Clinton's promised substantial cuts'.[26] 'Humanitarian intervention' was thus a convenient new pretext. The Acting Secretary of State, Lawrence Eagleburger, appeared to be referring to such reasoning when he noted that 'what we are seeing in Somalia does say that the US military may well have a new role'.[27]

National interests and human slaughter II: Indonesia and East Timor

The irrelevance of human rights to the leading Western powers remains an important dimension of contemporary international affairs. An important ideological modification is that a justification for supporting dictatorships and mass murderers can no longer be supplied by referring to the Cold War. The excuse that still worse atrocities would be committed if favoured states fell into the Soviet bloc is no longer available, which presents some dilemmas as to how to proceed. Another formulation is currently popular: that Third World states conducting mass repression and which happen to pursue economic policies favourable to Western business interests are somehow unable, for cultural reasons, to safeguard human rights (see below). Attempts by the West to impose high standards might be viewed as interference in their internal affairs (something that Western states surely could not contemplate) and therefore business should continue as normal.

Thus the actions of repressive governments can continue to elicit little response on the part of the leading Western powers if their 'national interests' remain unaffected by such policies. One of the clearest current examples of this is the case of Indonesian violence in East Timor, a former Portuguese colony subject to decolonisation in 1975 but invaded by Indonesia in that year and incorporated as its '27th province'. A brief consideration of the recent history of British, and US, relations with Indonesia is useful in further gauging contemporary national interests.

The current Indonesian military regime under General Suharto assumed power following the overthrow of President Sukarno in 1965. Britain and the United States were especially keen to see the fall of Sukarno's non-aligned, independent nationalist regime and, according to a CIA memorandum of June 1962, Prime Minister Macmillan and President Kennedy, at a meeting in April that year, 'agreed to liquidate President Sukarno, depending on the situation and available opportunities'. The CIA officer who wrote the memo noted further: 'it is not clear to me whether murder or overthrow is intended by the word liquidate'.[28] A highly placed MI6 officer at the time later denied knowledge of the discussion and denied also that the use of the word 'liquidate' meant that Sukarno was to be killed, but was reported as saying, 'However, they might well have discussed the best way of getting rid of this awkward fellow.'[29]

When the opportunity did arise, in 1965, for Sukarno to be overthrown, the Indonesian army engaged in mass killings to consolidate the new Suharto regime. At least 500,000 people are believed to have been killed by the army in an attempt to eradicate support for the Indonesian Communist Party (PKI). Declassified US documents reveal that not only did the United States support the slaughter but it actively aided the Indonesian army in conducting it. In October 1965 the US embassy pondered whether Suharto would 'have [the] courage to go forward against [the] PKI', with the US ambassador in Jakarta noting that 'we do think [the] army will go on trying, possibly not always as directly as we would like, to keep matters moving in [the] direction we would wish to see'. As the killings began and Washington and the US embassy in Jakarta were kept informed of the gruesome details, US Secretary of State Dean Rusk cabled the Jakarta embassy that the 'campaign against [the] PKI' must continue and that the military 'are [the] only force capable of creating order in Indonesia'. Moreover, Indonesian generals could count on US help for a 'major military campaign against [the] PKI'. The US ambassador, meanwhile, 'made it clear that Embassy and USG[overnment] [are] generally sympathetic with and admiring of what [the] army [is] doing', at a time when it was understood that the army was attacking the PKI 'ruthlessly' and 'wholesale killings' were taking place. When Indonesian generals approached the United States for arms to kill PKI supporters, the United States quickly promised covert aid, with the CIA recognising that the 'destruction' of the PKI was at stake and the US ambassador observing that 'carefully placed assistance' 'will help [the] Army cope with [the] PKI'.[30]

At the same time, the CIA was giving the Indonesian army a hit list of 5,000 PKI supporters, including party leaders, regional committee members and heads of labour, women's and youth groups, who were hunted down and then killed. A US embassy official who spent two years drawing up the hit list noted that it was 'a big help to the army'. 'I probably have a lot of blood on my hands, but that's not all bad. There's a time when you have to strike hard at a decisive moment.' Authority for drawing up the list came from the US ambassador, who stated that the United States had 'a lot more information' on the PKI than the Indonesian army. US officers ticked off names on the list as they were murdered.[31]

Leading US foreign policy analyst Gabriel Kolko comments that 'the "final solution" to the communist problem in Indonesia was certainly one of the most barbaric acts of inhumanity in a century that has seen a great deal of it' and that 'it surely ranks as a war crime of the same type as those the Nazis perpetrated'. Kolko notes further:

No single American action in the period after 1945 was as bloodthirsty as its role in Indonesia, for it tried to initiate the massacre, and it did everything in its power to encourage Suharto, including equipping his killers, to see that the physical liquidation of the PKI was carried through to its culmination.[32]

With the Suharto regime having assured 'stability' in the country and instigating a state of permanent terror to keep the population in check, Western business interests could move in. 'With its one hundred million people and its three-thousand-mile arc of islands containing the region's richest hoard of natural resources,' Richard Nixon wrote in 1967, 'Indonesia constitutes the greatest prize in the Southeast Asian area.'[33] According to Kolko, Japan and the United States, 'working through consortia and the multilateral banks, used aid as a lever to rewrite Indonesia's basic economic legislation'. US-trained technocrats took charge of the economy and, 'with the assistance of teams of American and European academics and business-men, quickly redefined the nature and direction of the economy'. Indonesia rejoined the IMF and the World Bank and issued an investment law making it 'a haven for foreigners'. The consequence was that landlessness increased as land ownership became more concentrated; the peasants were afraid to organise, and the prospects of fundamental economic changes preferential to the poor were successfully eradicated.[34]

Former Labour Foreign Secretary Michael Stewart recalled in his auto-biography that he visited Indonesia a year after the killings and was able to 'reach a good understanding with the Foreign Minister, Adam Malik', a 'remarkable man' who was 'evidently resolved to keep his country at peace'. Suharto's regime is 'like Sukarno's, harsh and tyrannical; but it is not aggressive', Stewart stated.[35] Malik later acted as a primary apologist for Indonesian atrocities in East Timor. In 1977, for example, he was reported as saying, '50,000 or 80,000 people might have been killed during the war in East Timor. ... It was war. ... Then what is the big fuss?'[36]

The Western condoning of Indonesia's domestic aggression has been matched by a similar condoning of aggression in East Timor, where over 200,000 people – around one third of the population – have lost their lives since 1975. Indonesia's illegal annexation of East Timor has been effectively (*de facto*) recognised by the major Western powers, although, apart from Australia, they have stopped short of *de jure* recognition.

Official documents reveal that Indonesia's invasion of East Timor in December 1975 was supported by the leading Western powers. In July 1975 the British ambassador in Jakarta informed the Foreign Office that 'the people of Portuguese Timor are in no condition to exercise the right to self-determination' and 'the arguments in favour of its integration into Indonesia are all the stronger'.

Developments in Lisbon now seem to argue in favour of greater sympathy towards Indonesia should the Indonesian government feel forced to take strong action by the deteriorating situation in Portuguese Timor. Certainly, as seen from here, it is in Britain's interest that Indonesia should absorb the territory as

soon and as unobtrusively as possible, and that if it should come to the crunch
and there is a row in the United Nations, we should keep our heads down and
avoid taking sides against the Indonesian government.[37]

As regards the US position, the Australian ambassador to Indonesia cabled
to Canberra in August 1975 that the US ambassador was 'under instructions
from [Secretary of State] Kissinger personally not to involve himself in
discussions on Timor with the Indonesians' and that the US position was
to 'keep out of the Portuguese Timor situation and allow events to take
their course'. The US ambassador told him that 'if Indonesia were to
intervene, the United States would hope they would do so "effectively,
quickly and not use our equipment"'.[38] The invasion took place a day after
President Ford and Kissinger completed a visit to Jakarta, having been
delayed so as not to embarrass the visitors. A few days after the beginning
of the intervention the US ambassador to Indonesia noted that the US
had 'not disapproved' of the invasion; within a month, a US State Department official stated, '... we are more or less condoning the incursion into
East Timor' since 'we regard Indonesia as a friendly, non-aligned state –
a nation we do a lot of business with'.[39]

An East Timorese Catholic priest stated two years after the invasion
that 'a barbarous genocide of innocent people goes on, apparently with
complete peace of conscience'. East Timor was being 'wiped out by an
invasion, a brutal conquest that produces heaps of dead, maimed and
orphaned'.[40] The population was subjected to aerial bombing, campaigns
of deliberate starvation and the wholesale annihilation of villages and
people. By 1985, up to half a million people had been killed or displaced,
according to Amnesty International, whilst 'disappearances' or deaths in
custody, the killing of prisoners who surrendered after being promised
amnesty, the torture and imprisonment of people suspected of being
disloyal to the Suharto regime were all common.[41] East Timorese Bishop
Carlos Belo later summed up the situation by stating. '... we are dying as
a people and as a nation.'[42]

Indonesian violence has been significantly aided by the leading Western
powers. The United States dramatically increased arms supplies to Indonesia after the invasion, delivering counter-insurgency aircraft which,
according to retired US admiral Gene La Roque, 'changed the entire nature
of the war'. US supplies of transport aircraft, armoured cars, rifles, mortars,
machine guns and communications equipment 'contributed significantly
to the military successes of the Indonesian Armed Forces in their 1977–
79 offensive', Budiardjo and Liong comment in their extensively documented study of the war in East Timor.[43] US arms sales continued to
Jakarta throughout the 1980s and 1990s.

The United States has also given significant aid to Indonesia at the
United Nations, where it has helped to block international efforts to take

action against this particular act of aggression. In April 1976, for example, the *Japan Times* reported that Japan and the United States reportedly were 'seeking to water down' a resolution calling on Indonesia to withdraw from East Timor and were trying to make it 'less offensive to Indonesia'.[44] Singapore's *Straits Times* similarly noted that the Security Council's Western members 'regarded a call for an immediate, unconditional withdrawal as impractical and unlikely to be acceptable to Indonesia'.[45] The United States subsequently either voted against or abstained on yearly General Assembly resolutions calling for an Indonesian withdrawal and self-determination for East Timor. The US representative to the United Nations, Daniel Moynihan, explained that in steering the international community away from effective action against Indonesia:

> The United States wished things to turn out as they did and worked to bring this about. The Department of State desired that the United Nations prove utterly ineffective in whatever measures it undertook. This task was given to me and I carried it forward with no inconsiderable success.[46]

In 1982 a State Department official was quoted as saying that 'our tradition-al position is and remains that we have accepted the incorporation of East Timor with Indonesia without recognising that there has been an act of determination'.[47] On a personal trip to Indonesia in 1981, former President Ford stated that the purpose of his visit was to 'renew old friendship ... notably with Mr Suharto'[48]; the following year, the US State Department described relations with Indonesia as 'close and friendly'.[49]

The British reaction to Indonesian aggression has also been instructive. Britain abstained on the first UN resolution condemning the invasion, supported two others (though these were widely acknowledged to be weakly worded and watered down[50]) and abstained on all subsequent ones. By 1992, a spokesman for the East Timor independence movement termed Britain 'the single worst obstructionist of any industrialised country' over international action against Indonesian violence in East Timor.[51]

Britain has provided significant support to the Suharto regime in the area of arms sales. In April 1978 British Aerospace announced an export order to Indonesia for eight Hawk jet trainer aircraft, Rolls-Royce engines, spares and training of pilots and engineers.[52] Britain refused to give assurances that the aircraft would not be used in a combat role, whilst the then Labour Foreign Secretary David Owen stated in November 1978 – the massacres in East Timor having reached near-genocidal proportions – '... we believe that such fighting as still continues is on a very small scale.'[53] Subsequent sales of Hawks and three contracts worth over £200 million (signed in 1984, 1985 and 1986) for the Rapier air defence system followed, whilst the Royal Navy supplied three frigates worth £27 million to the Indonesian navy in 1984. According to the *Financial Times*, the 1984 Rapier deal, which was backed by the British government's Export Credit

Guarantee Department, included 'various agreements on training and transfer of technology'. It also noted that 'many Indonesian military officials will be going for training in Britain while BAe personnel will be closely involved in back-up and other services in Indonesia'.[54] By 1987, Rolls-Royce was signing a technical cooperation agreement with Indonesia's state-run aerospace company involving possible joint venture manufacturing and servicing of various engine parts. Thorn EMI was reportedly aiming to sell a radar system, and Vickers a light tank.[55]

Hawk aircraft supplied by Britain are believed to have been used in Indonesian offensives against East Timorese. Oxford academic Peter Carey noted in 1992 that 'it is well-known these aircraft are readily adaptable for ground-attack and counter-insurgency operations. ... 15 are already in service with the Indonesian air force from earlier deals ... and some of these have been seen at Baucau airfield in East Timor where they have been used against' the resistance.[56] John Pilger has interviewed a number of Timorese who saw Hawk aircraft in action in East Timor in the early 1980s; one of the Timorese noted: '... they fly in low ... and attack civilians, because the people hiding in the mountains are civilians. Four of my cousins were killed in Hawk attacks near Los Palos.'[57] British supplies of frigates, submarine communications equipment and surveillance radar have also helped the Indonesian military to isolate East Timor from the outside world through a naval blockade.[58] Saladin, Saracen and Ferret armoured vehicles supplied by Britain, meanwhile, have been used for repression in Indonesia itself and are also available for use in East Timor.[59]

In relation to another of Indonesia's wars – in Irian Jaya – the *Observer* reported in 1979 that 'most of the weaponry Indonesia deploys against the rebels comes from Britain and the United States'. As the massacres in East Timor were mounting, Indonesia was also conducting 'intensive bombing raids' against rebels in Irian Jaya 'using American-supplied Bell helicopters and OV-10 Bronco counter-insurgency aircraft'. In one attack, in July 1977, '1,279 villagers were killed by napalm and anti-personnel cluster bombs'. Over 20 per cent of Indonesia's oil comes from the territory of Irian Jaya, and two thirds of the wells were owned by three US oil companies; US nickel and copper companies also operate there.[60]

The arms deals with Britain were signed against the background of continuing terror in both East Timor and Indonesia. In 1983–85, as the contracts for the Rapier air defence system were being signed, 3,500–4,500 people were murdered by army death squads in Indonesia. Similarly, on the same day in 1991 that a co-production agreement between British Aerospace and Indonesia for the Hawk fighter-trainer and a light attack fighter was reported, the US press observed that 'foreign human rights investigators and Western diplomats in Jakarta now estimate that up to 5,000 people have been killed or have "disappeared"' in Aceh province (in Indonesia) in recent months. 'Although there has been killing on both sides,' the report continued, 'human rights activists say most of it appears to originate with the Indonesian army.'[61] Amnesty International estimated that 2,000 people had died from 1989 to July 1993, 'most of the victims' having been 'ordinary villagers living in areas of suspected rebel activity'. The Indonesian military commander in Aceh province was quoted as saying in November 1990, 'I have told the community, if you find a terrorist, kill him. There's no need to investigate him. ... If they don't do as you order them, shoot them on the spot, or butcher them.'[62]

Warm diplomatic exchanges between Britain and Indonesia have also continued. Suharto visited the Queen in 1979, by which time the body count in East Timor was reaching into the hundreds of thousands. British Aerospace signed a contract worth £16 million in 1985 for the sale of a jet specifically for the use of President Suharto.[63] In December 1992, meanwhile, *Indonesian News* (published by the Indonesian embassy in London) reported that Margaret Thatcher had been presented with an honorary medal from the Indonesian Engineering Association (PII) by President Suharto at the State Palace in Jakarta. Referring to the award from the PII, Thatcher said, 'I am proud to be one of you.'[64] In September 1991 the same source reported that British Defence Minister Tom King met with his Indonesian counterpart, Benny Murdani, to discuss 'improving military cooperation between the two countries'. Murdani had organised and commanded the first invasion of East Timor in 1975.[65] He had also previously, in 1983, issued a message to resistance leader Xanana Gusmao to the effect that 'there is no country on the globe that can help you. Our own army is prepared to destroy you if you are not willing to cooperate with our republic,' before declaring that he would show 'no mercy' to resistance forces in East Timor.[66]

Close relations continued after the massacre in Dili, capital of East Timor, in November 1991, when the Indonesian army killed hundreds of people demonstrating against the occupation. The announcement of the British sale of a navy support ship to Indonesia was delayed in January 1992 because of the international outcry over the massacre, but the sale went ahead the following month. Britain had also offered places in military training programmes for three Indonesian army officers.[67] Their boss — the chief of the armed forces and later Indonesian Vice-President, General Try Sutrisno — had formerly promised to 'wipe out all separatist elements'.[68]

In April 1993, Foreign Secretary Hurd visited Indonesia and signed an agreement for a £65 million British loan to the country. On the day he arrived in Jakarta, a UN special envoy expressed his desire to meet Xanana Gusmao, the captured leader of the East Timor resistance movement, who was eventually sentenced to life imprisonment after his 'trial' in Indonesia.[69] Whilst Hurd was in Indonesia, the Antara news agency provided this report:

Referring to human rights issues, Hurd said that Western countries cannot export Western values to developing nations without making adjustments to local economies and cultures. Differences in cultural life and economic level are decisive factors for the adoption of Western values by developing countries, he said.

The news agency continued: 'what is done by Indonesia is proof of its recognition that basic freedom such as freedom for union, freedom to express opinion and press freedom is a fundamental right, he [Hurd] said'.[70]

It was in the context of such high-level apologetics that two months after Hurd's visit, in June 1993, British Aerospace signed a £500 million contract to sell twenty-four Hawk aircraft (along with £50 million worth of engines from Rolls-Royce) to Indonesia. The managing director of BAe Defence declared that the deal builds on the 'strong business relationship which has evolved' between BAe and Indonesia, whilst British Defence Minister Malcolm Rifkind stated the sale would 'enhance the existing good relations between the United Kingdom and Indonesia'.[71] 'Indonesia is a very exciting part of the world,' a representative of Rolls-Royce had observed the previous year, when Britain was on the verge of signing a deal for forty Hawks, becoming Indonesia's second largest arms supplier.[72]

Two months before the June Hawk deal, Indonesian Air Marshal Sibun noted that 'the planes will be used not only to train pilots, but also for air-to-ground attacks in cases of emergency. In fact the Hawks were made specially for air-to-ground assaults.'[73] In December, notwithstanding this admission, Britain's Air Marshal visited Indonesia and it was revealed that the Indonesian air force was to begin negotiations with British Aerospace to purchase a further sixteen Hawk aircraft. The same month saw a visit to Indonesia by British Trade Minister Richard Needham, who pledged to double trade with Indonesia over the next two or three years. This was followed by a visit in early 1994 by Kenneth Clarke, the Chancellor of the Exchequer, who offered financial services to Indonesia and explored the possibility of further British investments in the country.[74]

The Indonesian military commander responsible for the Dili massacre in November 1991 was promoted in early 1994 to become Minister of Research and Technology, where he will be in charge of matters related to weapons.[75] There, he will enjoy continuing close relations with the British government, whose 'military contacts' with Jakarta are 'reasonably extensive and gradually increasing, with some training in the UK', Douglas Hurd noted in February 1994.[76] At the same time, Foreign Office Minister Mark Lennox-Boyd noted that 'some Indonesian public officials trained under our aid programme may subsequently serve in East Timor'.[77] In the same month – February 1994 – a UN Human Rights Commission report noted that 'East Timor continues to be particularly affected by violations of the right to life perpetrated by the Indonesian security forces.' The perpetrators of human rights violations enjoy 'virtual impunity' and, 'with very few exceptions', those responsible are 'neither prosecuted nor condemned'. The report continued by declaring that 'there has been no significant improvement in the human rights situation on the ground and unless concrete measures are taken no such improvement can be expected in the near future'.[78]

Britain's apologetics for Indonesian violence have been accompanied by those from the United States, whose State Department described Indonesia's official investigation into the Dili massacre as 'serious and responsible'.[79] The investigation had concluded that 'about 50' people had been killed and that the army had acted in 'self-defence' and 'under no command', all of which was denied by eyewitnesses. An *Observer* report, for example, noted that 'the massacre was a meticulously planned operation aimed at killing the principal protesters against the occupation'.[80] *Indonesian News* could state that the US Under-Secretary of Defence 'reaffirmed that Washington believed the Dili incident was unplanned and that the US was satisfied with the initiatives being taken by Jakarta in the wake of the riot'.[81] The same source quoted President Clinton as saying at a US banking conference, '... we have a lot of opportunities in the country. ... I would like to talk to [Suharto] about our willingness to become a partner of Indonesia.'[82]

As well as providing a significant market for Western arms sales, Indonesia under Suharto has consistently offered other Western business interests the opportunity to benefit from the country's political 'stability', most notably in the exploitation of the country's vast mineral resources. A few months before the invasion of East Timor, a Confederation of British Industry (CBI) report noted that Indonesia presented 'enormous potential for the foreign investor' and that, according to one press report, the country enjoyed a 'favourable political climate' and the 'encouragement of foreign investment by the country's authorities'. 'The [CBI] mission acknowledges that investing and operating in Indonesia is not without its problems,' the press also noted.[83] RTZ, BP, British Gas and Britoil are some of the companies that have since taken advantage of Indonesia's 'favourable political climate'. In the mid-1980s it was reported that Britain was to 'break with recent policy' and offer aid on 'soft loan terms' to Indonesia; at the time, British aid to the country was larger than to any other in East Asia. Britain reportedly 'finally agreed to meet a requirement laid down by President Suharto' that soft loans should be granted at low interest rates, repaid over twenty-five years and with a seven-year grace period. The deal was worth £130 million and made Indonesia the world's second-largest recipient of British soft loans.[84]

In recent years, leading Western aid donors have continued their economic support for the Suharto regime, with agreements to provide £2.8

billion in 1991, £2.6 billion in 1992 and £3.4 billion in 1993; Britain's Minister for Overseas Development, Lynda Chalker, praises the country for having 'a well-deserved reputation for sound macro-economic management'[85] – meaning it provides a favourable economic climate for Western business interests. A US Department of Commerce publication similarly states that Indonesia offers 'excellent trade and investment opportunities for US companies' under a headline reading 'Indonesia: trade opportunities here too good to be ignored'.[86]

At the same time, the lowest 20 per cent of earners account for only 9 per cent of total household income, whilst the top 10 per cent account for over one quarter of all income. 'Indonesia's income per head', the *Economist* notes, 'is only $550. But the richest 10 per cent of Indonesians spend about as much as the average consumer in Portugal.'[87] Provided Indonesia maintains these conditions, there is little likelihood of significant international pressure on Indonesia over East Timor. In the extremely unlikely event that Indonesia was to adopt economic policies preferential to its poor – thus threatening the right of international capitalism to exploit the nation's resources – the historical record suggests that Western leaders would suddenly discover human rights to be a relevant issue in their relations with Jakarta and start condemning Indonesia's brutal aggression as an outrageous act intolerable by any civilised standards.

As well as Indonesia, East Timor itself offers Western business interests the prospects of substantial profits; here, Australia has led the way. A year after the invasion of East Timor the *Japan Times* reported on negotiations between an Australian oil company and Indonesia on extracting the vast oil resources in the Timor Sea, whose '200-mile stretch of water constitutes the only gap in the resources line agreed between Australia and Indonesia'. An Australian official commented that, with the dispute over East Timor, 'Australian access to a potentially good oil area remains in doubt'. 'Until the East Timor issue is out of the way and fully resolved,' he commented, 'there is little we can do publicly'.[88] Australia subsequently attempted to ensure the issue was 'out of the way' by recognising Indonesian incorporation of the territory. Prime Minister Malcolm Fraser noted in 1976 that the invasion of East Timor 'introduced some strain in our relations' with Indonesia but said '... we should look forward rather than backwards.'[89] In December 1989 the resources issue was finally resolved with a joint agreement to exploit the Timor Sea, involving Australian, British and US companies, amongst others. A month after the Dili massacre, in December 1991, the Australian government approved with Indonesia eleven oil production contracts for exploitation of a jointly controlled area of the sea.

Australia has continued its apologias for Indonesian barbarity in East Timor. In a 1991 interview, Foreign Minister Gareth Evans noted the 'ongoing human rights problems that crop up from time to time in East

Timor' and that 'the sovereign reality of that incorporation of East Timor is something that our country has accepted since the late 1970s'. He added, 'We simply can't lend ourselves to an exercise which is premised on the non-acceptance of a sovereign incorporation of East Timor into the Republic of Indonesia.' The Timor Gap Treaty was, he explained, 'an enormous economic opportunity' for both Australia and Indonesia.[90] By November 1992 Foreign Minister Evans was speaking of 'a new high point in the relationship' with Indonesia in trade and economic matters.[91]

In some US circles, there have been some recent signs of willingness to put pressure on Indonesia over human rights abuses in East Timor. In 1992, Congress halted the US–Indonesia military training programme and in July 1993 the United States blocked the transfer of four warplanes from Jordan to Indonesia. In September 1993, the Senate Foreign Affairs Committee voted for an amendment to the Foreign Appropriations Bill which asks the President to consult with Congress to determine whether improvements in the human rights situation have taken place before approving arms sales.[92] However, this amendment was opposed by the Clinton administration, and the State Department made clear that the decision to block Jordan's proposed sale of aircraft to Indonesia was 'not a precedent for other arms transfer decisions'.[93]

As talks on East Timor at the United Nations between Portugal and Indonesia continue under the auspices of the UN Secretary-General, there are currently few indications, even given the US moves on arms sales noted above, that Britain and other Western states are willing to press Indonesia sufficiently to change its policy on East Timor and prepare the territory for self-determination, in line with international law. International awareness of the plight of the Timorese is greater than it has ever been, however. After the issue had been effectively buried in the mainstream media following the 1975 invasion, increased public awareness of the issue was brought about largely by a remarkable TV documentary by John Pilger, which was based on a secret visit to East Timor and shown around the world in early 1994. Pilger also wrote a series of press articles which, along with the film, exposed to a wide audience – probably for the first time – the complicity of the British and other governments in Indonesian violence. It is clear from the evidence of the past twenty years that such public pressure will be the sole way of encouraging a change in British policy towards Jakarta. British and Western policy towards Indonesia will otherwise continue to be dictated by commercial interests which – with numerous precedents – override considerations about human rights and international law. The leading Western states would prefer to profit from the socio-economic conditions offered by the Indonesian military regime despite the fact that, in the words of Amnesty International, 'disregard for human life is an integral part of the Indonesian security forces' approach to its work' and 'in the quarter of a century since it came to power, the government of Indonesia has been responsible for a staggering range of violations of human rights'.[94]

Structural war: controlling the Third World

In the 1990s, Third World populations can continue to be disciplined into accepting economic policies which promote Western business interests in the usual ways: political repression and, if this is not sufficient, sheer terror. Western states are on hand to provide arms to regimes, ostensibly for defence against external threats, but in reality often for such internal repression. Even where there is no direct use of imported arms for internal repression, arms sales tend to legitimise governments both internationally and domestically and reinforce the position of the military within society, thus narrowing the options of those opposing repression. Arms sales also help to play the crucial role of solidifying the relationship between Northern and Southern elites, in a system where the latter benefit by acting as the local managers of Third World resources under the overall control of the world's powerful states and their business corporations.

The primary means by which structural control is exercised over Third World societies and resources is the organisation of the international economy. The collapse of the Soviet Union and its removal as a major power – and as an alternative model of Third World economic development or means of financial support for alternative development – more fully opens up the Third World playing field to Western business interests. A primary goal of postwar planning can now be realised virtually without hindrance. A dominating fact of current British policy towards the Third World, and one of its main contributions to contemporary horrors, is its full participation in the structural economic exploitation of the Third World currently taking place on a scale with little historical precedent.

In the earlier postwar period, Britain played a key unilateral role in organising the Third World appropriately. That it is now one actor among many emphasises the degree to which its national power has declined. Yet Britain is still a highly significant player in the international economy, as is evidenced in its membership of the G7 grouping and in its influential role in the IMF and the World Bank, whose structural adjustment programmes (SAPs) now determine domestic economic policy in much of the Third World. Britain is the fifth-largest shareholder in the World Bank group, and is one of only five countries entitled to appoint its own Executive Director who represents that country alone, rather than, as is the case for other member governments, representing a large coalition of member governments. Many of Britain's transnational corporations are also some of the most powerful actors in the international economy and it is largely in the interests of the Northern transnationals that the economic order functions.

One traditional means of exerting control over the international system – military intervention – is by no means obsolete, as testified in the war against Iraq. Yet it is the level of structural control over the international economy achieved by the Northern powers that might be regarded as the chief prize of 'winning' the Cold War. In a telling comment, Lawrence Summers, US Treasury Under-Secretary for International Affairs, notes that the regional development banks in the Third World are 'as important to the new world order as the regional security organisations were to the old one'.[95] Contemporary SAPs and the international debt and trade regimes can be regarded as means of warfare equivalent to military intervention and subversion in the earlier postwar period. Indeed, the economic 'development' programmes now being forced upon the Third World – primarily through SAPs – result in the pursuit of virtually identical policies as those that followed Western, including British, military interventions in the earlier period. These include a reduction in the role of the state in the economy, and severe cutbacks in government spending on the basic needs of the population, in a context where foreign investment is encouraged and the economy is organised to benefit domestic elites and transnational corporations.

Development specialist Susan George comments that 'we must be honest and recognise that [the Western powers'] goal is not, and never was, to feed today's undernourished or starving millions, but to perpetuate poverty and dependence for altogether "valid" political and economic reasons'.[96] She notes further that Western methods of development have 'not produced a single independent and viable economy in the entire Third World' and adds crucially, 'and in fact were not meant to'. So-called development, she continues, 'has been the password for imposing a new kind of dependency, for enriching the already rich world and for shaping other societies to meet its commercial and political needs'.[97]

This view fits squarely with the evidence accumulated in this study as to the motivations behind, and the effects of, British foreign policy in the Third World since 1945. Policy in, for example, Malaya, Kenya, British Guiana and Iran was geared towards organising Third World economies along guidelines in which British, and Western, interests would be paramount, and those of the often malnourished populations would be ignored or further undermined. Similarly, US interventions overseas – in Vietnam, Nicaragua, the Dominican Republic, Cuba, Chile, etcetera – were designed to counter threats to the Western practice of assigning the Third World to mere client status to Western business interests. British and US military forces have acted as mercenary – and often extremely violent – mobs intended to restore 'order' in their domains and to preserve the existing privileges of elites within their own societies.

To state that – in the light of the mass poverty that still exists in the Third World – Western 'development' strategies there have 'failed' misses the point: they have been singularly successful. A 1992 UN report, for example, notes that the gap between rich and poor has doubled in the last thirty years with the world's richest fifth receiving 150 times the income of the poorest fifth. Since 1960, the countries where the richest 20 per cent of the world's people live have increased their share of gross world product from 70 per cent to 83 per cent, making those states sixty times better off than those where the poorest 20 per cent live.[98] The international debt regime has been particularly successful since the early 1980s, enabling a vast transfer of resources from poor to rich to take place. Between 1982 and 1990, for example, resource flows from OECD countries to the Third World amounted to $927 billion, while Third World countries paid $1,345 in debt service alone to the creditor countries: $418 billion in the Northern countries' favour. During this 'crisis', Western banks received high rates of return on their loans, averaging 13.6 per cent from 1982 to 1989.[99] A former executive director at the World Bank commented that 'not since the conquistadores plundered Latin America has the world experienced a [financial] flow in the direction we see today'.[100]

Control over the Third World has therefore been successfully reasserted after the limited gains made by the Third World in the 1970s, particularly in the establishment of a number of agreements amongst commodity producers in the context of calls for a New International Economic Order. If the 1980s – especially with regard to the debt crisis – was a period of transition in which Third World economies were increasingly squeezed and Northern financial institutions earned windfall profits, the 1990s is the period of the strategy's final success. 'What we have seen in countries like Zambia since 1975 is a reversal of the gains made since independence,' John Martin of the World Health Organisation notes. The effects are severe:

> A combination of debt problems and IMF Structural Adjustment Programmes has led governments to cut expenditure on health and the result is increasing infant mortality rates, declining immunisation levels and a frightening marginal-isation of the poorer social groups.[101]

Real economic power in the international system lies with the giant transnational corporations and their supervisors in the G7 states – in which the largest of the transnationals are nearly all based. Transnationals control around 70 per cent of world trade and the largest 100 manu-facturing and service transnationals accounted for world assets valued at $3.1 trillion in 1990. The processing, marketing, distribution and transport of Third World commodities – upon which the majority of the world's poorest nations still rely for their export earnings – are largely in their hands. The most powerful British transnationals include Tate & Lyle – one of only two companies which process most of sub-Saharan Africa's sugar; Unilever – the world's largest tea packer; and British American

Tobacco (BAT) – one of a handful of transnationals that dominate the African tobacco industry. Other British companies play leading roles in controlling the trading and/or processing of Third World primary commodities; these companies include Allied Lyons and Brooke Bond in tea, and Cadbury-Schweppes and Rowntree-Mackintosh in cocoa. The result of such transnational control is that only around 15 per cent of the final retail value of products made from the main primary agricultural commodities accrues to the producing country in the Third World. Even this figure includes many direct and indirect costs, so the individual producer receives a far smaller proportion. For some products the proportion is even lower than 15 per cent: for example, 4–8 per cent for raw cotton, 6 per cent for tobacco, 14 per cent for bananas.[102]

The IMF's structural adjustment programmes are the currently favoured method of exercising overall control, now applied to dozens of countries in the Third World. The IMF has been described by Nancy Alexander, of the US nongovernmental organisation Bread for the World, as 'really a centralizing economic power in the world'.[103] 'You either eat at the IMF's table, or you don't eat at all,' says a leading London-based international financial adviser.[104] The results of SAPs have been virtually identical everywhere: spending on social services such as health and education has been cut back, inequality of income has increased, poverty levels have risen, whilst macro-economic performance has often enriched small ruling elites and the foreign enterprises associated with them. SAPs are merely an extension of traditional so-called development programmes foisted on the Third World in the postwar period and presided over by elements in the Third World only too pleased to enrich themselves whilst currying the favour of Northern governments.

Mexico, for example, was reported in 1992 as having torn down its trade barriers, embarked upon a major programme of privatisation, and adopted economic measures 'aimed at restoring the confidence of investors, both local and foreign'. Impressive growth rates of 4 per cent a year were recorded. 'Despite three years of economic growth,' Michael Reid reports, 'real incomes for most Mexicans have yet to recover from the 1980s slump, when they plunged by up to half.' And 'many of the reforms have had the effect of exacerbating the highly unequal distribution of income', whilst 'daily life in Mexico has yet to improve substantially for the majority'.[105]

Similarly, the *Economist* noted in November 1991 that the Peruvian government 'has released an avalanche of 126 economically liberal and politically repressive decrees this month'. It then noted that 'visitors from the International Monetary Fund and the World Bank ... helped devise' the decrees, and it explained that the new laws meant that the labour market would become 'flexibilised'. 'Laws to protect Peruvian workers from dismissal and to put them on management boards have been drastically weakened,' it noted further. The President's aim, the *Economist* noted, 'is to transform Peru into a haven for investors'. This was written in a context where the minimum legal wage in the capital, Lima, was $35 a month, with a family needing at least eight times as much to buy its basic food and services, according to the UN.[106] The number of Peruvians living in extreme poverty, meanwhile, had doubled in the previous three years to 13 million.[107]

Great profits can be made from countries that open up their economies. The *Economist* reported in June 1992 that international banks were 'making pots of money in unlikely places: in Latin American countries that cannot pay their debts, and in Africa's impoverished economies'. The Hong Kong and Shanghai bank accrued 'profits in Asia [which] had helped the bank weather disastrous ventures in more developed economies'. Bank of Boston was hit by recession in the United States in 1990 and 1991 but its branches in Argentina and Brazil enabled it to earn $130 million in those two years, 'a spectacular average return on assets of 2.6%'. 'Another beneficiary', the *Economist* noted, was US bank Citicorp, which 'made $444m from corporate banking in the Third World last year'. 'Economic chaos', the *Economist* continues, 'has been another big source of profit, especially in Latin America.' 'When inflation is roaring and interest rates are high, banks suck up deposits through their branches and lend them out, to local companies, which have few sources of finance other than local banks.'[108]

The GATT accord, finalised in December 1993, contributes firmly to the new international economic order, as a partner in 'development' to SAPs. As a result of the agreement, the world's poorest region – sub-Saharan Africa – will lose an expected $2.6 billion a year. By contrast, the EU is expected to gain $61.3 billion, the US $36.4 billion and Japan $27.0 billion a year. Thus 60 per cent of the estimated $212 billion in annual gains in world income will accrue to these fourteen countries.[109]

In the GATT negotiations in the early 1990s, a central EU and US aim was to eliminate Third World barriers to 'free trade' in agriculture, that is, to remove still further any obstacles to the near-complete control of international trade exercised by agribusiness corporations. A US proposal (the 'zero option') sought to eliminate all forms of state intervention in agriculture. 'Were this demand to be conceded,' the general secretary of the Catholic Institute of International Relations (CIIR) comments, 'developing countries would lose policy sovereignty in the key area of food security' and 'self-sufficiency in food' would suffer. 'Without wishing to venture into the realms of conspiracy theory,' he notes further, 'this appears to be what Washington – and the giant trading corporations which drew up the "zero option" – has in mind'.[110] Tim Lang of Parents for Safe Food and Kevin Watkins of the CIIR, and later of Oxfam, similarly note that 'the most disturbing aspect' of the GATT negotiations is the 'emerging US–EC agricultural trade compromise' requiring Third World states to reduce state support for food producers and phase out restrictions on cheap imports. 'By contrast,' they note, 'the dumping of cheap food in developing country food markets by the US and the EC will continue unabated.' 'Stated simply,' they note, 'this is a recipe for mass hunger. It is intended to open up developing country food markets to giant US-based corporations.'[111]

Watkins notes that the GATT final accord 'has created a new world trade order geared to the interests of the industrial countries and powerful transnational companies, consigning the world's poorest countries to a future of deepening poverty in the process'. The agreement 'will allow for the pursuit of trade war by diplomatic means'. 'In recent years,' Watkins continues, 'US trade policy has been guided more by the principles of gunboat diplomacy perfected by Palmerston, than by GATT principles of multilateralism,' since countries refusing to open their markets to US banks and insurance companies have been the principal target of US sanctions. But, after the GATT accord, 'the [US] administration can dry-dock its trade gunboats' and instead 'it can wave the GATT agreement at recalcitrant foreign governments'. Under the accord on services, it can force Third World governments to deregulate their markets and remove controls on foreign investment, including controls on profit repatriation.[112]

The new agreement on intellectual property rights under the GATT accord is particularly indicative of the trend towards further entrenching Northern control over Third World resources, by introducing a patenting system for technology products and opening the door to the patenting of life forms such as micro-organisms and genetic materials. Mohamed Idris, a Coordinator of the Third World Network in Malaysia, comments thus:

> Unlike the colonialism of the past, this new colonialism is more subtle, more invisible and therefore more dangerous. The rich countries and their corporations have already taken most of the Third World's natural resources, minerals, trees and soils, as raw materials for their industries. Now that these resources are almost gone, they want to take away the Third World's rich and diverse biological materials, seeds and genetic resources.[113]

Martin Khor, Research Director of the Third World Network, notes that the North's motives for introducing intellectual property rights were 'to enable their firms to capture more profits through royalties and the sale of technology products; and to place stiff barriers preventing the technological development of potential new rivals from the South'. He makes the important point that this agreement showed that the 'free trade' and 'liberalisation' pushed by the North were merely 'nice slogans' made to push the negotiations forward. 'Free trade', Khor notes, in reality means 'the vastly expanded freedom and powers of transnational corporations to trade and invest in most countries of the world, whilst correspondingly governments now have significantly reduced powers to restrict their operations'.[114] Third World economies are thus being transnationalised, which is diminishing the power of Third World states to manage and intervene in their own economies.[115]

The human consequences of this recolonisation are severe. A 1993 World Bank report notes that the number of people living in absolute poverty is increasing by around 2 per cent a year – or over 20 million people – with even the percentage (as well as the absolute number) of the population living in absolute poverty increasing in sub-Saharan Africa and Latin America.[116] A study by the International Fund for Agricultural Development (IFAD) analyses the causes of poverty in twenty sub-Saharan African countries and finds that 'international processes' – declining export commodity prices and dependence on foreign countries for income and employment – contribute to poverty in fifteen of them. IFAD notes that 'if a comprehensive strategy to combat [rising poverty] is not pursued by all developing countries, with assistance from the donor community, the number of rural poor could grow to 1,310 million by 2000'.[117]

The chances of this 'comprehensive strategy' being pursued are somewhat less than minimal. For example, UNICEF estimates that half a million children die each year as a result of Third World attempts to meet debt repayments.[118] Yet two analysts at the Institute of Development Studies at the University of Sussex note that the OECD countries are 'not highly concerned' with a cure for the debt crisis 'since the world financial market has averted the risk of major collapse, after the banks made contingency provisions and the debtors were offered partial alleviation under the Baker Plan and Brady Plan'.[119]

Similarly, the World Bank continues to encourage and enforce economic policies on Third World countries which its own reports stress have failed (in the conventional sense). Early 1994, for example, saw the publication of two major World Bank reports. In the first, consideration was given to the fall in commodity prices, which reduced Third World countries' incomes by around $100 billion in the decade to 1993. The 'major cause' of the decline in commodity prices, the World Bank notes, was 'the sharp increases in the aggregate supply of commodities on world markets'.[120] The second report nevertheless continues to urge the standard World Bank medicine which helps to cause this situation. In a sub-section entitled 'Putting exporters first', the World Bank urges that 'because exports are so beneficial for growth, countries should consider the needs of exporters carefully and apply an "exporters first" rule'.[121] As a former World Bank senior adviser commented, Africa's reliance on exporting primary commodities to increase export earnings – and the effect on prices when several countries do this at the same time – is like 'cutting its own throat'.[122]

As for the likelihood of a 'comprehensive strategy' being pursued by the 'donor community' – as IFAD urges in the report cited above – the chances are again less than minimal. Amongst the leading industrialised states, it is simply a truism to state that there is no institutional interest in reducing poverty in the Third World, or in promoting economic development outside of their overall control, as the historical record – partly documented in this study – clearly reveals. The term 'aid', for example, is more properly understood in an Orwellian sense since the benefits are intended to accrue to the donor rather than the recipient. The British 'aid' programme is a case in point. Around 70 per cent of Britain's bilateral 'aid' programme is tied to the purchase of British goods and services, meaning the money is spent in Britain rather than the Third World. As regards the multilateral programme, a Foreign Office minister has noted that for every pound spent the return is £1.40.[123] Furthermore, the United Nations Development Programme estimates that just 6.6 per cent of Britain's bilateral 'aid' is spent on human priorities, such as basic education, primary health care and the provision of safe water – the areas that would be prioritised if poverty reduction were a serious concern.[124]

The British government has been explicit about the aims of its 'aid' programme. 'The UK provides aid for two broad reasons,' the government notes. The first is that 'the government believes it is right that a part of the nation's wealth should be used to help poorer countries and their peoples improve their standard of life'. This, however, hardly constitutes an explicit 'reason' for providing 'aid'. The second reason is clearer. The government states that 'the provision of aid to poorer countries is one of the instruments for helping to pursue the government's wider international policy objectives'. By enhancing 'sustainable development', the 'UK's trading interests can be advanced and the risks of political instability reduced'. 'Aid' can also be a 'valuable tool for strengthening the UK's commercial and political relations with particular countries', the report continues.[125]

Stark realities

This study has attempted to highlight some of the facts about British foreign policy towards the Third World, by showing the underlying motivations and effects of that policy in a number of countries. In the contemporary world it is surely hard to conceive of a more serious area of enquiry than that of analysing the policy motivations of the world's most powerful states, and in particular the degree of control they exercise over the fate of poor nations and peoples. Britain bears considerable responsibility for many of the horrors which have afflicted people in the Third World throughout the postwar era. These policies have been based not on whims – or on the delusions of malevolent individuals. Rather they are the consequence of the rich states' pursuit of their straightforward 'national interests'. In the same way, the current unprecedented scale of exploitation of Third World societies and resources is structural, rather than *ad hoc*, going right to the heart of the organisation of the international system.

One basic fact – of perhaps unparalled importance – has permeated a number of studies and is well understood: that the mass poverty and destitution that exist in much of the Third World are direct products of the structure of the international system.[126] Moreover, an elementary truth is that the world's powerful states have pursued policies with regard to the Third World which knowingly promote poverty. It is clear that the policies they have encouraged or imposed on the Third World – in the earlier postwar period following military intervention and in the later period through the international financial institutions – have betrayed no institutional interest in eradicating poverty or in promoting a form of economic development meaningful for the poor. Rather, policies have been imposed with the understanding that they will not contribute to these ends. It is hardly open to question, for example, that the basic framework adhered to by the Northern states for allegedly promoting development in the Third World – a framework of 'free trade' and 'liberalisation' – cannot do this. This framework has hardly been adhered to by those states that have largely extricated themselves from membership of the Third World, such as the Asian Tigers, most notably South Korea. These countries are more correctly understood as command capitalist regimes, in which the state has played a commanding role in the economy not only by putting in place trade and investment regimes favourable to domestic enterprises but also by engaging in production itself.[127] Susan George correctly comments thus:

> The only underdeveloped countries that have either solved the food problem for their own people – or are on the way to solving it – have used some kind of central planning and have devised means for involving the people ... in turning the tide against hunger.[128]

This central planning, however – often formerly termed 'communism' – has necessarily been viewed as heretical by the West throughout the postwar era and remains so in the current economic orthodoxy. The consequences are well understood and documented.

There are other notable examples from postwar history of states that successfully embarked upon poverty reduction programmes and allowed the poor in their countries to make significant advances. Yet a key leitmotif of that history is that comprehensive attempts in the Third World to alleviate poverty have been met by destabilisation, terror or outright invasion, as in Vietnam, Cuba, Nicaragua and elsewhere. That these countries not only made such attempts but also made significant, demonstrable gains in social welfare made their achievements the more problematic to the Northern powers.

The evidence suggests that the basic facts about the motivations and effects of British and Western foreign policy cannot be expressed in mainstream media and academic circles. As I have tried to document above, the systematic contribution to postwar horrors made by various British governments lies buried in professions as to Britain's benign intentions and masked by the portrayal of British actions in a convenient ideological shroud. Mainstream media and academic commentators are therefore unable to comment on the structural war waged against the poor of the Third World which has been taking place continuously throughout the postwar period and which has recently entered a new, perhaps unfettered, phase. Thus, there can be little attention given to the need for a major reordering of international society.

This view touches on an issue outside the scope of this enquiry: namely that improving the lot of the subject peoples of the Third World requires fundamental structural changes within Northern societies. A recognition that the pursuit of elementary 'national interests' leads to, if not requires, mass impoverishment, leads to the conclusion that the present structure of society in the North is incompatible with the achievement of meaningful development and the fulfilment of human rights in the Third World. If foreign (and domestic) policy is dictated by the requirements of business corporations and small ruling elites within the societies of the North, human needs will continue to be sacrificed on the altar of narrowly defined 'economic interests'. If these appear to be elementary, obvious truths to some, it is worth repeating that they are inexpressible in the 'independent' circles that promote the ideological agenda.

These questions are closely related to democracy at home: a 'democracy', that is, in which citizens play no meaningful role in policy-making and where, every few years, they are required to take seriously public relations exercises and choose between parties that offer increasingly similar policies and effectively represent the same interests. If Third World societies are becoming increasing 'transnationalised' with sovereign power being increasingly reduced, a similar process is evident in the industrial countries, where decisions about investment, job creation and macro-economic policy are increasingly subjected to international economic forces that lack any democratic accountability. A political charade necessarily goes on with none of the mainstream parties concerned to attempt to dismantle the underlying structures that control domestic and international society.

The propaganda system is as much a crucial element here as it is in concealing from the public British foreign policy's consistent role in the world's horrors. In this situation, it would not be surprising if the public as a whole were uninspired to work towards structural change. Indeed, as with foreign policy, they would be unable even to formulate what is wrong.

Notes

1. Amnesty International, *Repression Trade (UK) Limited: How the United Kingdom makes torture and death its business*, AI, London, January 1992, pp. 14, 16, 19–20, 25, 31–2 for the following citations.

2. Ibid., p. 25.

3. Ibid., p. 26.

4. John Pilger, *Distant voices*, Vintage, London, 1992, p. 191. See also David Munro, 'Cambodia: A secret war continues', *Covert Action Information Bulletin*, No. 40, Spring 1992.

5. Ibid., p. 215.

6. 'Return to year zero', Channel 4 TV, 20 April 1993.

7. *Independent*, 4 May 1990.

8. Ruby Ofori, 'Ecological terrorism', *West Africa*, 19 November 1990.

9. Ian Traynor, David Hearst and Yigal Chazan, 'US and Russia at odds as Serbs batter Gorazde', *Guardian*, 22 April 1994.

10. Mark Tran and Ian Traynor, 'US throws weight behind move to lift arms embargo', *Guardian*, 30 June 1993.

11. Andrew Marshall, 'Serbia offered sanctions trade-off', *Independent*, 23 November 1993.

12. Douglas Hurd, 'Keeping our heads in a nightmare', *Guardian*, 1 July 1993.

13. Médecins Sans Frontières, *Life, death and aid*, MSF/Routledge, London, 1993, p. 89.

14. Ian Traynor, 'Villains of the peace in the Balkans', *Guardian*, 2 September 1993.

15. See, for example, House of Commons Official Report, *Parliamentary Debates*, Vol. 233, No. 2, 19 November 1993, Col. 119.

16. Ian Traynor and John Palmer, 'Muslim leader thrust aside over partition', *Guardian*, 23 June 1993.

17. Ed Vulliamy, *Guardian*, 13 September 1993.

18. Christopher Bellamy, 'Bosnian army finds more proof of Zagreb troops', *Independent*, 8 February 1994.

19. David Fairhall, 'Pentagon's aim entirely punitive', *Guardian*, 18 January 1993; David Kay of the IAEA and a former UN weapons inspector also noted, the US press reported, that 'as a result of a mid-1991 UN inspection and subsequent UN actions, there was no longer any activity at the site that could be helpful to an atomic weapons programme' (Paul Horvitz, '40 to 50 "smart" weapons hit a plant near Baghdad', *International Herald Tribune*, 18 January 1993).

20. Patrick Wintour, 'Britain backs use of cruise', *Guardian*, 18 January 1993.

21. Simon Edge, 'Clinton's double-edged sword', *Middle East Economic Digest*, 16 July 1993. For the alleged plot against Bush, see also 'Iraqi plot against Bush "not proved"', *Guardian*, 25 October 1993.

22. Nikki Knewstub, 'Labour lists catalogue of objections to "dubious" raid', *Guardian*, 29 June 1993.

23. Deborah Pugh, 'Arab dismay greets raid', *Guardian*, 28 June 1993.

24. Rakiya Omaar, 'For mercy read murder', *Guardian*, 15 June 1993.

25. *Africa Confidential*, Vol. 34, No. 14, 16 July 1993; Mark Huband, 'Aideed allies test UN plan for Somalia', *Guardian*, 22 July 1993.

26. *Africa Confidential*, Vol. 33, No. 24, 4 December 1992.

27. European Wireless File, News Alert, 'Somalia effort offers chance to "make a difference"', 6 December 1992.

28. CIA memorandum of 18 June 1962, cited in Blum, p. 219.

29. 'Liquidating Sukarno', *Times*, 8 August 1986.

30. Kolko, *Confronting the Third World*, pp. 180–81.

31. Christopher Reed, 'US agents "drew up Indonesian hit list"', *Guardian*, 22 May 1990.

32. Kolko, *Confronting the Third World*, p. 181.

33. Quoted in Carmel Budiardjo, 'Indonesia: Mass extermination and the consolidation of authoritarian power', in Alexander George (ed.), *Western state terrorism*, Polity Press, Cambridge, 1991, p. 181.

34. Kolko, *Confronting the Third World*, pp. 184–5.

35. Michael Stewart, *Life and labour: an autobiography*, Sidgwick and Jackson, London, 1980, p. 149.

36. Carmel Budiardjo and Liem Soei Liong, *The war against East Timor*, Zed, London, 1984, p. 49.

37. G. Munster and J. Walsh, *Documents on Australian defence and foreign policy, 1968–75*, Hong Kong, 1980, pp. 192–3.

38. Munster and Walsh, pp. 199–200.

39. Budiardjo, 'Indonesia', p. 200.

40. Jonathan Mirsky, 'War by famine kills 200,000', *Observer foreign news service*, 20 November 1979.

41. Michael Simmons, 'Amnesty says atrocities are continuing in East Timor', *Guardian*, 26 June 1985.

42. 'ET bishop reports persecution', *International Herald Tribune*, 16 February 1990.

43. Budiardjo and Liong, p. 27.

44. 'UNSC draft bid seeks Indonesian withdrawal', *Japan Times*, 23 April 1976.

45. 'UN bid for "quit Timor" order to Indonesia', *Straits Times*, 22 April 1976.

46. Cited in Budiardjo, 'Indonesia', p. 203.

47. R. Chakrapani, 'Irritants in focus as Suharto meets Reagan', *The Hindu*, 13 October 1982.

48. *Straits Times*, 19 March 1981.

49. 'Jakarta's strategic role big factor for US aid', *Straits Times*, 11 October 1982.

50. See Budiardjo, 'Indonesia', pp. 203–4.

51. John Gittings, 'East Timorese accuse Britain of blocking action on Indonesia', *Guardian*, 17 June 1992.

52. *Financial Times*, 5 April 1978.

53. Budiardjo, 'Indonesia', p. 205.

54. Kieran Cooke, 'Why Indonesia bought British Rapiers', *Financial Times*, 3 January 1985.

55. John Murray Brown, 'Britain eyes defence market in Indonesia', *Financial Times*, 11 November 1987.

56. Letter from Peter Carey, *Guardian*, 1 July 1992.

57. John Pilger, 'On Her Majesty's bloody service', *New Statesman and Society*, 18 February 1994.

58. John Taylor, *Indonesia's forgotten war: The hidden history of East Timor*, Zed, London, 1991, p. 275.

59. Letter from Stephen Chappell, Campaign Against the Arms Trade, *Guardian*, 12 July 1985; letter from Peter Carey, *Guardian*, 18 February 1992.

60. Peter Tatchell, 'West Papua's guerilla war', *Observer foreign news service*, 22 August 1979.

61. David White, 'BAe in Indonesia fighter pact', *Financial Times*, 21 June 1991; 'In Sumatra uprising, army is said to execute hundreds', *International Herald Tribune*, 21 June 1991.

62. *Amnesty International Newsletter*, Vol. XXIII, No. 7, July 1993.

63. Kieran Cooke, 'BAe "signs contract for Suharto jet"', *Financial Times*, 24 May 1985.

64. *Indonesian News*, Vol. 20, No. 42, 20 December 1992.

65. *Indonesian News*, Vol. 19, No. 17, 1 October 1991.

66. Budiardjo and Liong, pp. 47–8.

67. *TAPOL Bulletin*, No. 112, August 1992, p. 2.

68. *International Herald Tribune*, 10 December 1991.

69. *Summary of World Broadcasts*, FE/1656, A1/1, 6 April 1993.

70. *Summary of World Broadcasts*, FE/1658, A1/2, 8 April 1993.

71. Rebecca Smithers, 'Hawk deal provokes human rights row', *Guardian*, 11 June 1993.

72. *TAPOL Bulletin*, No. 112, August 1992, p. 1.

73. Rosie Waterhouse, 'UK sold £260m arms to government accused of atrocities', *Independent*, 23 February 1994.

74. See *TAPOL Bulletin*, No. 121, February 1994, pp. 7–8.

75. 'Leader of massacre promoted', *Diario de Noticias*, translated in *Internet* service, 7 April 1994.

76. Memorandum by the Secretary of State for Foreign and Commonwealth Affairs to the House of Commons Select Committee on Foreign Affairs, February 1994.

77. House of Commons, Parliamentary Debates, *Hansard*, Written answers, 10 February 1994, Col. 457.

78. 'Human Rights-Indonesia: Jakarta under scrutiny over East Timor', *Internet*, 24 February 1994; Jeremy Wagstaff, 'Human rights still under attack', Reuters, *Internet*, 21 February 1994.

79. Adam Schwarz, 'Burden of blame', *Far Eastern Economic Review*, 9 January 1992.

80. Hugh O'Shaughnessy, 'Mourners walked into bloody ambush', *Observer*, 17 November 1991; see also John Gittings, 'E. Timor killings "covered up"', *Guardian*, 28 December 1991.

81. *Indonesian News*, Vol. 20, No. 35, 24 July 1992.

82. *Indonesian News*, Vol. 20, No. 9, 20 June 1993.

83. 'Opportunities in Indonesia', *Daily Telegraph*, 21 July 1975; Peter Hill, 'CBI says UK neglects trade with Indonesia', *The Times*, 21 August 1975.

84. Chris Sherwell, 'Britain to offer Indonesia soft loans', *Financial Times*, 4 June 1985; Alain Cass, 'Britain to offer Indonesia loans', *Financial Times*, 19 June 1986; 'UK, Indonesia sign loan deal', *Financial Times*, 18 July 1986.

85. Cited in *TAPOL Bulletin*, No. 112, August 1992, p. 4.

86. Karen Wilde Goddin, 'Indonesia: Trade opportunities here too good to be ignored', *Business America*, Vol. 114, No. 8, 19 April 1993.

87. 'Asian adventures', *Economist*, 30 May 1992.

88. Ingo Hertel, 'Australia eyes Timor oil areas', *Japan Times*, 17 October 1976.

89. 'Timor: "No lasting Aussie enmity"', *Straits Times*, 4 November 1976.

90. Interview with ABC TV, in *Indonesian News*, Vol. 19, No. 2, February 1991.

91. *SWB*, FE/1541, A2/3, 18 November 1992.

92. *TAPOL Bulletin*, No. 119, October 1993, pp. 1–2.

93. See Human Rights Watch, *Human Rights Watch World Report 1994*, HRW, New York, 1993, p. 168.

94. *Amnesty International Newsletter*, Vol. XXXIII, No. 7, July 1993.

95. Stephen Fidler, 'US policy switch on economic reform', *Financial Times*, 13 April 1994.

96. Susan George, *How the other half dies: The real reasons for world hunger*, Penguin, Harmondsworth, 1991, p. 19.

97. Ibid., p. 17.

98. Victoria Brittain, 'The rich get richer, and the poor get poorer, poorer', *Guardian*, 24 April 1992; 'Why the poor don't catch up', *Economist*, 25 April 1992.

99. Susan George, *The Debt Boomerang: How Third World Debt Harms Us All*, Pluto, London, 1992, pp. xv, 86.

100. Cited in Walden Bello, *Dark Victory: The United States, structural adjustment and global poverty*, Pluto, London, 1994, p. 67.

101. Quoted in Edward Luce, 'WHO switches to inequality fight', *Guardian*, 25 April 1994.

102. See Michael Barratt Brown and Pauline Tiffen, *Short Changed: Africa and world trade*, Pluto, London, 1992, p. 97; World Bank, *Global economic prospects and the developing countries*, World Bank, Washington DC, 1994, pp. 41, 100–2, 194.

103. 'IMF addresses poverty in Structural Adjustment Programs', *IMF Survey*, 10 January 1994, p. 9.

104. Cited in Philip Gawith, 'A growing trend towards Africa', *Financial Times*, 17 January 1994.

105. Michael Reid, 'Salinas strives to maintain the momentum of change', and 'The will to compete is winning ground, but miracles take time', *Guardian*, 20 July 1992.

106. 'Looking to authority', *Economist*, 23 November 1991.

107. James Brooke, '"Bands of iron" throttle Peru', *International Herald Tribune*, 12 November 1991.

108. 'A bundle in the jungle', *Economist*, 27 June 1992.

109. 'GATT: Who wins what?', *Guardian*, 15 December 1993, using OECD/World Bank estimates.

110. Letter from Ian Linden, *Guardian*, 14 July 1990.

111. Letter to the *Guardian*, 8 March 1991.

112. Kevin Watkins, 'Package "to make the poor poorer"', *Guardian*, 16 December 1993.

113. Mohamed Idris, 'The new biological colonialism', in *Development and Cooperation*, No. 2, 1994, p. 19.

114. Martin Khor, 'The South at the end of the Uruguay Round', *Third World Resurgence*, No. 45, May 1994, p. 36.

115. See Chakravarthi Raghavan, 'South to face new "trade-related" threats', *Third World Resurgence*, No. 45, May 1994, pp. 18–19.

116. See Shaohua Chen, Gaurav Datt and Martin Ravallion, 'Is Poverty Increasing in the Developing World?', World Bank, Working Papers, June 1993.

117. IFAD, *The state of world rural poverty: A profile of Africa*, IFAD, Rome, 1993, pp. 1, 17–23.

118. 'Loan sharks', *New Statesman and Society*, 13 September 1991.

119. Prabirjit Sarkar and H.W. Singer, 'Debt crisis, commodity prices, transfer burden and debt relief', Institute of Development Studies, Discussion Paper No. 297, February 1992, pp. 23–4.

120. World Bank, *Global Economic Prospects*, p. 12.

121. World Bank, *Adjustment in Africa: Reforms, results and the road ahead*, OUP, New York, 1994, p. 11.

122. Cited in Barratt Brown and Tiffen, p. 25.

123. Mark Lennox-Boyd, *Hansard*, Vol. 217, No. 110, 27 January 1993, Col. 636.

124. UNDP, *Human Development Report 1994*, UNDP, New York, 1994, p. 74.

125. Foreign and Commonwealth Office, *The Government's expenditure plans, 1994–95 to 1996–97*, Cm. 2502, HMSO, London, March 1994, p. 51.

126. See, for example, Susan George, *How the other half dies* and *Ill fares the land: Essays on food, hunger and power*, Penguin, Harmondsworth, 1990; Frances Moore Lappe and Joseph Collins, *World hunger: Twelve myths*, Grove Weidenfeld, New York, 1986; Teresa Hayter, *The creation of world poverty*, Pluto, London, 1982; Samir Amin, *Maldevelopment: Anatomy of a global failure*, Zed, London, 1990.

127. Bello, p. 72.

128. George, *How the other half dies*, p. 18.

INDEX

Pezzullo, Lawrence, 165
Philippines, 23, 211
Pilger, John, 212, 222, 227
Pinochet, Augusto, 129–36
Piotrowski, Harry, 149
Pirouet, Louise, 138–9
Poland, 48, 172
Portugal, 217, 219
Poverty (see Economic development)
Powell, Colin, 186, 187–8, 204
Pratt, Cranford, 16
Prowse, Michael, 199
Pye Telecommunications, 211–2
Propaganda system, 1, 4–6, 116–7,
  235–6; and Chile, 131–2, 135–6; and
  Diego Garcia, 118–9; and Falklands
  War, 118–9; and 1991 Gulf War,
  194–206, and Malaya, 58–9, 61,
  63–4; and the Middle East, 193; and
  Nicaragua, 165–74; and the Soviet
  Union, 22, 29–39, 43–8, 58, 59, 76,
  78–9, 148–9, 155, 163–5, 167–71,
  217; and Uganda, 139–40; and
  Vietnam, 148–9

Qadafi, Muammar, 10, 157
Qasim, Abdul Karim, 106–8
Queen, The, 78, 156, 206, 223
Quinlan, Michael, 187

Reagan, Ronald, and Britain, 162, 180;
  and Chile, 135; and El Salvador, 161;
  and Guatemala, 161; propaganda
  system on, 168, 170, 171, 173; and
  Nicaragua, 159, 164, 165; and South
  Africa, 125
Red Cross, 101
Reed Report, 186–7
Reid, Michael, 231
RENAMO, 120, 126–7
Reporter, Shahpour, 93
Reynolds, David, 36
Rhodesia, 122, 125
Ridley, Nicholas, 133, 155
Rifkind, Malcolm, 138, 224
Rogers, Paul, 189
Rolls-Royce, 221–2, 224
Rowntree-Mackintosh, 231
Royal Institute of International Affairs
  (Chatham House), 35, 94

Royal Air Force, 99, 100, 101, 190, 192
Royal Navy, 2, 188, 221, 223
RTZ Corporation, 122, 225
Rubin, Barry, 93, 95
Russia, 183, 216 (see also Soviet Union)

Sana, Hassan, 96
Sandhurst, Royal Military Academy at,
  101
SAS (see Special Air Service)
SAVAK, 96
Saudi Arabia, 13, 21–2, 31, 100, 101,
  193
School of Oriental and African Studies,
  91
Schultz, George, 164
Schwartzkopf, Norman, 205, 206
Scotland Yard, 62
Scotsman, 62
Searle, Chris, 155
Serbia, 206, 213–5 (see also former
  Yugoslavia)
Seychelles, 117
Shah of Iran, 87–96, 100
Sharjah, 101
Shell, 99, 105–6
Shuman, Michael, 193
Sierra Leone, 14
Singapore, 56, 60, 64–5, 221
Smuts, Jan, 19
Somalia/Somaliland, 10–11, 48, 183,
  200, 216–7
Somoza, Anastasio, 157–8, 159, 163,
  166
South Africa, 19, 116; and Angola, 48,
  120, 121; and Britain, 6, 119–29; and
  Mozambique, 120, 126–7;
  Sharpeville massacre, 120–1;
  Simonstown agreement, 123–4; and
  the UN, 122, 124–5; and the USA,
  123, 125
Southeast Asia, 13, 20, 30, 32, 34, 39,
  57–9, 128, 146–52 (see also individual
  countries)
Southern African Association, 128
Soviet Union (see also Russia), 10, 23;
  and alleged 'Soviet threat', 22,
  29–39, 43–8, 58, 59, 76, 78–9, 148–9,
  155, 163–5, 167–71, 217; and
  Britain, 12, 13, 15, 48; and British